UNDERSTANDING HUMAN ECOLOGY

This book examines the domain of human agency–environment interaction from a multidimensional point of view. It explores the human–environment interface by analysing its ethical, political and epistemic aspects – the value aspects that humans attribute to their environment, the relations of power in which the actions and their consequences are implicated and the meaning of human actions in relation to the environment. The volume delineates the character of this domain and works out a theoretical framework for the field of human ecology.

This book will be a must-read for students, scholars and researchers of environmental studies, human ecology, development studies, environmental history, literature, politics and sociology. It will also be useful to practitioners, government bodies, environmentalists, policy makers and NGOs.

Geetha Devi T. V. is Project Coordinator (Honorary), Institute for Social and Ecological Studies (ISES), an NGO based in Kozhikode, Kerala, India, and an independent researcher. She began her academic career in the sciences and completed her postgraduate degree in botany. Subsequently, she moved into the field of human ecology and completed both her MPhil and PhD degrees from the School of Social Sciences, Mahatma Gandhi University, Kottayam, Kerala. She was Lecturer (temporary) of Human Ecology at the Social Sciences department for postgraduate and MPhil programmes. She became an affiliated scholar at the Interuniversity Centre for Social Science Research and Extension (IUCSSRE), M. G. University, for one-and-a-half years and submitted a working paper titled 'Sustainable Development and Environmental Policy Making: A Review'. She gained insights in Geo-spatial technology from the Dr. R. Satheesh Centre for Remote Sensing and GIS at the School of Environmental Sciences, M. G. University, and continued research to examine the role of GIS tools in environmental studies and completed training programmes at the National Remote Sensing Centre, Hyderabad. Her research interests include natural resource management, environmental studies, human ecology, the environment–development interface, sustainable development and political ecology. Her other interests include music and Indian philosophy.

'This is an epistemologically sound and methodologically unassailable study of the domain and dimensions of Human Ecology, a fast-growing interdisciplinary field of convergence research with thermodynamic depth and truth of entropy. Delving deep into the meaning of "value" as raised and deliberated upon across the existing thought systems like reform environmentalism, deep ecology, ecofeminism and social ecology, the study underscores the homologous processes of techno-economic development and the inevitable consequence of ecological degradation.

Unlike eco-philosophical literature bound by questions of human–nature dualism or scientific works confined to causal explanations, the present study focuses on the human agency–environment interface. It entrenches the irreducibility of value, politics and knowledge as three fundamental dimensions of human ecology. Quite convincingly the present study informs that human ecology is best understood by recognising the ontological inseparability of these dimensions, generally treated as independent facets in the extant literature. A brilliant combination of analysis and description, this work is eminently readable and educative.'

– **Rajan Gurukkal**, former Professor and Vice Chairman, Kerala State Higher Education Council, Thiruvananthapuram, India

'Bringing together the ethical, political and epistemic dimensions of human ecology that define a knowledge area, this book challenges the conventional wisdom on environmental challenges that we face today. Suggesting a critical new orientation towards environmental policies in a democratic framework, the author suggests new ways of understanding development that will be ethically justified. This justification finally comes out of a new politics that does not make a binary choice between ecology and development.'

– **P. Sanal Mohan**, Director, School of Social Sciences, Mahatma Gandhi University, Kottayam, India

'The book presents the complex interconnections between human agency and the environment. It is clearly written and well-argued. The critique at the beginning and the new proposals and claims that come at the end of the book are both firm and well-grounded. The interesting aspect of this book lies in its interdisciplinary approach; integrating both theory and case studies and closely analysing both failures and successes in environmental movement.'

– **A. Raghuramaraju**, Professor, Department of Humanities and Social Sciences, Indian Institute of Technology Tirupati, India

'A concise but critical effort to explicate human ecology as a disciplinary practice at the intersection of the natural and social sciences. A careful and sustained attention to the field is the primary approach used – one that the author characterises partly as a "textual analytic method" – and the effort is to develop the domain of human ecology along the constitutive dimensions of "value, politics and knowledge". It is not only a successful academic effort to transpose the terms of the author's own disciplinary location in natural science; it also creatively inserts itself into a pedagogic situation where environmental studies are approached as a cross-disciplinary terrain.'

– **Sasheej Hegde**, Professor of Sociology, University of Hyderabad, India

UNDERSTANDING HUMAN ECOLOGY

Knowledge, Ethics and Politics

Geetha Devi T. V.

Routledge
Taylor & Francis Group
LONDON AND NEW YORK

First published 2019
by Routledge
2 Park Square, Milton Park, Abingdon, Oxon OX14 4RN

and by Routledge
52 Vanderbilt Avenue, New York, NY 10017

Routledge is an imprint of the Taylor & Francis Group, an informa business

© 2019 Geetha Devi T. V.

The right of Geetha Devi T. V. to be identified as author of this work has been asserted by her in accordance with sections 77 and 78 of the Copyright, Designs and Patents Act 1988.

All rights reserved. No part of this book may be reprinted or reproduced or utilised in any form or by any electronic, mechanical, or other means, now known or hereafter invented, including photocopying and recording, or in any information storage or retrieval system, without permission in writing from the publishers.

Trademark notice: Product or corporate names may be trademarks or registered trademarks, and are used only for identification and explanation without intent to infringe.

British Library Cataloguing-in-Publication Data
A catalogue record for this book is available from the British Library

Library of Congress Cataloging-in-Publication Data
A catalog record for this book has been requested

ISBN: 978-1-138-05563-6 (hbk)
ISBN: 978-0-367-14020-5 (pbk)
ISBN: 978-0-429-02978-3 (ebk)

Typeset in Bembo
by Apex CoVantage, LLC

To my mentor
Prof (Dr) T. K. Ahmed Nizar
who showed me the path of Truth

CONTENTS

List of abbreviations ix
Preface and acknowledgements xi

PART I
Human ecology: the domain and its dimensions   1

   Introduction   3

PART II
Ethics   13

  1 Environmental scenario of the twentieth century: a historical sketch   15

  2 'Value' dynamics in the environmental thought systems   28

PART III
Politics   81

  3 'Environment' in the 'development' context: a historical inquiry   83

  4 The question of 'political' in environmental thought systems, movements and as a political process   100

PART IV
Knowledge   151

   5 The making of human ecology: a historical perspective   153

   6 'Human ecology' as a discipline: methodological reflections   181

PART V
Ethics, politics, knowledge: a multidimensional approach   199

   Conclusion   201

Bibliography   *207*
Index   *222*

ABBREVIATIONS

BNR   Bali Nirwana Resort
CPM   Communist Party (Marxist)
DGSS   *Dashauli Gram Swarajya Sangh*
EDF   Environmental Defense Fund
EPA   Environmental Protection Agency
FLCs   Forest Labour Co-operatives
FMG   Five-Member Committee
GPCB   Gujarat Pollution Control Board
GTCs   General Trading Companies
HEP   Human Exceptionalism Paradigm
ITTO   International Tropical Timber Organization
IUCN   International Union of the Conservation of Nature
JATAN   Japan Tropical Forest Action Network
KFRI   Kerala Forest Research Institute
KPL   Karnataka Pulpwood Ltd.
KSEB   Kerala State Electricity Board
KSSP   *Kerala Sastra Sahitya Parishad*
MAF   Million-acre feet
MIC   Methyl isocyanate
MNCs   Multinational Companies
MoEF   Ministry of Environment and Forests
MOSOP   Movement for the Survival of the Ogoni People
MP   Madhya Pradesh
NASS   *Narmada Asargrasta Sangharsha Samiti*
NBA   *Narmada Bachao Andolan*
NCA   Narmada Control Authority
NCEPC   National Committee on Environmental Planning and Coordination

Abbreviations

NDS	*Narmada Dharmagrastha Samiti*
NEP	New Environmental Paradigm
NEPA	National Environmental Policy Act
NGNS	*Narmada Ghati Navnirman Samiti*
NSP	Narmada Sagar Project
NWDT	Narmada Water Dispute Tribunal
NWDTA	NWDT Award
OBR	Ogoni Bill of Rights
PASS	*Parisara Asoothrana Samrakshana Samiti*
SPS	*Samaj Parivartan Samudaya*
SSP	Sardar Sarovar Project
SSV	Save Silent Valley
SVSPC	Silent Valley Scheme Protection Committee
UCC	Union Carbide Corporation
UCIL	Union Carbide India Limited
UNDP	United Nations Development Programme
WWF	World Wildlife Fund

PREFACE AND ACKNOWLEDGEMENTS

This book is a modified version of my doctoral thesis, for which I was awarded a degree in 2009. I completed my graduate and postgraduate work in the scientific discipline of botany, and this training in science has helped me to have a good scientific knowledge about the environmental issues around us. However, a concern about society and its problems prompted me to shift to the wider terrain of social sciences for my MPhil studies. My later engagement in the Social Sciences department at Mahatma Gandhi University, Kottayam, encouraged me to undertake a deeper enquiry into environmental issues, which culminated in this interdisciplinary study for my doctoral research. An inquisitiveness that evolved out of understanding human beings, nature and environment philosophically directed me to this study.

The in-depth lectures on social science methodology and critical social theories that I received at the School of Social Sciences from eminent scholars during my course work and in subsequent years helped me get a thorough foundation in interdisciplinary research. In later years, my teaching experience in human ecology and environmental history including guidance of postgraduate and MPhil dissertations at the School of Social Sciences helped expand my knowledge field to varied issues transcending disciplinary boundaries. The doctoral thesis was an attempt to understand the human–environment interacting sphere (the domain of human ecology) from a multidimensional framework. In this volume, two chapters (one and three) are added anew to situate the themes historically with clarity. The book covers a wide range of theoretical approaches that emerged in the latter half of the twentieth century and outlines a human ecological framework from a 'development' perspective. Thus, the book brings forth a new outlook in understanding and dealing with environmental issues. Prof. Bernhard Glaeser (president of German Society for Human Ecology), one of the evaluators of my PhD thesis, pointed out the potential of the thesis to be a book. I gratefully acknowledge him on this occasion.

Now, as the doctoral thesis has evolved into a book, I remember several faces with gratitude and I take this opportunity to acknowledge them here. My teachers at the School of Social Sciences need special mention. I express my deep gratitude to my professor and research supervisor as well as mentor, Dr T. K. Ahmed Nizar. Prof. Nizar always revealed to students through his own life how to be a perfect teacher, researcher, learner and, above all, a compassionate human being, rather than acting as a mere adviser. He taught me how to look critically not only at the research problem but at our own lives and our own ways of thinking as 'humans', which prompted me to go beyond the perceptions I had about the world and ourselves, which were founded merely on 'ego'. This 'critical eye' guided me in unfolding the analytical ability of my mental faculty that helped me to produce this volume.

I remember with much pleasure my acquaintance with Dr P. Sanal Mohan, who was first my teacher and then my colleague and friend later during my teaching period at the School of Social Sciences. He always remained a high-spirited scholar who inspired me through these years. I am extremely grateful to him for the great encouragement and support rendered to me in the preparation of this book at each stage and for the genuine interest shown in my career. I extend sincere thanks to my Professor Dr Rajan Gurukkal, with utmost respect, who has shown great interest in my career and who advised me to rewrite my thesis into a book. Dr S. Raju introduced me to the field of 'development' studies and I acknowledge him with gratitude. I need to mention the late Dr Muraleedharan, who showed his genius through mind-blowing classes and took care of his students with much affection. I remember with gratitude Ms Radhika, P., for the additional care in his absence.

I extend whole-hearted thanks to my friend Sheeba Vijayakumar for reading this book with a critical eye and for suggesting stylistic improvements. Above all, she has remained with me sincerely all through my difficult times. I gratefully acknowledge and appreciate the warm support rendered by the staff of Mahatma Gandhi University library and the departmental libraries of Social Sciences and Environmental Sciences (special thanks to Mr Gireesh, Ms Vidhu and Mr Abubacker) and TMAM library, Manganam, in the second phase of library work during book preparation.

I would like to express deep love towards my dearest ones – Unnimaya, Shalumon and Athulya – who instilled in me the warmth of life during the most difficult moments. Big thanks to my close friends Susan Simon, Anish R, Saji, Harsha Oommen, Poornima, Abeetha, Sr Prabha and Brahmaputhran for their unconditional support and motivation in this endeavour. I also remember gladly my friends, Nancy, Saju Y, Jubin, Elizabeth, Lalcy aunty, Anns, Indu, K and Binu Abraham, who always encouraged my research efforts. I am indebted to the Director of Pope John Paul Bhavan, Athirampuzha, Fr Jose Parappillil for providing me accommodation and facilities during the preparation of the book and to the Warden, Sr Sicily and Sr Rosy for treating me with motherly affection. I am obliged to my parents and other family members for all kinds of support rendered to me through these years, especially to my late father, who greatly helped improve my writing skills earlier in my career.

PART I
Human ecology
The domain and its dimensions

INTRODUCTION

The book is an attempt to characterise the domain of human agency–environment interaction (i.e., the domain of human ecology) from a multidimensional point of view. The emergence of innumerable environmental problems due to human interaction with nature has made it imperative to understand this domain. The domain of human ecology can be defined as one which human ecology as a science purports to explain. In other words, this domain provides a representation of a world of interconnected events, for example, real situations of environmental changes created by humans that take place in the ecosystem or have the possibility of happening in the future. This domain can also be represented in terms of the features that limit the possibilities of the events that may occur there. The nature of these events is largely determined by the kinds of intersection formed by the relation between human agency and environment. The notion of human agency mentioned here is to be understood in terms of the capacity of human actions to produce adverse or beneficial effects in the domain. As effective human actions are largely bound to the structures of the social systemic life of human beings, human agency is a complex notion. Thus, when human actors function as government officials, corporate bodies, legislators, members of communities and so on, they become part of those institutions, and such institutional roles and positions form human agency. What influences human actors as individuals or as social agents is not directly evident in many cases. These questions can be explored only through a characterisation of the domain under investigation. However, since human ecology as a science would limit the notion within the boundaries of explanation, it will not be able to fulfil the purpose of this inquiry, that is, to characterise the domain in the sense just detailed. The meaning of human actions, the value humans attribute to their environment, the relations of power in which the actions and their consequences are implicated – all make the domain so complex as to demand a more comprehensive approach to understanding it. Thus, the book proposes imagining the domain of human–environment interaction from a multidimensional perspective. In this attempt, the ethical (value questions) and the political find equal emphasis alongside the scientific in the characterisation of this domain.

A basic assumption of the book is the idea of interconnectedness, mentioned earlier. An understanding of this notion would help the inquirer to relocate the significance of the social life of human beings as forming part of a larger ecosystem. In other words, it underscores the ecological significance of human actions. A realisation of this role of human beings would require a redefinition of the notion of human agency, which has many implications as far as environmental issues are considered. That is, the socially mediated actions of humans need to be treated at another level as interventions in an ecosystem involving non-human members, with the potential to bring about changes in the ecosystem that cannot be understood from a social perspective alone.

In addition, most environmental issues with ethical and political implications generally arise in the 'development' context; understanding it from that perspective is of utmost importance. Development ideas pervaded the world consequent to the adoption of economic policies worldwide in the twentieth century, especially those of neo-liberalisation and globalisation policies, which have serious adverse environmental consequences. Thus, how human actors deal with environmental situations is highly influenced by the economic and political ideologies followed worldwide. Hence, a serious inquiry into human-induced environmental issues (that is, the human–environment intersecting area) cannot be delimited to the boundaries of a specific region or a particular nation.

The present work examines the following aspects pertaining to the domain of human–environment interaction:

(1) The dynamics of the questions of 'value' as raised and deliberated upon in existing thought systems, such as reform environmentalism, deep ecology, ecofeminism and social ecology.
(2) The 'political' dimension of the issues arising from the domain, as is evident in the lived experiences of the affected people and their expressions in various environmental movements.
(3) The nature of explanations provided by various multidisciplinary theoretical efforts that broadly agree with the goals of what can be termed human ecology.

Through these points, the book aims to establish the irreducibility of the dimensions of value and politics to each other and both of these to a scientific account of the events.

The attempt to view the three dimensions of value, politics and knowledge as characteristics of the domain that human ecology as a discipline addresses, and to integrate these aspects to inform an adequate understanding of the domain, can be claimed to be a novel approach in comparison to the existing studies on the area. The treatments accorded to these aspects in the available works present them as independent, rather than mutually exclusive fields of study. The eco-philosophical literature centres around questions regarding value judgement that have a bearing on the debates on human–nature dualism. These works adopt either a human-centred approach or a nature-centred one, to which the former is attributed an instrumental value and the latter intrinsic. The studies addressing the political aspect of environmental problems generally fail to contextualise the political struggles in terms of human agency–environment interaction, or in other words, these accounts overlook the political intricacies arising from these situations as determined by power relations among human (social) agents that will have a bearing on the environment. Scientific works in the area of human ecology confine themselves to the discovery of causal connections in order to provide an explanation of the process under study. The present study identifies the three dimensions and represents them as the defining features of the domain that intersects the human agency–environment. Another point of divergence relates to the status of human ecology. Human ecology as presented in the historical literature provides us with some ideas constructed from the sociological and the geographical viewpoints with a biological orientation. While these ideas throw some light on the nature of the domain theoretically, they do not qualify for providing an explanatory framework adequate to the domain. The present work tries to situate human ecological theorising within the theoretical works by other disciplines of similar or related concern. This is to locate the discipline reasonably in the interdisciplinarity formed by inquiries with family resemblances among each other.

This study proposes to conduct a conceptual level research and follows, in part, a textual analytic method. The philosophical literature of the 1960s and 1970s, study reports of NGOs and various descriptive accounts of environmental movements that have emerged in and around India, Asia and worldwide form the textual material for the study. The study also relies on actual research works conducted in the areas of ecology, some versions of human ecology and natural history, with a view to developing a larger theoretical framework for situating the discipline of human ecology. The choice of the studies is guided by the idea of what constitutes the domain of human ecology. The analysis is aimed at culling relevant, social scientific and ecological insights that would give the direction in delineating the features of the domain that may characteristically enter into the definition of the discipline of human ecology. The book presents ideas in such a way that arguments are analytically examined by first surveying all available debates about them, followed by an account that summarises the author's observations at the end of each part: the nature of human–nature relationship in each thought system that represents the ethical dimension (in Part II), analysis of the conflicts of human living in various life contexts that elicit the political dimension (in Part III) and a critical analysis of the development of the idea of ecology and human ecology that forms the epistemic dimension (in Part IV).

As a prelude to this study, it is relevant to familiarise the readers with the concepts that guide the discussion. The terms 'nature' and 'environment' are generally used interchangeably; it is a contested area. In this study, there is reference to 'nature' as an all-encompassing entity, but the main focus here is on 'environment', which is defined as *any part of nature, including biosphere, atmosphere, hydrosphere and lithosphere, that forms the living and non-living surroundings of all living beings, where human (or social) agents come to interact with, directly or indirectly, and transform it for human purposes, in the process of which human beings themselves or other living beings can be adversely affected.* Another term that needs elucidation is 'environmental problem' (environmental issue), which is a concept that directs the study; hence, the question of how to perceive it is of much importance here. In the context of human agency–environment interaction, an 'environmental problem' is conceived as *any disturbance created in the living and non-living environment of human beings by the harmful activities of human (or social) agents that will have repercussions in the lives of beings such as plants, animals and human beings themselves and also in those parts of nature such as mountains, rocks, rivers, wetlands, lakes and so on.* With this background, the author presumes that all instances of human action that can have an adverse impact on the habitat of other living beings and on the environment will be addressed by the domain of human ecology. This conversely means that instances of any natural calamity, which are not traceable to human actions, will not fall within the purview of human ecology.

Situating the book

In this section, only literature that either claims to take an integrated approach to the domain of human ecology or focuses particularly on the human–environment interacting sphere is included. Works that undertake a theoretical endeavour on the human–environment interacting sphere are very limited in number, and the available works do not adequately address this domain. Though many researchers have placed emphasis on understanding the domain in an interdisciplinary manner, these attempts end up in identifying it as science or social science discipline; the actual point of establishing linkage of human agency with environment is not evident in these works. Moreover, although many researchers begin their inquiry with environmental problems as the reference point, most of them fail to make a proper theorisation of the domain.

Marten (2001) conceives human ecology as science and understands human–environment interaction as the interaction between the human social system and the rest of the ecosystem. While the social component of human is identified, it is termed a social system, which is defined as everything about people, their population and the psychology and social organisations that shape their behaviour; however, this is not developed further. He focuses on how people and the environment function together by tracing chains of effects through ecosystems and human society; hence, the book forms a practical guide to human actions, as claimed by the author. Bennett's (1996) book also falls into this category. He recognises environmental problems as the result of human behaviour, where the realm of interaction with nature (or dependence on nature, as he conceives) is identified as complex 'socio-natural systems'. The study by Dyball (2010) belongs to this category of science; it approaches the 'wicked' problems in the environment from the perspective of a human ecologist, that is, from a transdisciplinary perspective. In other words, it takes up the methodological challenge of blending knowledge from different disciplinary sources and other ways of knowing as well to produce a coherent new knowledge that differs from the sum of its parts. Moreover, it adopts the accepted notions of human ecology – that it is about the interrelationships between humans, their cultures and their ecosystems. However, the study recognises the normative aspect that distinguishes it from other branches of science and the power dimension of all decision-making and human action. The study is illustrated by an example of the Snowy Mountains Programme, which used the methods of human ecology and the key principles of a transdisciplinary inquiry such *complexity*, *realism*, *partiality*, *pluralism*, *provisionally*, *ethical* and *critical*.

Moran's (2010) book, titled *Environmental Social Science*, focuses on human–environment interaction and realises it as a cross-disciplinary area. As observed before, an effort to theorise the domain is lacking, and the book rather makes accessible the theories, methods and concepts from both social science and natural science disciplines, across disciplines. Though Kormondy and Brown (1998) also take an integrated approach to human ecology, they end up in blending biological ecology with social sciences approaches. The book edited by Lopes and Begossi (2011) tries to link human beings to their environment through social, cultural, economic and ecological processes in the context of the accelerating negative changes currently being witnessed on our planet. The approach taken in this book claims to be only one of many ways of defining human ecology. Case studies from different branches of human ecology are shown as feasible alternatives to understanding the interactions of human culture and behaviour with the natural environment from all parts of the world. Along with this, theoretical aspects are included and examined in every case, including the evolution of culture, values and webs of information within cultures.

The article by Rasmussen and Finn Arler (2010) deviates and focuses on the problems involved when one tries to study the issues that lie at the human–environment interface. The authors identify problems at three levels – sociological, institutional and epistemological – that make the study of interdisciplinary studies difficult. The study focuses on exposing the inability to carry out interdisciplinary studies at the human–environment interface but does not advance any constructive suggestions. While the paper emphasises the differences between disciplines in terms of methodology, ontology and epistemology, it fails to put forward feasible suggestions for solving the issues. Williams et al. (2012) claim to have taken a radically new direction in their edited book, compared to the existing perspectives, to study the relation between natural and social environments. This book is concerned with intercultural and indigenous approaches and explores the power of indigenous and traditional people's epistemologies both to critique and to complement insights from modernity and post-modernity. This book seems to take an alternative and unique approach for understanding and tackling environmental issues.

The book by Glaeser (1995) goes in line with the present one to a certain extent as far as the orientation of the book is considered. He begins his inquiry with environmental problems as the thrust of the research. Moreover, the author recognises human ecology as an area of research that can be placed between natural and social sciences and characterises the area with a definite social science component. He also distinguishes this research area from the conventional academic scientific research disciplines. However, the book does not construct a theoretical framework for the domain of human agency–environment in the manner the present one does; rather, the book focuses on the philosophical and social science aspects of human ecology. Further, it tries to find out the relationship between environmental ethics and environmental policy and also to explore what ecologically sustainable development is with the support of case studies.

Thus, we can see a lacuna while examining studies that are pertaining to the human–environment interacting sphere in particular. Works that lie on par with the present volume are not available when the main objective of the present book (i.e., perceiving the domain of human ecology in an in-depth way) is considered. The actual point of establishing linkage between human agency and environment is missing in most of the works, and the novelty of the current work lies in establishing this connection in a reasonable manner. This can be verbalised in the following way. Various kinds of modern institutions give rise to human agency, through which diverse modes of human–environment interactions take place in different fields of life. Hence, the structure and nature of these institutions will determine the role of human agency pertaining to each field. This is referred to in this book as the 'socially mediated actions of humans'. Those actions of humans that are capable of making (adverse) impacts on the environment result in environmental issues. Hence, this attempt to understand the domain that human ecology addresses, from a multidimensional point of view, seems to be a promising one, considering the scope it has in tackling environmental issues and in making decision-making and policy drafting more effective.

Chapter presentation

The book consists of five parts, including an introductory part. The first and fifth parts stand alone, while each of the other three parts contains two chapters. The second part examines existing literature that emerged in the 1960s and 1970s, such as reform environmentalism, deep ecology, ecofeminism and social ecology, which were offered as various socio-economic and political critiques of modern ways of living and have resulted in large-scale exploitation of nature and unintended consequences in the functioning of the ecosystem. This literature is largely philosophical in nature, and different schools of thought raise important value-oriented questions in their approaches to the issues that emerge in human–environment interaction. The attempt here is to elucidate the value dynamics inherent in each system of thought, which would provide us with analytical tools for identifying and analysing the value orientation as reflected in the actions of human agents in any conceivable environmental setting. Reform environmentalism considered humanity as part of the ecological system and followed an anthropocentric perspective. While the conservation and preservation movements of earlier times highlighted the importance of nature for its wilderness, the reformist group showed a concern for 'quality-of-life issues', which reflected the shift in the way life was conducted by people in the late modern period and the corresponding value system. Deep ecology attributes intrinsic value to all human and non-human life on Earth and conceives of all beings in nature as having equal right to live and blossom. Deep ecologists base their principles of analysis and norms of judgement on the notion of intrinsic value. Ecofeminism advances a value-oriented approach to nature and women by arguing for their liberation from dominant forces like patriarchy and capitalism. The political overtone in their analysis is only subtly presupposed by the alternative value system they propose. In some cases, at least explicit mentions of 'feminine' virtues like care, friendship and love etc. are made as opposed to the values of the male-dominated social world. Social ecology emphasises the processes of natural evolution and finds value in culture (called 'second nature') supposed to have evolved from the (first) nature's evolutionary processes. It traces nearly all present ecological issues to deep-seated social ramifications like hierarchy, dominance, patriarchy, classes, the State and others. Therefore, the ways human beings deal with each other as social beings are shown to be crucial to addressing the ecological crisis. Social ecology advances an ethics of complementarities in which human beings must play a supportive role in perpetuating the integrity of the biosphere, as potentially, at least, the most conscious products of natural evolution. Part II is divided into two chapters (1 and 2). Chapter 1 tries to situate these approaches in the larger schema of environmental scenarios of the twentieth century. These thought systems emerged as part of the response to modern developmental activities and consequent environmental deterioration. In this context, Chapter 1 provides an account of the conservation and preservation movements that started from the eighteenth century, transition to the idea of environmentalism after World War II and the pragmatic changes that took place in the political arena corresponding to the shift in environmental concern. Chapter 2 elicits the value dimension inherent in the thought systems or approaches mentioned above.

Part III presents a descriptive account, randomly selected, of environmental movements worldwide by letting this account naturally highlight the political dimension involved in environmental issues, that is, of the events that occur in the domain that human ecology addresses. It focuses on the nature of political intricacies involved in the actual, concrete situations of social conflicts centred on environmental issues. Selected case studies belonging to four different classes of issues are analysed here. They are (1) concern for protecting biodiversity and endangered species of plants and animals, (2) the case of governments or other external forces denying the people their rights to use forests and other natural resources, on which they depend for sustenance, (3) displacement of local or indigenous people by governments in the name of development activities and (4) exploitation of water and other resources of a region by multinational companies, putting the lives of local people in trouble or denying their right to hygienic environments necessary for their well-being. The distinctive feature of this perspective is identified as the presence of a 'power factor' that controls the relations between people in a specific manner. The complexity of any social conflict seems to be determined by the nature and number of powerful agents, who have access to wealth or the capacity for political lobbying, involved in it. When the numbers of these social agents are numerous and the relations between them take on multifarious dimensions as determined by power, it results in irreparable consequences in both people's lives and the natural environment. Thus, the movements that arose from this crisis demand political solutions designed to ensure the protection of individual rights as assured by the constitution in a democratic set-up. As a result, governments are forced to intervene in issues in order to resolve them, though sometimes government itself form a party in generating the issues and often resorts to strategies such as rearrangements in existing institutional structures, modifications to policy frameworks and enactment of laws. Thus, the political dimension of environmental issues, which these movements address, forms a distinguishing feature of the sphere of human–environment interaction. It is also important to enquire into the circumstances that caused these environmental movements to emerge worldwide in the 1970s. These movements are a response to the relentless pursuit of economic growth that started in the mid-twentieth century, which can be traced to the idea of 'progress', the eighteenth-century precursor of the notion of the 'development' idea. This part comprises two chapters (3 and 4). Chapter 3 traces the history of the 'development' idea and the debate that links issues of 'environment' to those of 'development'. The fourth chapter provides an account of environmental conflicts in India and worldwide, followed by an analysis of these case studies.

In Part IV, an effort is made to characterise the domain of human–environment interaction from an explanatory point of view by situating it in available theoretical and empirical frameworks of the ecology and social science disciplines, for the purpose of acquiring objective knowledge of the domain. Alternatively, it addresses the question of explaining the events or phenomena that occur at the intersection of humans and the environment. With this purpose, we examine the theoretical efforts (of an interdisciplinary character) made by a number of scholars, including social scientists – that is, the various proposed definitions of human ecology that are historically given by sociologists, biologists and geographers as well as ecologists. The methodological and conceptual issues, the methodological shift and theory building in ecology and references to its developmental history, are all examined for developing the methodology for studying the processes at human agency–environment interacting sphere. The questions related to methodology and the subject matter of the discipline are debatable issues in ecological science. Some ecologists point towards the importance of studying natural patterns rather than individual facts or models. The revival of natural history studies is also an important recommendation. Observation as followed in field ecology is highlighted as an important way of understanding patterns in ecology. This study takes seriously the suggestion for pattern finding, the concern being different from that of natural history studies, the predecessor of ecology. While ecology focuses on concepts like ecological succession, dynamics of communities, food chains, food webs, ecological niches and so on, this study applies pattern finding in a larger unit that interconnects flora, fauna and geographical and other physical features. That is, our attempt here is to reconstruct natural history studies based on the key idea of 'ecosystem'. By tracing these entire factors, one can presuppose the historical connections resulting in the changes (natural) that occurred in relation to any specific natural happenings, for example, any catastrophe, extinction of species, desiccation of river and others. The effort here is to connect the changes created in the environment due to human actions in order to find out certain patterns. Two groups of case studies, one from natural history and the other from human ecological inquiries drawn from different disciplines (such as archaeology, geology and geography), are exemplified. A consideration of the general methodological orientation and the specific discipline-based methods employed in these works may contribute to imagining the discipline of human ecology on a broad base and recognising the inherently interdisciplinary character of human ecological endeavours. With regard to theorising on human agency, innumerable factors that are conventionally considered in isolation in inquiries of independent social science disciplines enter into the account of human actions. A third major component of human ecology is the 'historical'. The historical method will be an essential part of its methodology since any relevant data in human ecology is spread along a very long timescale. This part has two chapters (5 and 6). Chapter 5 is an analysis of theoretical insights provided by several scholars – social scientists as well as ecologists – in the form of definitions of human ecology. The sixth chapter is a discussion on the construction of the methodological underpinnings of the discipline of human ecology, taking insights from the case studies discussed.

On the basis of analysis carried out in the foregoing parts of the book, Part V recommends a multidimensional approach to studying events in the domain of human ecology as well as solving problems arising thereof. In a sense, it aims to arrive at a theory of understanding of the happenings in the domain by integrating the dimensions of value, politics and knowledge into a holistic perspective. These three aspects are internal to any problem that arises in the human–environment interface. Therefore, a correct representation of environmental problems should culminate in an integrated account of these three aspects.

It is presumed that these dimensions can be accounted for in the policy making processes of the government while dealing with the issues that might affect the environment. The inadequacies that arose from insufficient policy guidelines often resulted in drastic environmental issues that have many ethical and political implications on a wider scale. Therefore, it is argued that the issues belonging to the development–environment interface (or human agency–environment intersection) need to be addressed from a different perspective, one that will take into account these concerns. That is, if the questions regarding the value dynamics and political aspects of environmental problems, adequately informed by the explanatory part, get translated into environmental policies and laws and their implementation by the democratic structures of the government is ensured, then one can hope to solve such problems in an assured manner. In conclusion, the multidimensional framework that this book brings forth will be a viable platform for approaching environmental problems in the future.

PART II
Ethics

This part presents value-orientation as one of the salient features that characterises the domain of human–environment interaction. In human engagement with nature, whenever a harmful event occurs in the ecosystem as a consequence of human activities (e.g., large-scale destruction of natural resources such as forests, water and land, modification of natural areas for construction purposes, pollution of atmosphere and so on), the context advances a fundamental question of value embedded in that activity. The question of value in this context may lead to a reflection on the character of the social practices humans interweave with nature and the implications these have in their immediate surroundings or in natural settings at large. Thus, the domain opens up the question of evaluating human actions, to the extent these can adversely affect beings. The dimension of value in the sphere of human–environment interaction is irreducible to other dimensions. Therefore, reflections on this dimension deserve independent consideration.

It is both necessary and sufficient for an inquiry in this area to evaluate existing strands of thought that provide an idea of the moral status of any situation involving humans and nature. The sources of such an inquiry lead to the literature that emerged in the 1960s and 1970s, which represent a particular stage of response to highly industrialised and urbanised ways of living, especially the twentieth-century environmental scenario in the United States. These works consist of various socio-economic and political critiques of modern ways of living that have resulted in large-scale exploitation of nature and unprecedented damages in the functions of the ecosystem. The major sources of this literature include reform environmentalism, deep ecology, ecofeminism and social ecology, which are philosophical in nature. These literatures uphold the environmental concern of the period as necessitated by then-existing political and cultural circumstances. The emergence of different thought systems or approaches in solving the issues from the field seems to emanate from the ideas of nineteenth-century conservation and preservation movements. These approaches have varied theoretical positions based on certain value-oriented assumptions about the sphere of human–environment interaction. The value perceptions of these thoughts differ according to the basic principles that guide their ethical thinking.

Reform environmentalism represents a period of shift in concern towards nature that resulted from changed perceptions of value in social life in the second half of the twentieth century. Deep ecology evaluates a situation by emphasising the 'intrinsic value' of all natural beings, while ecofeminism attributes equal value (status) to men and women that will have a bearing on their relation to nature. Social ecology puts weight on the scientific explanation of evolutionary theory and finds moral value in imagining the social world as emanating from natural evolution. Though these viewpoints differ from each other in terms of the approach adopted in their analysis of human–environment contexts, all of them conceive of human agents as moral agents under obligation to fulfil their duty towards nature and other beings.

To contextualise these thought systems in the environmental scenario of the twentieth century, this part begins with an outline of the early conservation and preservation movements, followed by a shift to the idea of environmentalism in the first chapter and an account of the literature on reform environmentalism, deep ecology, ecofeminism and social ecology in the second chapter. By analytically following the arguments put forward by these different approaches, these chapters aim to identify recurrent themes and propose showing that these themes converge on the question of value despite divergence among the approaches.

1
ENVIRONMENTAL SCENARIO OF THE TWENTIETH CENTURY

A historical sketch

1.1 The nineteenth-century conservation movement

The history of human concern with nature or environment starts roughly in the eighteenth century, beginning with conservation and preservation activities, gradually shifting to environmental campaigns in the late nineteenth century[1] and then moving to mass movements in the last decades of the twentieth century and in the early twenty-first century. The ways in which human beings of earlier centuries viewed interventions in nature and the measures they adopted to minimise or regulate the use of natural resources have much significance in an inquiry about the twentieth-century environmental scenario. Earlier perceptions about the protection and conservation of nature and ways of utilising natural resources have greatly influenced twentieth-century environmental philosophy, ideologies and political positions, among others.

There are varying opinions among historians as to the origin of the conservation movement[2] and origin of the term 'conservation'. One observation is that it was first used in English in the 1700s to refer to the 'conservancy' of London's Thames River (Krech et al., 2004: 262). Some scholars refer to the publication of George Perkins Marsh's *Man and Nature: Or, Physical Geography as Modified by Human Action* in 1864 as the clearest beginning of the movement. Marsh was also considered the first environmental historian; in *Man and Nature*, he asserted that overcutting of forests led to erosion, loss of soil fertility and an unchecked destruction of civilisation (262). Mumford refers to *Man and Nature* as 'the fountain-head of the conservation movement' (1931: 78). However, some historians have noted that conservation measures were adopted by colonial administrations much earlier than the publication of *Man and Nature* and that Marsh's theories were greatly influenced by early findings about deforestation, especially in the tropical areas subjected to European colonisation from the fifteenth century onward (Krech et al.,

2004: 262). Marsh's correspondence with Dietrich Brandis, the German forester who in 1864 founded the Indian Forest Department, serves as evidence of colonial precedence in conservation activities (262).

There is a general perception that the conservation movement emerged in the late eighteenth century with the appearance of a significant political concern for the environment, which prompted governments in Europe and North America to begin to establish institutions and policies aimed at conserving natural resources. This was a response to the dramatic changes that occurred all over the world as a result of industrialisation and urbanisation, referred to as environmentalism.[3] Global industrialisation altered the natural world through new methods of resource extraction, production and transportation (Guha, 2000: 4). European economic growth also impacted the natural environments of Asia, Africa and North America and led to major changes in the rural economy (4). History says that it is European settlers who encountered the relatively pristine environment of the Americas in the 1600s and turned it into a world of agriculture, industry and urbanism (Koppes, 1988: 230). By the 1890s, there was widespread recognition that old patterns of economic development needed drastic change. Koppes observed that the American environment in 1900 reflected three reigning assumptions about the use of natural resources that had existed since the early 1600s (231). Firstly, Americans believed that an abundance of natural resources existed in an unclaimed state. Secondly, they believed that natural resources were exhaustible. The depletion of natural resources in the early period exemplifies this, though there were shortages of firewood as early as 1638 in Boston and by the 1700s in most Eastern cities, but one could get it from other mountain ranges. It was in the late 1800s, in the context of the shortage of natural resources like timber, that a serious threat was felt and an economic imperative was created for conservation.[4] Thirdly, Americans believed that it was best to use natural resources immediately. The basic assumption of this belief was that people who had done the hard work of converting the wilderness into usable resources should reap the benefit of their labour as soon as possible. Conserving for future generations was not an accepted philosophy, especially when capitalism's emphasis on turning a quick profit worked against long-term calculations (231–2).

Compared to Europe, conservation groups in the United States were among the pioneers in conservationism. Though rapid industrialisation occurred in Britain in the late eighteenth and early nineteenth centuries, there was little opposition to this development.[5] The precedence of America in conservation matters was strengthened by the argument that conservation in fact was an American 'invention',[6] though it is also argued that American conservation was heavily influenced by German forestry and conservation policies in other parts of Europe and even in India and South Africa.[7] In the United States, the second half of the nineteenth century marked a vital transition from a pre-industrialised society to the modern world of cities, mass consumption, cars and so on (Hjelmar, 1996: 75). Americans tended to regard everything around them – the land, its natural resources and their own labour – as potential commodities that might fetch a profit in the market. The Homestead Act of 1862 (by which one could acquire title to 160 acres simply by making it productive) forms an important statement of this discourse (74). Hjelmar points out that in this turbulent period the cultural conduciveness towards conservationism grew and the cognitive basis for conservation organisations was formed (75). 'Prior to the 1890s, natural resource use was based upon the principles of economic laissez-faire and Social Darwinism and had flourished upon the contemporary myths of resource super abundance and the manifest destiny of the American people' (O'Riordan, 1971: 156). By the end of the nineteenth century, the demand for reform had increased, and it soon became evident that society could not reduce the social and environmental ills of industrial society without using the power of the central state (Hjelmar, 1996: 78). Consequently, the conception of the state changed in this period, which was later labelled as 'the progressive era'.[8]

Three ideas were dominant in Progressive era conservation thinking – efficiency, equity and aesthetics (Koppes, 1988: 233–5). The efficiency school resorted to modernising and managerial techniques to manage natural resources against the short-run practices of the past. Equity advocates stressed that natural resources, which belonged to all the people, should be retained in public control in order to ensure that the benefits of resource development were fairly distributed. Supporters of aesthetics campaigned to preserve great scenic wonders from ruinous development. Although most Progressive era conservationists subscribed to all three ideas, they differed on their emphases, and these approaches often proved incompatible. The developmental ethos of the efficiency and equity schools co-existed uneasily with aesthetics, the desire to preserve areas of natural beauty or scientific importance (237).

American conservationism was greatly inspired by nineteenth-century romanticism. American poets like Emerson and Thoreau, and British poets like Ruskin and Wordsworth, influenced people through their poems to have a wilderness-oriented view of nature for its beauty and potential for spiritual enlightenment. The first organisation based on conservation ideas was the Williamstown Alpine Club, founded in 1863 in Massachusetts; it was followed by similar organisations, all with the principal mission of protecting specific areas for their aesthetic and recreational qualities (Hjelmar, 1996: 75). Other such groups were the Commons, Footpaths and Open Spaces Preservation Society (founded in 1865) and the National Trust (founded in 1895) in Britain (Sandbach, 1980: 21). In France, the first preservation group was founded as early as 1857, while in most other countries conservation groups were founded around the turn of the century (Hjelmar, 1996: 99, note 3). The writings of Wordsworth, Ruskin, Morris and Carpenter helped inspire the establishment of an array of environmental societies in the late nineteenth century.

> These included the Commons Preservation Society, begun in 1865 to prevent the encroachment of cities on woodland and heath used by communities for recreation; the Society for the protection of Ancient Buildings, founded by William Morris himself in 1877; the Lake District Defence Society, stoutly in the Wordsworth-Ruskin lineage, which was formed in 1883; the Selborne League, created in 1885 for the protection of rare birds, beautiful plants and

threatened landscapes and named for the great eighteenth century naturalist Gilbert White of Selborne and the Coal Smoke Abatement Society, influenced by Edward Carpenter's writings and started in 1898 as an independent pressure group to make the government enforce pollution control laws on errant factories. Preceding all of these was the Scottish Rights of Way Society, formed in 1843 to protect walking areas around the city of Edinburgh.

(Guha, 2000: 16)

It was in the 1880s and 1890s that conservation movements really became powerful and several organisations were formed, such as American Ornithological Union in 1883, the Audubon Society in 1886 and the Sierra Club in 1892 (Hjelmar, 1996: 75). In 1886, George Bird Grinnell took the initiative to form the country's first bird preservation organisation, the Audubon Society. It was formed against the fact that, at the beginning of the twentieth century, there were no laws to control the hunting of birds and animals. Problems such as the destructive effects of predators and habitat destruction also concerned the Society. The first Audubon Society lapsed in 1888 but formed a corporation, National Audubon Society, in 1905 for the Protection of Wild Birds and Animals. This happened as a consequence of the outrage of a group in Massachusetts, the majority of them women, against the continued killing of birds for making women's hats; this got its legislative victory in 1910 (Conkin, 2007: 230).

The Sierra Club was a San Francisco-based organisation concerned with preserving the redwoods and high peaks of the Sierras (Benton and Short, 1999: 114). John Muir was the co-founder,[9] President of the Sierra Club and the leading ideological force in the organisation around the turn of the century. Muir questioned the supremacy of man in nature as taught by the Industrial Revolution; this belief soon became the cornerstone of the organisation and continued to be a vital part of the ideology of the Sierra Club (Hjelmar, 1996: 75). The exploration and mapping of the Sierra was a primary concern of the Club. Their concern was that wilderness areas should be conserved and reserved for recreational purposes. The membership of the Sierra Club was 20,000 in 1959, rose to 54,000 in 1970 and had increased to over 500,000 by 1995 (Benton and Short, 1999: 114). Muir authored innumerable articles and lectures about the American wilderness and was, in the early twentieth century, instrumental in the establishment of some of America's greatest national parks, including General Grant, Sequoia and Yosemite (Kuzmiak, 1991: 269).

Another influential wilderness thinker since Muir was Aldo Leopold, the author of *A Sand County Almanac* (1949). He became a cornerstone of the conservation movement. An advocate of wilderness preservation, he was instrumental in establishing the Gila Wilderness Area in New Mexico during the 1920s (Kuzmiak, 1991: 270). This was the first national forest–wilderness system. He helped found the Wilderness Society in 1935, an autonomous pressure group that embraced both a philosophical credo and a practical programme to protect wild areas and keep them untouched by mining, industry, logging, roads and other such threats (Guha, 2000: 55); the Society also focused on protecting public lands in the United States (Kuzmiak, 1991: 270).

Another important aspect with a significant role in the formation of conservationism as a body of thought was the emerging scientific discourse (Hjelmar, 1996: 76; also, see Guha, 2000: 6, 25–43). The branch of science coined as ecology by Ernst Haeckel in 1866 soon spread to American natural science. On the one side, the new science developed a better understanding of the fragility of the natural system and an increased capacity for precise measurement of environmental dynamics; however, on the other, it meant that science could exercise an even greater authority in man's dealings with nature (Hjelmar, 1996: 77). A large number of the people who founded the Sierra Club were natural scientists, and they saw it as an opportunity to enhance the possibilities for drawing maps, collecting samples and organising the scientific community in order to establish a library for geology (76–7). Scientific conservation, which aims to manage nature and natural resources efficiently in the long run, chose to go along with industrial society by taming its excesses, out of the realisation that without careful and expert guidance, industrialisation would rapidly use up resources (Guha, 2000: 6). By the middle of the nineteenth century, the centralisation of political authority and the formation of nation–states allowed experts to intervene more broadly, on a national scale, in the planning and management of natural resources (Guha, 2000: 27). Internationally, a number of Acts were passed based on the ideology of scientific conservation in this period (28). They are as follows: (1) in 1859, the government of the Cape Colony of Southern Africa passed the Forest and Herbiage Protection Act, allowing the state to intervene and take over areas of veld and forest threatened with destruction, (2) in 1860, the governor–general of colonial Java formed a committee to plan forest legislation for the island, the epicentre of the Netherland's overseas empire; laws protecting Java's forests and affirming state control over them were passed in 1865 (also the year of the first Indian Forest Act), (3) in 1862, the French promulgated the first of a series of ordinances designed to create forest reserves in their colonies in Cochin China (present-day Vietnam) and (4) the 1870s witnessed a flurry of forest-related activities in the British colony of Australia. Thus, the province of Victoria appointed a Royal Forestry Commission in 1871, and South Australia passed a Forest Tree Act in 1873 (28). In 1872, by an Act of Congress, the first national park in the US, Yellowstone National Park, was created with the recommendation that it become a natural outdoor laboratory for the study of earth and life sciences (Hjelmar, 1996: 77). Hjelmar points out that scientific discourse also played an important role in this decision.

Conservationists established a foothold in American politics in 1901, when President Theodore Roosevelt delineated plans to Congress for resource management.[10] Conservation became the dominant resource strategy of the government during Roosevelt's tenure, as illustrated by the policies of the new governmental agencies (Gottlieb, 1993: 24). Roosevelt, who was fascinated by nature, did more than any other President before him to elevate environmental issues to the national level (Kuzmiak, 1991: 269). During his administration, the word 'conservation' came into official use at a time when there was not enough reforestation, vast quantities of top soil were being washed into the sea, lakes and rivers were being polluted by mining operations and the passenger pigeon, Carolina paroquet and heath hen were almost extinct. From 14 March 1903 to 4 March 1909, Roosevelt recognised 51 wildlife refuges (269).

Gifford Pinchot, who was considered the father of American conservation,[11] acquired his early training abroad, at the French Forestry School at Nancy, and later through travels to Germany and Switzerland; he influenced the President to expand the federal government's conservation programme (Krech et al., 2004: 265). As a result, a number of conservation measures were taken over the next few years. They included:

(1) The National Reclamation Act, in 1902, which authorised the Secretary of the Interior to construct reservoirs in the arid regions of the West and to sell the resulting irrigated cropland to settlers (265); the Reclamation Service promoted scientific methods like irrigation, storage, power generation and flood control (Gottlieb, 1993: 22).
(2) In 1905, the Forest Service was created with Pinchot as its first Chief Forester; it combined the supervisory and enforcement responsibilities for the forest reserves that had been scattered previously through several offices into a single bureaucracy (Krech et al., 2004: 265).
(3) The establishment of Yale Forestry School in 1900, in recognition of the government's growing need for scientifically trained foresters (265).
(4) The 1906 American Antiquities Act, authorising the President 'to declare . . . objects of historic or scientific interest . . . situated upon the lands owned or controlled by the Government of the United States to be national monuments' (266); shortly after signing the act into law, Roosevelt created Devil's Tower National Monument in Wyoming and the Petrified Forest National Monument in Arizona (266).
(5) In 1907, the Inland Waterways Commission, a task force dedicated to improving inland navigation in the United States, was inaugurated (266).
(6) In 1908, the National Conservation Commission was created (266).

The institutional set-up through which these movements functioned reflected their concern towards nature. When conservationists implemented their policies by making laws for management of nature through various state departments, the non-profit organisations like the Audubon Society, Izaak Walton League, Wilderness Society, Sierra Club and others, which embodied the preservationist ideology, tried to make people aware of the value of wild nature in the United States. Examples of such organisations from other parts of the world included the Royal Society for Nature Conservation, the Royal Society for the Protection of Birds (est. 1889), the Swedish Society for Nature Conservation, the Danish Conservation Society, the Norwegian Conservation Society, the Finnish Association for Nature Conservation, the Dutch Society for the Protection of Natural Resources, the German Society for the Protection of Birds and so on (Hjelmar, 1996: 123).

1.2 Conservation and preservation movements

The conservation movement discussed in the earlier part was characterised by a mix of wilderness orientation, scientific management of natural resources and conservation of destructed natural areas. Nevertheless, two distinct tendencies gradually emerged among the early conservationists: a pragmatic 'utilitarian' wing led by Pinchot (Utilitarian Conservationists) and an idealistic 'preservationist' wing represented by naturalist Muir (Preservationist Conservationists) (Krech et al., 2004: 267). A disagreement on the necessity of a reservoir in Hetch Hetchy, a valley located in Yosemite National Park (San Francisco), culminated in the separation of Muir and Pinchot into two different movements – Conservation and Preservation (266). This division became all the more marked when Pinchot redefined conservation as 'the greatest good to the greatest number for the longest time', following utilitarianism, in his book *The Fight for Conservation*, in 1910. This definition elevated the term conservation from forestry circles to popular discourse and also gave the misleading impression that conservation was a new movement, when in fact the term described a process that was already well under way (266).

O'Riordan observed that the first American conservation movement (1890–1920) was essentially developmental rather than preservationist in nature (1971: 157). For him, preservation of environments for their own sake was never regarded as a very practicable alternative during a period of rapid economic growth. Man's right to control nature in order to advance economic and social opportunity was never seriously questioned; rather, what was questioned was the manner of this control and the subsequent distribution of benefits (O'Riordan, 1971: 158). The conservationists focused on the prudent stewardship and sustainable utilisation of natural resources like timber, water, soils and minerals, in pursuit of the 'greatest good of the greatest number for the longest time'.[12] The conservation movement gave birth to such professions as forestry, agronomy and game (wild life) and fisheries management. It was represented by federal government agencies such as the US Forest Service, Soil Conservation Service, US Fish and Wild Life Service, Bureau of Land Management, Bureau of Reclamation and US Geological Service and by State-level counterparts in all 50 states (Beck and Kolankiewicz, 2001). Conservationists emphasised the efficient use and development of physical resources to combat inefficient land management.[13] They put forth a developmental strategy based on efficiency, scientific management, centralised control and organised economic development (Gottlieb, 1993: 24). This strategy was exemplified by management systems, which were created to emphasise the balance between immediate and long-term production necessary to sustain a continuous yield (Hays, 1997: 102). The preservationists focused on a love of the outdoors and on preservation of natural areas and wildlife for their own intrinsic value as well as for the enjoyment and spiritual nourishment of present and future generations.[14] According to Muir, it was wrong to view wilderness as simply resources for human consumption; rather, wilderness had an independent value as a 'fountain of life' (Gottlieb, 1993: 24). Muir's philosophy embodied natural land management through the 'right use' of wilderness resources. On the contrary, they viewed the traditional conservationist strategies of 'right use' and efficient land management as promoting industry needs (Gottlieb, 1993: 24).[15]

However, by the end of the 1920s, cultural conduciveness towards conservation claims was reduced and the movement lost much of its momentum, though the concept did not disappear. The decade was dominated by a suspicion of anything that interfered with capitalist expansion (Hjelmar, 1996: 83). Priority was given to business interests, not welfare and conservation issues. The 1930s, the period of Great Depression, was marked by the worst environmental disasters of the century. The drought from 1934 to 1939 caused serious erosion of the Great Plains (approximately 500,000 square miles) and made more than a million tenant farmers virtually homeless (Worster, 1977: 224). These events were perceived as caused by human activities, their interferences in nature or manmade disasters. In other words, this was a period that recognised the relationships within natural processes and the interaction of these processes with man's activities (O'Riordan, 1971: 159). As a result, ecology grew strongly in this period and became the dominant frame of reference for conservationists (Hjelmar, 1996: 86). The political atmosphere also turned favourably towards the conservationists under the administration of Franklin D. Roosevelt (86). The New Deal politics of Roosevelt favoured measures that would reduce the influence of the market and enhance government's role as a counterweight to the power of private interests. Conservation organisations had a larger influence on resource planning, preservation schemes and so on in this period (86). The aesthetic phase of the conservation movement gained power during the New Deal (Koppes, 1988: 246). Economic failure encouraged Americans to recapture spiritual and community values. The aesthetic/ecological attitude found expression in policy through the growth of preserved areas and a change in their orientation (247).

According to O'Riordan, the period from 1933 to 1943 (referred to as the 'second conservation movement') also emphasised development with the idea of man exerting control over his environment rather than being in harmony with nature's forces (1971: 159). The conservation activities in this period included soil conservation and watershed management practices that were designed to encourage nature's own healing powers in order to result in greater productivity (159). By the end of World War II, New Deal conservationists had greatly expanded the scope of the efficiency doctrine, especially through their dam-building activities (Koppes, 1988: 246). By harnessing the river, floods could be controlled, cheap power generated, fresh water supplies for urban agricultural use provided and large stretches of navigable river created to provide low-cost transport of raw materials and finished goods upon which America's future economic prosperity was believed to rest (O'Riordan, 1971: 159). In the 1950s, the efficiency school of conservation was dominant, and its programmes brought substantial environmental change to the country, particularly in the West (Koppes, 1988: 251).

1.3 From conservation/preservation to environmentalism

The 20 years after World War II, that is, the 1960s and the latter decades, were known as the 'development decades' and called for a more intensive use of nature and natural resources (Guha, 2000: 65–6). The period was suffused with the optimism of the technologist, and the prospect of unending economic growth, modelled on America, was held out to the people of the North and also to the underdeveloped world (66). This was a period that realised the inability of the early preservationist/conservationist scheme to incorporate newer environmental concerns and scientific ecologists within its boundaries (White, 1985: 310). Dowie points out that though the adherents of the new environmental movement considered wilderness preservation and environmental aesthetics worthy, they overemphasised values.[16] In the United States, the 1960s created the political and cultural atmosphere for the sudden rise of environmentalism consequent to the negative effects of industrialisation and rapid urbanisation in the 1950s and 1960s (Hjelmar, 1996: 125). This period was a highly creative one that carried new ideas about fundamental social issues into Western society such as gender, peace and civil rights. The ideas of ecology, that is, the 'Earth as an ecosystem', also contributed to this shift (124). The unlimited urban and industrial development caused issues of pollution, which raised questions of 'health concerns' from the 1960s onwards.

The period witnessed the emergence of various kinds of writings on the harmful effects of unlimited economic growth, like *Silent Spring* (Carson, 1962), that helped to raise the consciousness of the people. This period also witnessed the emergence of radical ways of looking at humans' relation to nature, like deep ecology, ecofeminism, social ecology and so on. Moreover, many accidents (manmade disasters) around the world also emphasised the necessity of monitoring and checking various development activities. In these circumstances, conservation organisations, which emerged in large numbers in the United States, played a major role in protecting the environment by functioning as pressure groups and influencing governments. The legacy of the conservation movement formed the platform for the easy transition to the environmental movement[17] in the United States.[18] In the 1960s and 1970s, traditional organisations underwent modifications according to the needs of the time (Sandbach, 1980: 16).

There was another turning point in the early 1970s, when the conservation/preservation dichotomy came under attack. Scholars debated whether rational planners and preservationists were the same people, operating in different contexts.[19] According to Dowie, early environmentalism (the conservation and preservation organisations) was not a social movement but rather an attempt by privileged classes to preserve a place for outdoor recreation.[20] Members of these groups were generally wealthy, white, Anglo-Saxon males who enjoyed outdoor activities such as hunting, fishing and camping. Working-class individuals and ethnic minorities were generally excluded from conservation and preservation organisations (Dowie, 1995: 2). According to Gottlieb, there is an utter lack of diversity among these early organisations, which comprised anti-urban and class biases, and their debates were primarily 'disputes among elites – between those who wished to leave the natural environment in a pristine state and those who viewed it as a place for recreation and pleasure' (1993: 29–31). Worster characterised the preservationist and conservationist ideas as holding Arcadian and imperialist tendencies, respectively.[21] White observed that the new ecology 'transformed nature into a reflection of the modern, corporate, industrial system' and has relegated the Arcadian strain to popular environmentalism (314).

The 1980s and 1990s have seen a reassertion of 'grass root' involvement and a revitalisation of environmental groups, for example, 'Group Ten'[22] in the United States (Kuzmiak, 1991: 276). Scholars distinguish environmentalism from conservation by a number of features: its popular appeal, its concern with threats to the human body and its consumerist rather than producerist orientation towards nature (Krech et al., 2004: 267). Though the environmental movement emerged in the 1950s and 1960s in the United States, it had a late start in Europe, that is, around the 1970s. The institutional and cultural background that stimulated the environmental movement to come into existence differed widely between these two regions (Hjelmar, 1996: 125–6). Firstly, Europe had a relatively weak conservation movement and highly regulated urban and industrial development. That is, the environmental movement in northern Europe did not have the same favourable mobilisation conditions compared to those of the United States. Secondly, the environmental problems were often not as visible in northern Europe as in the United States. Hence, environmental issues entered public perception only gradually in the former. Another difference between the organisations in both countries is related to the different political opportunity structures. In the United States, the organisations had a great deal of access to decision-making centres, that is, lobbying, constitutional challenges and litigation were used much more frequently than in Europe but lacked the necessary resources to effectively pursue their goals (126).

The nature of environmental movements was varied in Third World countries. Compared to the North, environmentalism emerged at a relatively early stage in the industrial process in the South in countries such as India (Guha and Martinez-Alier, 1997: 17). Nature-based conflicts were at the root of environmental movements in these countries. That is, in Southern movements issues of ecology were often interlinked with questions of human rights, ethnicity and distributive justice (Guha, 2000: 105; Guha and Martinez-Alier, 1997: 18). Ecological degradation, such as the drying up of water sources, decimation of forests and erosion of land, and various developmental activities, such as commercial forestry, oil drilling, the damage created by large dams and so on, constitute a threat to rural livelihoods and create the circumstances for the emergence of resistance movements. Usually, opposition to these interventions by the victims took the form of environmental movements (Guha, 2000: 105). Based on this, some salient differences between the North and South can be noticed in the nature of environmental movements (Guha, 2000: 122; Guha and Martinez-Alier, 1997: 18):

(1) While Southern movements are more strongly rooted in material conflict and poorer communities' rights to natural resources, Northern movements

originate outside the production process and call for a change in attitudes (towards the natural world) rather than a change in systems of production or distribution; thus, Southern movements have to work for cultural change and a change in production systems.
(2) Southern environmental groups have tended to be more adversarial with regard to their government by opposing laws and policies, but Northern groups have more often had a constructive side to their programmes, working with their governments to promote environmentally benign laws and policies.

Developments in environmental concerns in North America and Europe in the 1960s and early 1970s, including the creation of different Acts and Laws, were generally known as the 'modern environmental movement'. This forms one of the themes for Chapter 2 and is analysed in detail under the part 'Reform environmentalism'.

Notes

1 Environmental campaigns were the earliest form of environmental activity and can be traced back to the late nineteenth century, when Europe and North America experienced growth in social movements. Social concerns, including issues of worker's right, gender equality, opposition to war (Vietnam) and the like, were linked to environmental concerns on nuclear testing and chemical pesticides. Haq, G. and Paul, A. 2012, *Environmentalism Since 1945*, New York: Routledge, 4.

2 John Reiger points out that conservation movements began with a concern for wild life exhibited by organised American sportsmen. He anchored conservation as a non-utilitarian concern for wild life. Reiger, J. 1975, *American Sportsmen and the Origins of Conservation*, New York: Winchester Press, 21, cited in White, R. 1985, 'American Environmental History: The Development of a New Historical Field', *Pacific Historical Review*, 54(3), 310.

The conservation movement is so broad and varied that one cannot find a single starting point for it. See Krech, S., Mc Neill, J. R. and Merchant, C. 2004, *Encyclopaedia of World Environmental History*. Vol. I, London: Routledge, 262.

3 The term 'environmentalism' has been interpreted in various ways: as a social movement, a set of ideas based on ecology, a 'back-to-nature' philosophy or just a greater interest in environmental affairs. See Sandbach, F. 1980, *Environment, Ideology and Policy*, Oxford: Basil Blackwell. The periodisation of environmentalism varies according to different sources. For Guha, the initial period of response to the onset of industrialisation in the eighteenth and early nineteenth centuries belongs to first wave environmentalism and the transformation from intellectual response to mass movement after 1960 forms second wave environmentalism. See Guha, R. 2000, *Environmentalism: A Global History*, New York: Oxford University Press, 3–4, 6. Some scholars consider the period from the late 1960s to the early 1970s as first wave and from the late 1980s to the early 1990s as second wave environmentalism. See Krech et al., 2004: 477. O'Riordan talks about three conservation movements in America, the first from 1890 to 1920, the second from 1933 to 1943 and the third after 1960. See O'Riordan, T. 1971, 'The Third American Conservation Movement: New Implications for Public Policy', *Journal of American Studies*, 5, 155, 160.

4 Cronon, W. 1983, *Changes in the Land: Indians, Colonists and the Ecology of the New England*, New York: Hill and Wang, 121–2, cited in Koppes, C. R. 1988, 'Efficiency, Equity, Esthetics: Shifting Themes in American Conservation', in Worster, D. (ed.), *The Ends of the Earth: Perspectives on Modern Environmental History*, Cambridge: Cambridge University Press, 231.

5 Gould, P. C. 1989, *Early Green Politics: Back to Nature, Back to the Land, and Socialism in Britain, 1880–1900*, Brighton: Harvester Press, 156, cited in Hjelmar, U., 1996, *The Political Practice of Environmental Organizations*, England: Avebury, 74.
6 Worster, D. 1977, *Nature's Economy: The Roots of Ecology*, San Francisco, CA: Sierra Club Books, 261, cited in Hjelmar, 1996: 74.
7 McCormick. J. 1989, *Reclaiming Paradise: The Global Environmental Movement*, Bloomington, IN: Indiana University Press, viii, cited in Hjelmar, 1996: 74.
8 Hofstadter, R. 1963, *The Progressive Movement: 1900–1915*, Englewood Cliffs, NJ: Prentice-Hall, cited in Hjelmar, 1996: 78.
9 John Muir and Robert Underwood Johnson founded the Sierra Club together.
10 Gottlieb, R. 1993, *Forcing the Spring: The Transformation of the American Environmental Movement*, Washington, DC: Island Press, 23, cited in Silveira, S. J. 2001, 'The American Environmental Movement: Surviving Through Diversity', *Boston College Environmental Affairs Law Review*, 28(2), Article 7, 499–500.
11 See O'Riordan, 1971: 158.
12 Pinchot, G. 1947, *Breaking New Ground*, New York: Harcourt Brace, 320 in Strong, D. H. 1988, *Dreamers and Defenders–American Conservationists*, London: University of Nebraska Press, 83, cited in Beck, R. and Kolankiewicz, L. 2001, 'The Environmental Movement's Retreat from Advocating U.S. Population Stabilization (1970–1998): A First Draft of History', June. www.mnforsustain.org/beck_environmental_movement_retreat_long3_causes2.htm.
13 Hays, 1997, 'From Conservation to Environment: Environmental Politics in the United States Since World War II', in Miller, C. and Rothman, H. (eds.), *Out of the Woods: Essays in Environmental History*, Pittsburgh, PA: University of Pittsburgh Press, 102, cited in Silveira, 2001: 499.
14 Nash, R. 1967, *Wilderness and the American Mind*, New Haven, CT and London: Yale University Press, cited in Beck and Kolankiewicz, 2001.
15 Pinchot's conservation movement was part of a more general progressive movement fighting the laissez-faire, monopolistic social Darwinism characteristic of much of nineteenth-century American economic life. Progressives held that natural resources should benefit all citizens, not just the wealthy few who privately owned vast amounts of property. Government policy should serve this goal by preventing waste, limiting monopolistic control, providing economic opportunity for the many and keeping prices low. See Des Jardins, J. R. 2001, *Environmental Ethics: An Introduction to Environmental Philosophy*, Canada: Wadsworth, 42.
16 Dowie, 1995: 127, cited in Beck and Kolankiewicz, 2001.
17 Benton and Short are of the opinion that the term 'environmental movement' is something of a misnomer. They find it more accurate to talk about it as a number of different organisations, groups and movements motivated by differing objectives. See Benton, L. M. and Short, J. R. 1999, *Environmental Discourse and Practice*, Wiley-Blackwell, 113.
18 Petulla put forward a different view. He adopted a new tripartite division of the movement into biocentric (preservationist)/economic (conservationist)/ecological components and argued that people in the third category provided much of the intellectual basis for and leadership of current environmentalism. See Petulla, J. M. 1977, *American Environmental History: The Exploitation and Conservation of Natural Resources*, San Francisco, CA: Boyd & Fraser Publishing Co., cited in White, 1985: 312.
19 Various literature shows that the whole conservationist/preservationist dichotomy was questioned in the 1970s and thereafter. In 1972, Lawrence Rakestraw revealed the difficulty of differentiating preservationists from conservationists. See Rakestraw, L. 1972, 'Conservation History: An Assessment', *Pacific Historical Review*, XLI, 273. Susan Schrepfer also noticed that rational planners and romantic preservationists could be the same people operating in different contexts. See Schrepfer, 1983, *The Fight to Save the Redwood: A History of Environmental Reform, 1917–1978*, Madison, WI: University of Wisconsin Press, cited in White, 1985: 310.

20 Dowie, M. 1995, *Losing Ground: American Environmentalism at the Close of the Twentieth Century*, Cambridge, MA: MIT Press, 2, cited in Silveira, 2001: 502.
21 Worster, *Nature's Economy*, 291–338, cited in White, 1985: 314.
22 Group Ten includes Sierra Club, Natural Resources Defence Council, National Audubon Society, Izaak Walton League, Wilderness Society, National Wildlife Federation, Friends of the Earth, National Parks and Conservation Association, Sierra Club Legal Defence Fund and Environmental Defense Fund. See Kuzmiak, D. T. 1991, 'The American Environmental Movement', *The Geographical Journal*, 157(3), 275.

2
'VALUE' DYNAMICS IN THE ENVIRONMENTAL THOUGHT SYSTEMS

Even though the two movements discussed in the last chapter were active simultaneously in the same period, they were constructed on different value systems. Conservationists found value in the 'wise use' rather than exploitation of natural resources. Thus, as they try to conserve nature in its wild form for human purposes, conservationists argued for the instrumental value of nature. However, preservationists valued nature for its wilderness, which by its mere existence contributes to the well-being of the human spirit. Hence, they attribute intrinsic value to the former, which has nothing to do with the question of human needs. Now, the concern of the new liberal movement of reform environmentalism was for 'quality-of-life issues', primarily motivated by scientific concerns about human health being negatively impacted by toxins and pollution. This shift from conservation and preservation movements to one as represented by the reformist group reflects the shift in the way of life and the corresponding value orientation of society in the 1960s.

2.1 Reform environmentalism

The modern environmental movement has its roots in the United States in the 1960s, when a range of developments after World War II made environmental consciousness an imperative. There was a population boom as a result of medical advances in both Africa and Asia, which created unprecedented demands on basic resources (Conkin, 2007: 232). In North America, Europe and Japan, a dual development added even more demands on resources. The baby boom in the United States from 1950 to 1970 and, to a lesser extent, Western Europe, along with an economic boom, set the stage for an emerging environmental outburst. Rising incomes and consumption created steadily growing demand for basic resources such as energy and a dramatic increase in waste products and pollution; the green revolution spread to all parts of the world, accompanied by chemicals like fertilisers, insecticides, fungicides and herbicides (232). There was a shift in production from products directly derived from nature to new, science-based and synthetic production systems like plastics. These synthetic products brought many new environmental hazards (Hjelmar, 1996: 93). Society was becoming even more urbanised and people were forced to face manmade problems. Cars, having developed into a common commodity, and coal-fired power plants were polluting the air. Problems with air quality were noticed in Los Angeles as early as 1943, and by 1957, it had been authoritatively traced to car exhaust (93). The symptoms of Los Angeles 'smog' – choking, coughing and weeping – were found in most large cities (O'Riordan, 1971: 160–1). The nation's waterways showed steady deterioration both in health and amenity aspects, and most major rivers failed to meet federal water quality criteria (161). In addition, immoderate consumption created mountains of waste and rivers of sewage. Poisonous waste was left or buried in the desert and contaminated drinking water and crops were drowned in pesticides. In this period, ecology that had been developing into a particular branch of biology began to influence human perceptions of their relationship with nature. Thus, the popularisation of ecological ideas also gave countless citizens a new perspective on the risks of transforming and manipulating nature.[1]

Silveira attributed the reasons for the emergence of new environmentalism to two major social changes that occurred in American culture (Silveira, 2001: 505). Firstly, citizens began to search for improved standards of living and amenities, beyond necessities and conveniences, due to increased personal and social 'real income' (Hays, 1997: 108). Rising standards of living allowed Americans to view nature as an essential provider of recreational activities (109). Secondly, increasing levels of education spawned values associated with personal creativity and self-development, including involvement with the natural environment (108). According to Silveira, both these changes allowed individuals to think broadly about the natural habitat in which they lived, worked and played (Silveira, 2001: 505). She characterised this shift in thinking as the infusion of particular social values into the public arena and the widespread expression of those values in the environmental arena. By the late 1960s, activists had begun to link destruction of the natural environment to the complex interplay of new technology, industry, political power and economic power (Gottlieb, 1993: 96).

Sandbach noticed two different types of reactions under the banner of environmentalism (1980: 22). The first was an ecological or scientific brand of environmentalism. This emphasised sustaining a viable physical and biological environment; any technological or economic changes were to be determined by this principle. The second was less concerned with environmental systems and more with whether or not science and technology were compatible with humanistic principles. This standpoint had been more influenced by the New Left, anarchism and counter-culture (22).

A number of scholars had contributed through their writings to creating awareness among the public about environmental factors in the 1960s and 1970s. The 'holistic' or 'systems' approach to science became a major theme in the popular environmentalist literature (Sandbach, 1980: 24). The status of science was not questioned; rather, the greater authority of ecology was emphasised (25). The New Left and anarchists both saw the problem of alienation and social control as a product of science and technology (26). People like Robert Owen, Peter Kropotkin, William Morris and Lewis Mumford were the few among them who contributed to the debate.

The publication of Rachel Carson's *Silent Spring* in 1962 marked the beginning of modern environmentalism (Dowie, 1995: 23). This book was particularly influential in bringing environmental health into public consciousness. In this book, Carson warned about the overuse of pesticides and attributed the increasing rate of cancer to the excessive use of insecticides (Carson, 1962). The seemingly minute levels of persistent pests could be concentrated in food chains and hence become a serious environmental problem. The book condemned the US pesticide industry, particularly for its use of DDT and possible damage due to the spreading of pesticides, and called for government intervention and restraint (Hjelmar, 1996: 93). Hjelmar observed that Carson re-conceptualised the relations between 'nature' and 'society' by viewing them as two sides of the same coin rather than considering nature as a separate realm outside society (94). She stressed the interactions and interdependence of the two. In this sense, Carson was one of the leading political intellectuals in the environmental movement in the 1960s. She also criticised the politics of science and the exclusion of the public from information about the risks of chemicals (94).

Another work, *The Quiet Crisis*, was a landmark in modern environmental thinking. In this book, Udall warned of the dangers of pollution and threats to America's natural resources, stressing that the concept of conservation had to be expanded to meet the problems of the new age (1963). This was followed by Barry Commoner's *The Closing Circle* (1971) and *Only One Earth* by Rene Dubos and Barbara Ward (1972). Commoner's widely quoted four principles were: every separate entity is connected to all the rest, everything has to go somewhere, you cannot get something for nothing from it and nature knows best (Sandbach, 1980: 23). He considered Americans to be the unwitting victims of ignorance and explored the reasons for the American environmental crisis in his works (Kuzmiak, 1991: 272). Commoner espoused New Left politics with a strong strain of socialism and argued that environmental problems were actually caused by the unfair distribution of resources and by profitable technologies (Beck and Kolankiewicz, 2001). He found the locus of solutions to environmental problems in a democratic process of reform of social, economic and political structures.[2] *A Blueprint for Survival* (Goldsmith et al., 1972) laid emphasis on Commoner's principles and stressed the importance of returning to 'natural' mechanisms (Sandbach, 1980: 23). Its recommendations were:

> 'natural' control of pests as opposed to the use of artificial pesticides; the use of organic manure instead of inorganic fertilizers; the use of ecologically sound alternative technologies; the decentralisation of the economy to make

reasonably self-sufficient communities possible and a reduction of the British population to a level sustainable by indigenous renewable resources.

(23)

A number of other writings came from the Right, reviving the Malthusian theory on population (*Essay on the Principle of Population*, 1798). Samuel Ordway's *Resources and the American Dream* appeared in 1953, warning the world about the limits of growth and the dangers of overpopulation and over-consumption. Garret Hardin wrote an essay, 'The Tragedy of the Commons', in 1968, arguing that most environmental problems arise from a single cause, that is, the misuse of resources that are owned in common.[3] Paul and Anne Ehrlich wrote *The Population Bomb* in 1968, which raised fears about the environmental impact of exponential increases in human population. Calculating the doubling time of the human population, they warned that the world's population would continue to grow as long as the birth rate exceeds the death rate (Ehrlich and Ehrlich, 1968: 17–35). The period was enriched by a debate between Ehrlich and Commoner regarding whether population growth or technology was responsible for the environmental crisis. Commoner's argument rested on the growth of harmful technologically advanced products increasing at a rate greater than population growth, while Ehrlich's case was strongest in relation to the pressure of a rapidly increasing population on resources (Sandbach, 1980: 30). However, most of the literature generally argued that the roots of environmental problems were overpopulation, excessive resource consumption and pollution.

As the above discussion discloses, the shift in the concern about nature to one of human health issues points towards a changed value orientation in the ways in which people were living. The various writers, who dealt with social and environmental situations, generally adopted a problem-oriented approach, which indicated a shift in the question of value either in the mode of living of people or in the functioning of institutional structures. For example, Ehrlich and others problematised the issues of population increase and over-consumption in light of knowledge about the finiteness of natural resources. By examining the ecological impacts of hazardous substances like pesticides that pollute both natural and human environments, Carson fundamentally altered the way Americans perceived the environment and the dangers of toxins to themselves (Dowie, 1995: 21). Thus, she placed her study in the context of changed value perception in American social life. As a solution, the leaders of the new environmentalist group, such as Barry Commoner, Aldo Leopold, Garret Hardin and others, including Carson, tried to manage nature with a view of 'appropriate technologies for appropriate ends', an idea that is a mark of the utilitarian tradition (White, 1985: 311).[4] In analysing the problems associated with the industrial society, Carson exposed the fact that science and technology had been effectively removed from any larger policy framework and insulated from public input and opinion (Gottlieb, 1993: 86). In addition, many activists linked environmentalism with novel values that could restructure society and form alternative institutions and lifestyles (97). Several New Left ecology collectives were organised in the late 1960s to focus on the waste issue and were pivotal in the formation of community-based recycling centres (96).

Along with the rich source of writings mentioned, various other factors triggered an unprecedented rise in public concern and set the stage for political activism over the environment. A series of environmental catastrophes were reported in the 1960s that revealed the urgency of taking necessary steps to prevent further environmental deterioration. The first major oil spill in Britain occurred when the super tanker *Torrey Canyon* struck a reef between the UK mainland and the Isles of Scilly in March 1967 (Haq and Paul, 2012: 3). The tragedy resulted in the deaths of tens of thousands of birds. Other major events included the 1965 power blackout and garbage strikes of New York City, the 1969 burning of the Ohio River along the industrial sections of Cleveland and the 1969 Santa Barbara oil spill in California (Gottlieb, 1993: 102–3). In the 1960s, Lake Erie was killed by excessive eutrophication resulting from pollution and there was the Japanese Minamata tragedy following mercury poisoning of fish (Sandbach, 1980: 30). Environmentalists responded to these events by demanding government protection from environmental degradation and pollution (Dowie, 1995: 23). As a result, a number of environmentally significant laws were drafted, such as the Wilderness Act (1965), the Clean Air Act (1967), the National Trails Act (1968) and the Wild and Scenic Rivers Act (1968) (23).

In 1970, 20 million people concerned with the environment united to celebrate the first Earth Day in the United States. This event was the direct result of the infusion of social values of the 1960s into environmentalism (Dowie, 1995: 23). A key question was whether Earth Day was the manifestation of a genuinely popular movement or the result of the manipulation of public opinion by elites in government, business and the media (Krech et al., 2004: 477). Earth Day was also considered a tool for enlisting youth in a constructive rather than violent and destructive crusade, rejecting mainstream environmental organisations and joining several radical environmental groups (Conkin, 2007: 239). The rise in public concern for the environment was also accompanied by the creation of new governmental institutions and legislation. However, in the United States, general legislation came earlier with the passage of the National Environmental Policy Act (NEPA) in 1969 (Sandbach, 1980: 18). NEPA was followed by significant pollution control legislation, notably the Clean Air Act 1970 and the Federal Water Pollution Control Act 1972. Another institutional response by the US government was the establishment of Environmental Protection Agency (EPA) in 1970 to address issues of water and air pollution, insecticides, waste management and radiation (Kuzmiak, 1991: 271). Different agencies responsible for regulating pollution were brought together by this move. These included Federal Water Quality Administration, the National Air Pollution Control Administration, the Bureau of Water Hygiene and the Solid Waste Management Programme (Sandbach, 1980: 19). The EPA had the duty of co-ordinating federal environmental programmes, monitoring pollution, enforcing laws and reviewing environmental impact statements (19). Other Acts that came into being in the decade were: the Coastal Zone Management Act 1972, the Endangered Species Act 1973, the 1972 ban on DDT (Kuzmiak, 1991: 272) and the Pesticides Act 1972 (Silveira, 2001: 509). The Coastal Zone Management Act was passed in direct response to concerns during the previous decade regarding dredging and filling, industrial siting and offshore oil development (Silveira, 2001: 509). Later in the decade, lead was removed from petrol after being cited as a major cause of air pollution, and the scientific and industrial communities began pondering the effects of acid rain (Kuzmiak, 1991: 272). In Britain, this involved the setting up of a central scientific unit on pollution, a standing Royal Commission on Environmental Pollution, working parties on refuse disposal, the creation of the Department of the Environment (DEO) and general legislation such as the Control of Pollution Act 1974, though its implementation was delayed (Sandbach, 1980: 17–18).

Among the literature produced during the 1960s and 1970s was 'The Limits to Growth', which appeared in 1972 as a report to the Club of Rome[5] and seemed to be unique due to the approach it adopted in analysing the environmental situation. The Club of Rome was established by a group of individuals who were close to decision-making points and were concerned about the apparent incapability of governments and the international organisations to foresee the consequences of substantial material growth that would affect the quality aspects of life in the future (King and Schneider, 1993: vii). From the beginning, the Club's thinking was governed by three related conceptual guidelines:

- Adopting a global approach to the vast and complex problems of a world, in which interdependence between nations within a single planetary system is constantly growing.
- Focusing on issues, policies and options in a longer-term perspective than is possible for governments, which respond to the immediate concerns of an insufficiently informed constituency.
- Seeking a deeper understanding of the interactions within the tangle of contemporary problems – political, economic, social, cultural, psychological, technological and environmental – for which the Club of Rome adopted the term 'the world problematique' (King and Schneider, 1993: viii).

The Club of Rome identified population explosion in the South and the macro effects of man on his environment as the two most dominant elements of the contemporary problematique (King and Schneider, 1993: ix). Other factors included changes in human behaviour; the emergence of seemingly irrational movements, including terrorism; and the growth of individual and collective selfishness, thrown up by a materialistic society. Human beings created the problematique and suffered its consequences. The problematique therefore demanded a systematic analysis that paid due attention to both rational behaviour and the instinctive and apparently irrational elements inherent in human nature that make for an uncertain world (ix).

The Club of Rome questioned the values upheld by a materialistic society and identified various dimensions of the problems it faced. Against the approach of localised and short-term treatment of problems by the materialistic society, the Club suggested perceiving the global and long-term effects of the problems and treating them accordingly. It also found value in understanding environmental problems as arising from the interaction of a number of problems rather than viewing it as single and separated from the contexts of other issues. Thus, it seemed to hold a holistic worldview. Besides material factors like population explosion, it probed into immaterial aspects like human behaviour. The Club found value only in the rational behaviour of the human species, which included selfless action that would ensure a balanced relation between nature and human beings. Selfishness is cited as a case of irrational behaviour by the human species and as a problem-generating factor. Therefore, it is also a call for transformation at the personal level.

The Club put forward the idea of 'world resolutique', which connoted a coherent, comprehensive and simultaneous attack, as the solution to resolve as many of the diverse elements of the problematique as possible (King and Schneider, 1993: viii). The word resolutique included the need to adopt certain values founded on the *collective values* of humanity that were sketchily emerging as a moral code for action and behaviour (87). These codes and values were to constitute the basis of international relations and the source of inspiration for decisions, with due regard for cultural diversity and pluralism. To find value in the collective values of humanity meant avoidance of individual self-interest in human behaviour, which characterised the materialistic society. The Club of Rome expected that if human beings belonging to different cultures or nations act on the fundamental value of humanity, it will make all the difference in the current situation of problems.

The Club of Rome also recommended structural changes for resolving the crisis. It found deficiencies in governance[6] that lay at the root of many of the strands of the problematique and warned that improved governance is an essential aspect of the resolutique (114). Primarily, what needed is the invention of instruments of governance capable of coping with change without resorting to violence and of maintaining the kind of peace that provides security, justice and fulfilling growth for individuals and societies (73). Secondly, instead of the monopoly of governments and their departments in decision-making, it tried to bring various partners into the process – business and industrial organisations – so that the widest possible experience and skill were made available. In addition to this, enlightened public support, where the public is aware of new needs and the possible consequences of decisions, would be essential (74).

In this recommendation for establishing institutions that will ensure security, justice and the growth of individuals and societies, the Club highlighted the value of peace instead of violence. Moreover, they found the co-operation of various institutional structures and the public, instead of the monopoly of governments, in the process of decision-making to be ethical. Thus, the Club also emphasised the fundamental value of immaterial qualities that were to be followed in governance.

The Club saw it as important to convince policy makers that it is possible for North and South to work together without the regional and global environment paying a high price (King and Schneider, 1993: 111). Along with this, measures were also required to find a policeable mechanism that would permit development without destroying much of world resources and other measures to condition market forces and to take into account long-term environmental quality and equity (112–13). However, they needed to be flanked by ethical mobilisation worldwide if the challenge was to be overcome (113). An ethical conception of international relations needed to evolve from inspiration at the national level and, finally, on the individual level as well (161).

The Club put forward their concept of 'development', which has implications for regional and global environments. It found value in a development that will not bring unrecoverable changes in the environment, demand excessive resource use or target market-oriented purposes and development, based on criteria that stressed long-term environmental quality and equity. Thus, the Club required us to bring an ethical dimension to behaviour at the individual and national levels.

In the period between 1960 and 1970, traditional organisations underwent modifications as circumstances required, and many new organisations were established, including the World Wildlife Fund in Switzerland (WWF; est. 1961; now the World Wide Fund for Nature) and, in North America, the Environmental Defense Fund (EDF; est. 1967), Friends of the Earth (FoE) (est. 1969), Natural Resources Defense Council (est. 1970) and Greenpeace (est. 1971) (Haq and Paul, 2012: 7–8; see also Conkin, 2007: 239). US environmental groups, campaigning for stricter national pollution control laws and the agencies with the power to enforce them, helped to achieve a number of legislative milestones (Haq and Paul, 2012: 8). For example, in 1971, the EDF, with support from the Izaak Walton League and National Audubon Society, battled for a national ban of DDT, which was implemented in 1972. During this period, US environmental groups quickly established a presence in Europe. In 1971 FoE took its first step to form an international network with representatives from countries like France, Sweden, United Kingdom and the USA (9). Older organisations such as the Sierra Club and Audubon Society mobilised the public, lobbied effectively for new legislation and litigated in courts to ensure enforcement of existing environmental laws (Conkin 2007: 232).

The mid-1970s met another environmental crisis, that is, the energy crisis – in particular, the spectre of an insufficient oil supply raised by the policy of decreasing exports and dramatically increasing prices initiated in 1973 by the Organization of Petroleum Exporting Countries (OPEC) (Krech et al., 2004: 479). In this period, environmentalists turned their attention to the question of energy resources. Amory Lovins was a key figure who significantly reformulated the energy problem by proposing a soft energy strategy (479). He found problems with inefficient energy use coupled with a lack of development of alternative energy sources. He pointed out that conventional energy production was both energy intensive and a source of substantial pollution (479).

2.1.1 Analysis

Reform environmentalism was founded on the natural sciences and on Jeremy Bentham's ideas of utilitarianism. It considered humanity as part of the ecological system and followed an anthropocentric perspective. The key components of reform environmentalism are: (1) natural systems are the basis of all organic existence, including that of humans, (2) humankind is an element within natural ecosystems, and hence human survival is linked to ecosystem survival, (3) ethical human actions (actions that promote the good life for humankind) necessarily promote action towards all life on Earth in an ecologically responsible manner and (4) proper use of the natural sciences can guide the relationship between humanity and its natural environment (Brulle, 2000: 173–4).

The basic idea of reform environmentalism as derived from these assumptions is that nature is to be protected for the sake of humans. That is, the human species is viewed as a species in nature, whose existence depends on other species; hence, ensuring the well-being of the latter is important for human survival. In other words, value is attributed to the natural world because it is necessary for human life. Hence, in the third component they warn human beings to perform ethically responsible actions, which will take care of all life on Earth. They rely on the knowledge of natural science in order to maintain a balanced relation between humans and the natural environment. Thus, the idea of reform environmentalism is not based on certain abstract principles, but rather on a utilitarian calculation of the consequences of human actions.

Reform environmentalism has been found less suitable as a framework for the articulation of value orientation towards the environment when compared to other approaches, discussed in the following part. Despite this, for Reform Environmentalism, the domain of human ecology is value laden, because there is right or wrong of human action in the ecosphere, whether such judgements proceed from a consequentialist criterion or not. For the present purpose, it suffices to point out that reform environmentalists would agree that value judgements about situations in the ecosphere are distinct from the explanation of it. The framework it provides for the articulation of value orientation, however, may not entertain any intrinsic value, as we may come across in some other frameworks.

2.2 Deep ecology

The deep ecology movement emerged in the 1970s as a reaction to the dominant reform environmentalist attitude of the 1960s, which had developed in turn as a response to the unfettered exploitation of nature during the global economic boom of the 1950s and 1960s. The concept of deep ecology is influenced by a number of traditions from around the world (Luke, 1988: 68; Fox, 1990: 66–7). The sources include Christian Franciscanism, the later philosophy of the twentieth-century Western philosopher Martin Heidegger, Eastern process philosophy (Taoism and Buddhism) – its principles of non-violence and relation to nature – Western process philosophy (Heraclitus, Whitehead[7] and Spinoza), European romanticism (Goethe, Rousseau, Blake, Wordsworth, Coleridge and Shelley), American transcendentalism (Emerson, Thoreau, Whitman and Muir), Murray Bookchin's social ecology, Aldo Leopold's ecosystem ethics and the ecological wisdom of various tribal cultures. Each of these cultural pieces is placed into the deep ecological conceptual mosaic in one way or another (Luke, 1988: 68). In this way, deep ecology serves as a 'global philosophy' in which influences from all world religions, cultures and philosophies converge.

Deep ecology[8] was developed as an alternative to viewing humans as the source of all values and ascribing only instrumental value to the non-human world. That is, treating humans as independent of and in isolation from the environment.[9] Deep ecologists summarised their viewpoints in the form of eight principles,[10] which they expect the humans to fulfil, in order to prevent the exploitation of nature and to solve environmental issues:

(1) The well-being and flourishing of human and non-human life[11] on Earth have value in themselves.[12] (Synonyms: intrinsic value, inherent worth).[13] These values are independent of the usefulness of the non-human world for human purposes.
(2) Richness and diversity of life forms contribute to the realisation of these values and are also value in themselves.
(3) Humans have no right to reduce this richness and diversity except to satisfy vital needs.
(4) The flourishing of human life and cultures is compatible with a substantially smaller human population. The flourishing of non-human life requires a smaller human population.
(5) Present human interference with the non-human world is excessive and the situation is rapidly worsening.
(6) Policies must therefore be changed. These policies affect basic economic, technological and ideological structures. The resulting state of affairs will be deeply different from the present.
(7) The ideological change will be mainly that of appreciating life quality (dwelling in situations of inherent value) rather than adhering to an increasingly higher standard of living. There will be a profound awareness of the difference between big and great.
(8) Those who subscribe to the foregoing points have an obligation directly or indirectly to try to implement the necessary changes (Devall and Sessions, 1985: 20–1).

As principle one points out, the basic assumption of deep ecology is that both human and non-human life have intrinsic value. According to Naess, intrinsic value implies that whatever characters each living being carries will form its intrinsic nature. These may be reflected in the different behaviours of both human and non-human entities. Therefore, by the term intrinsic value, he implies 'value objectivism',[14] as used in the philosophical circle (Naess, 1998a: 142). Thus, A is said to have a value, independent of whether A has a value for B. The value of A must therefore be said to have a value inherent in A (that is, A has intrinsic value) (143). Thus, the traits living beings possess do not form part of their intrinsic value so far as they are classified as 'good' or 'bad' in relation to any other being.

38 Ethics

The concept of intrinsic value is closely linked to the two ultimate norms of deep ecology, that is, Biospherical egalitarianism (also known as 'biocentric equality') and Self-realization (Devall and Sessions, 1985: 19).

> The intuition of biocentric equality is that all things in the biosphere have an equal right to live and blossom and to reach their own individual forms of unfolding and Self-realization within the larger Self-realization. The basic intuition is that all organisms and entities in the ecosphere, as parts of the interrelated whole are equal in intrinsic worth.
>
> *(20)*

The idea of spiritual growth envisaged in the norm of Self-realization tries to go beyond what is made possible by the modern Western self and by unfolding the inner essence that will enable one to rise above narrow contemporary cultural assumptions and values, and the conventional wisdom of time and place, facilitating an identification with the non-human world (20).

Principle one adds that to conceive the value of the non-human world in terms of its 'use' to humans will not form its intrinsic value. However, it is not clear whether this value is independent of the usefulness of non-human beings among themselves (for example, the natural tendency of species of birds and animals to be killed for food, for others, among themselves). In this sense, intrinsic value is not sufficiently articulated in the principle, and the norm of biocentric equality also does not justify this position. However, Naess agrees that though in principle it is true, in the process of living, all species use each other as food, shelter and so on, since mutual predation is a biological fact of life. Deep ecologists seem to take the position that an idea of 'use' cannot go with the concept of intrinsic value, because if human beings view the non-human world as a means of 'usefulness',[15] it will adversely affect the existence of the latter. In other words, the right of the non-human world to exist will be questioned. When one views the latter as possessing intrinsic value, there will not be any exploitation, since nature's own way of living will be the norm.

McLaughlin tries to restate the first principle, avoiding the concept of intrinsic value. According to him, we can care for the rest of nature without attributing any values. Such care can spring, for example, from a felt sense of relatedness to the rest of nature or a love of existence (1995: 86–7). Whether McLaughlin takes into account the concept of 'intrinsic value' or not, he also shares the same feeling that Naess conveys by this term. The emphasis is still on the *care* to be taken towards the non-human world, though the reasons are different.

Fox does not do away with the notion of intrinsic value. He replaces it with the notion of differential intrinsic value. That is, organisms may have differential intrinsic value depending on their complexity and, hence, capacity for richness of experience (Fox, 1984: 198). He refers to the class of value theory, which recognises the intrinsic value of the non-human world but ascribes differential intrinsic value to organisms depending on their complexity and, hence, capacity for richness of experience (198). According to this theory (as inspired by Whitehead's thought), humans are not posited as the source of all value, nor is it denied that organisms possessing nervous systems of comparable complexity to that of humans (such as whales and dolphins) also possess comparable intrinsic value. Moreover, it is not assumed or implied that organisms possessing greater intrinsic value have any right to exploit those possessing lesser intrinsic value (198). Rather, as Birch and Cobb[16] think, this theory considers as its central ethic that human beings have an obligation to act so as to maximise richness of experience in general – which includes the richness of experience of the non-human world.

However, Naess denies such grading of the particular intrinsic value living beings have 'simply as living being' (Naess, 1984: 202). Deep ecologists seem to negate any view based on qualities which will place living beings one above the other; rather they try to consider every being on equal terms, so that there will not be any chance for exploitation of the species at lower levels. They do not find it fair to categorise even human beings based on any characteristic. Thus, Sessions argued that

> the point is not whether humans do in fact have the greatest degree of sentience on this planet . . . (but that, for deep ecologists) the degree of sentience is irrelevant in term of how humans relate to the rest of Nature.[17]

Hence, deep ecologists are not in a position to accept Whiteheadian ecological ethics, which Fox suggested, as corresponding to 'ecological egalitarianism[18] – in principle'. Fox remarks that deep ecologists tend to conflate principle and practice when they make judgements such as this, though, in this case, this value theory does not contradict the norm of biocentric equality (Fox, 1984: 198).

Supporting his own view, Fox cites Naess's revelation that 'value conflicts can never be completely avoided in practice; the process of living entails some forms of "killing, exploitation and suppression"'.[19] Here Fox brings in the idea of degree of sentience, which becomes extremely relevant in terms of how humans relate to the rest of nature if they are to resolve genuine conflicts of value in a decent manner (Fox, 1984: 198). He alleges that the result of this deep ecology position, that is, confusing 'ecological egalitarianism – in principle' with 'ecological egalitarianism – in practice', is that they are forced into the position that they might as well eat meat as vegetables since all organisms possess equal intrinsic value (198).

It seems that deep ecology's norm of 'biocentric equality' logically entails that meat or vegetable makes no difference for the deep ecologists, so that meat can be used over vegetables as food without any hesitation. Nevertheless, in combination with another principle of deep ecology, that is, 'simple in means, rich in ends' (Devall and Sessions, 1985: 20) – the practical implication of this intuition or norm suggests that we should live with minimum rather than maximum impact on other species and on the Earth in general – it leads to a different conclusion, from which it follows that one should lead a life which will have a minimum destructive effect on other living beings.

However, Luke argues that in whatever way people try to reduce their needs and live with minimum rather than maximum impact on other species and the earth in general, humans' interrelation with nature will always remain anthropocentric given humans' technological powers and biological facts of life (1988: 82). He continues that rocks and trees do not use humans – except for their survival or Self-realization. Nevertheless, for the purpose of creating shelter, tools, food, medicines and so on, humans indulge in many activities in nature, such as crushing, chipping and chopping rocks, carving and burning trees and many others. Generally, in the process individual non-human entities or organisms are treated with less respect, equality and rights by humans. Even if humans try to change many of their ways of living, they would not be able to maintain a mutual dependence on nature. Luke asks,

> Will we allow anthrax or cholera microbes to attain self-realisation in wiping out sheep herds or human kindergartens? Will we continue to deny salmonella or botulism microorganisms their equal rights when we process the dead carcasses of animals and plants that we eat? In the end, people inevitably put themselves above other species and natural entities, as deep ecology accepts, 'simply to live'.
>
> *(Luke, 1988: 82)*

Foley also complains that this principle proclaims equality only 'in principle' and allows for use of one species by another in practice, when vital needs are at stake (Foley, 1988: 120). The animals may use animals, men may use other men and all men may use technology. He questions how strict egalitarianism must be in practice.

Naess would accept certain established ways of justifying different norms dealing with different kinds of living beings, and these do not necessitate grading the particular intrinsic value living beings possess simply as living beings (Naess, 1984: 202). It may be out of intuition that he proclaims that particular value to be ungraded, and it neither logically nor otherwise necessitates a norm of equal behaviour towards all living beings. Naess refers to his own experience; during a stay in the mountains for a long time, he could not avoid stepping on the little arctic plant *Salix herbacea* and never felt the need to justify such behaviour out of the feeling that the plant has less right to live and blossom, or less intrinsic value as living beings, than certain other living beings, including himself. Instead, he could admire these plants, acknowledging their equal right to live and blossom as his own right (1984: 202). Naess adds that his use of the term 'biospherical egalitarianism – in principle' in fact suggests a positive doctrine. 'The importance of the intuition is rather its capacity to counteract, the perhaps only momentary, but consequential, self-congratulatory and lordly attitude towards what seems less developed, less complex, less miraculous' (1984: 202).

Both Fox's and Luke's criticism are directed at the inability of deep ecology to escape anthropocentrism in practice, as discussed in the above cases. However, these allegations imply that to be anthropocentric is not good in itself as far as other living beings are considered, which indirectly means that taking care of the latter is the morally true position. Even in the absence of a clear-cut practical solution, the attempt of deep ecologists is to take a caring attitude towards non-human living beings, especially the often-neglected lower forms, and they continue to argue for the same. They take the stance that in this effort, even if one cannot follow the principles fully in practice, one can accept them as a motto of life.

The confusion regarding the norm 'biospherical egalitarianism – in principle' becomes more problematic when one tries to resolve such conflicts on the grounds of rights-based theory, that is, when one takes both parties in an issue as right holders. Jim Cheney argues that on such a view conflict is inevitable because 'conflict is structured into Naess's position in virtue of his rights-based theory, the equal right of all forms of life to live and blossom' (Cheney, 1987: 140). He points out that the theory provides no way to resolve the conflict, since, for example, the relationship between the vegetable carrot and him would end up in his eating the former, which would be a potential violation of the principle of biospherical egalitarianism, according to Naess. Cheney questions how to understand this situation, that is, as a moral conflict between the carrot's right to live and blossom and his right. If so, and if it is wrong to eat the carrot, the situation is consistent with Naess's norm. If it is not wrong to eat the carrot, then, although the carrot has moral standing, a moral hierarchy is seen here. If we consider that there is no moral conflict, then it is not wrong to eat the carrot; this may be because the carrot has no moral standing, but only for him, or it could be that the relationship between himself and the carrot is not one of moral conflict. Thus, Cheney finds that the conflict generated out of this norm of biospherical egalitarianism has no solution (1987: 140).

He argues that the rights view invoked in the first case, that is, where there is moral conflict, is by contrast a market economy notion (Cheney, 1987: 141). 'Possession of rights by individuals generates conflict among individuals and this conflict is typically resolved by establishing some sort of pecking order among the rights or ranking of interests which satisfies all the involved individuals' (141). In this case, the rights or interests of the human outweigh those of the carrot. Conflict is logically inevitable in such an understanding of morality (141–2). The kind of equality invoked in such a view is shown to be problematic, for equality fractures society and places on every person the burden of standing on his own feet.[20] Callicott[21] suggests that this conflict can be resolved by moving up a level and making good of the whole the standard for adjudicating the (otherwise equal) claims of the parts. But according to Cheney, by taking this step the claims of the constitutive parts are invalidated; that is, the 'right to live and blossom' no longer counts – what counts is the well-being of the whole. Here, either ethics is concerned with defending the rights of individuals (or species), or it is concerned with defending the rights of the ecosystem (1987: 131).

Cheney observes that the question of whether one is justified in eating the carrot is not to be decided by weighing its claims or interests against humans, not because the carrot has no moral standing (1987: 141) but because the moral issue here is the correct relationship to one's food. According to him, to understand what our obligations are and what is required of us, it is necessary to understand the individuals involved, their relationship to one another and their place in a complex community or ecosystem. Instead of simplifying the situation as a conflict, it is recommended that

> the actors in the dilemma are to be seen not as opponents in a contest of rights but as members of a network of relationships [. . .] the solution of the dilemma lies in activating the network by communication [. . . and . . .] the solution to the dilemma will follow its compelling representation.[22]

The above discussion emerges from a situation where all non-human beings are also imparted equal right as humans, by deep ecologists. When all beings have similar right claim, all take the position of moral agents. Hence, the questions are focused on the issue of how the moral claims of moral agents other than human beings can be maintained, since other beings are not able to make decisions on their own. Though each discussant seeks different ways to solve the issue, the concern of all is to avoid conflict, to protect the moral right of the non-human, living and non-living beings. Those who think in terms of conflict resolution or follow a relational dimension try to highlight the moral stand of the non-human beings to avoid being overrun by the human beings.

In Naess's opinion, the issues that emerged while practicing the norm of biospherical egalitarianism, in principle, cannot be resolved by formulating some rules. He points out that there are many different cultures and that the cultural setting is different for each being in each culture (1984: 202). There are only a few general norms and only vague guidelines that can be applied to all cultures. In addition, it is difficult to put forth ethical rules of conduct without taking feelings such as felt nearness[23] and limited capacities[24] seriously. When interests conflict, under symbiotic conditions there are rules, which manifest as two operating factors, 'vitalness' and 'nearness' (Naess, 1998a: 142). The more vital interest has priority over the less vital. The nearer has priority over the more remote in space, time, culture and species. Nearness derives its priority from our special responsibilities, obligations and insights. Another factor is 'the diversity of obligations' (Naess, 1984: 202) one has to keep in life – for example, special obligations towards one's own children. In most cultures, any animal may be killed in order to feed one's starving child. Obligations towards species that have been members of our life community for long periods are greater than towards accidental visitors. Suffering is another factor that has influence in relations. Naess tries to convey here that an ethics concerning differences between non-human living beings is of a comparable level of complexity to ethics concerning different people and groups (202). He points towards the impracticability of making general rules when there are different preferences in different cultures. Therefore, he calls for understanding the equal right (or intrinsic value) of all beings as the basic premise of the deep ecology principle, thereby encouraging people to change their attitude towards the non-human world, irrespective of cultures and their practices.

Devall and Sessions reveal that when one tries to put into practice the biocentric norm, it begins with the realisation that humans, at both the level of individuals as well as communities, have vital needs other than food, water and shelter for becoming a mature human being; they include love, play, creative expression, intimate relationships with a particular landscape or nature in its entirety as well as intimate relationships with other humans and the vital need for spiritual growth (1985: 20). Here, deep ecologists introduce an alternative set of vital needs, characteristically different from the one from which the issues of conflict emerge. As this account shows, deep ecologists value certain non-material factors as more important than or as vital as material factors like food, water and others. According to them, our vital needs are simpler than what we usually realise (Devall and Sessions, 1985: 20). But technocratic–industrial societies encourage people towards increased consumption of goods by creating feelings of false needs and destructive desires through advertisements and so on. This tendency actually diverts us from facing reality in an objective way and from beginning the 'real work' of spiritual growth and maturity (20).

Devall and Sessions point out that 'biocentric equality is intimately related to the all-inclusive Self-realization in the sense that if we harm the rest of nature then we are harming ourselves. There are no boundaries and everything is interrelated' (1985: 20). Naess explains this connection of biocentric equality to Self-realization through a process of identification. He defines identification as a spontaneous, non-rational process through which the interest or interests of another being are reacted to as our own interest or interests (Naess, 1998a: 139). For Naess,

> the process of identification is sometimes expressed in terms of loss of self and gain of Self through self-less action. Each new sort of identification corresponds to a widening of the self and strengthens the urge to further widening, furthering Self-seeking.[25]
>
> *(140)*

This widening of self occurs through union with higher and higher levels, that is, first identifying with 'one's nearest', then through circles of friends, local communities, tribes, compatriots, races, humanity, life and, ultimately, with the supreme whole, which Naess identifies as the highest level of unity (Naess, 1998b: 140). Deep ecologists suggest here the ways to arrive at the philosophy that one should attain in order to escape from the overly exploitative attitude of the current system of society. They show that the process of identification or widening of self helps human beings to narrow the gap one feels towards other creatures, including other humans. They suggest attitudes like love, intimacy and so on that they value the most and that would help one to overcome possible opposite feelings like enmity, cruelty and others.

However, a higher level of identification does not eliminate conflicts of interests (Naess, 1998a: 139–40). That is, humans' vital interests imply killing at least some other living beings. For example, even a culture of hunters, in which identification with hunted animals reaches a remarkably high level, does not prohibit killing for food. The implication is that humans have to depend on nature for satisfying their vital interests, even if this requires killing some species, though one attains Self-realization. Naess claims that a great variety of ceremonies and rituals has the function of expressing the gravity of the alienating incident and restoring identification (1998a: 140). But Luke alleges that these are only 'symbolic rituals of sacralization' (1988: 88). It can be seen that this term itself advances the question of value. For example, there are contexts in which people find certain kinds of intervention in nature inevitable but wish to avoid such activities. These situations are of moral importance, and they will face a moral question. In such cases, acknowledging the wrongness of action, people may interact with nature. Hence, there is no devaluation of the moral maxim, which Naess upholds throughout his philosophy. There may be some practical overriding reason that necessitated one to act in that particular way. That is, here the act is justified by making some compensation, as Naess points out, by expressing love and respect towards nature in the form of saying thanks or performing some rituals or ceremonies, which is only one way of doing it. What follows from this example is that one cannot put clear-cut limiting criteria on human's interaction with nature. One can only insist that the actions they perform should be judicious. Hence, Naess's suggestion of performing ceremonials or rituals can be viewed as acts that guide the moral action of human beings in the non-human world. But Luke argues that there is a working of a 'soft anthropocentrism' in nature sacralization (88). Even a ritual prayer, the right attitude of respect or compassionate loving gratitude will rationalise and legitimate the softer anthropocentric actions of human beings, and hence 'people will continue to cut and burn trees, kill and eat plants and animals, or isolate and kill germs to fulfil vital human needs or to protect the integrity of humanly defined eco-communities' (88). However, this allegation can be true only when one reads this suggestion of deep ecologists as standing independent of other principles. If it is understood in accordance with the norm that 'we should live with minimum rather than maximum impact on other species and on the Earth in general' (Devall and Sessions, 1985: 20), the implication would be to reduce interactions with the non-human world as much as possible.

Another criticism against biocentric equality raised by Trumbore is that it is misanthropic, anti-people, fearful and distrustful (1996). He points out that in this view human beings are demoted in value to just another species competing for food and shelter. Trumbore questions deep ecology's call to abandon our status at the top of the food chain and our power over the environment, for the good of the whole. Likewise, the native intelligence of the ecosystem is taken to be much greater by deep ecologists than humans' wisdom to strike a harmonious balance between different competing species. For example, Dave Foreman, founder of Earth First!, considers that the AIDS virus benefits the planet because it helps in thinning the human herd. Moreover, human beings are asked to reduce demands because of their capacity to understand the consequences of their own actions. According to Trumbore, a dimension of coercion is implied in this view, to which many would object. He asks who, in such a situation, will determine the appropriate role of human beings in the ecosystem? If the population becomes too large for any place by some environmental yardstick, who decides who can move here, who must leave and who may stay? Who determines if one can plough up one's own backyard or cut down a tree? (1996). In his opinion, the solution must come from inside, from a sense of environmental altruism, or from outside through government regulations, though he does not have faith in the latter. Trumbore alleges that deep ecologists avoid such questions regarding coercion by suggesting a change of heart in terms of a spiritual shift in the human race, which inspired the deep ecologists to change eco-destructive habits. He points towards the fact that the reality of being a creature of any kind is having competing desires that can be mutually incompatible. For example, a lion's hunger is not compatible with the gazelle's desire for peaceful grazing; climbing vines have no concern for the host they choke from the light; so too human beings' desire and aversion (1996). In his criticism, Trumbore argues for the rights of the human species; the contention here is against the negligence of the human species. Though Trumbore agrees with the intention of the deep ecologists to take care of species other than humans, he finds it unethical to compel the latter to act in favour of the former. Therefore, he argues that the human species has the right to enjoy the privilege they possess over the environment as the superior ones.

In the second principle, deep ecologists highlight the richness and diversity as indicators of intrinsic value. Against the evolutionary view, they consider simple, lower or primitive species of plants and animals as the life forms that contribute essentially to the richness and diversity of life. These have value in themselves and are not merely steps towards so-called higher or rational life forms (Naess, 1995a: 69). They understand evolution as a magnificent expression of a multitude of forms of life. In their opinion, cherishing diversity appreciates differences and rejects any single standard of excellence (McLaughlin, 1995: 87). Naess points out that diversity enhances the potentialities of survival, the chances of new modes of life and richness of forms (1998b: 135). The struggle for life and survival of the fittest, necessary steps in the evolutionary explanation, should be interpreted in the sense of the ability to co-exist and co-operate in complex relationships rather than the ability to kill, exploit and suppress. While 'live and let live' forms the ecological principle of the former, 'either you or me' forms that of the latter, which tends to reduce the multiplicity of kinds of forms of life and to create destruction within communities of the same species. Ecologically inspired attitudes, however, favour the diversity of human ways of life, cultures, occupations and economies (135).

The third principle is more of a norm; it is a restriction on the uncontrolled intervention of human beings in the non-human world, with the purpose of protecting it by introducing the idea of vital need. But there is ambiguity regarding the feasibility of the concept of vital need in human life. The important issue is how to distinguish between vital and other needs. Luke complains that deep ecologists offer few criteria or no standards for practicing these precepts. He puts forward a few cases of conflicts which cannot be resolved without certain standards regarding vital needs:

> can humans destroy viruses and bacteria to cure diseases, can humans eat all plants if game is meager and turn to any game animals, if crops or natural grazing food fails, can humans reduce the diversity of a river basin with dams to control floods that let rivers or rain become what they are, and allow crops to displace natural vegetation and alter nitrogen fixation cycles in the existing topsoil?
>
> *(87–8)*

Luke alleges that deep ecologists need substantive rational criteria for answering these questions and for choosing between alternatives, but what they seem to offer are new symbolic rituals of sacralization (88).

Luke points out the difficulty in identifying vital needs (1988: 87). Without providing any criteria, how can humans decide that their need is more vital than that of other, non-human beings? How can one know about the vital needs of the latter? There will always be confusion in deciding who should get preference: human or the non-human beings? All these questions arise from a concern regarding human life, the existence of which is dependent on the non-human world. According to Naess, 'the term vital need is deliberately left vague to allow for considerable latitude in judgement. Differences in climate and related factors, together with differences in the structures of societies as they now exist, need to be taken into consideration' (1995a: 69). McLaughlin supports this view with the argument that the distinction cannot be drawn precisely, since what is a vital need in one context may be a trivial want in another (1995: 87). He cites two instances in order to show the difference in the two contexts: in the first, an Eskimo wears the skin of a seal, out of necessity, and in the other, the skin is worn as a marker of social status in an affluent society. The deep ecologist position is that the case of a vital need can be realised only according to context, and no other standards can be offered. Referring to the complexity of current society, McLaughlin opines that

> the consumerism inherent in industrialism denies the distinction between vital and other needs. To lose sight of it is to become trapped within an endlessly repeating cycle of deprivation and temporary satiation. Making the distinction opens to the possibility of more enduring forms of happiness and joy.
>
> *(McLaughlin, 1995: 87)*

This account reveals that the argument raised is not against the human species per se; rather, the criticism is towards the instrumental approach taken in the consumerist way of living. In such a situation, the primary and the most important step is to put a limit to the overuse of natural resources, which would be possible only by distinguishing between real and other needs.

The fourth principle is a call to decrease the human population to allow the flourishing of both human and non-human entities. Deep ecologists observe that an overnight reduction in excessive interference with the non-human world is not possible (Naess, 1995a: 69). They realise the urgency to develop new strategies for the stabilisation and reduction of the human population and to make deep changes in order to prevent substantial decreases in richness and diversity (69). Deep ecologists point towards the need to curb population growth in developed countries considering the tremendous rate of consumption and waste production by individuals in those societies (Devall and Sessions, 1998: 148). Moreover, they represent a much greater threat and impact in the biosphere per capita than individuals in Second and Third World countries. McLaughlin notes that humans have already jostled many species out of existence, and there are signs of more extinction in the future (1995: 87). UN reports indicate that the current trends in population growth will involve converting about 80% of current nature reserves to human use.[26] This would drastically accelerate already alarming trends towards the extinction of myriad species of life.[27]

According to deep ecologists, the continuing increase in human numbers also condemns many humans to a life of suffering (McLaughlin, 1995: 87–8). Industrial societies prefer fewer children than more, hoping to give them a better life. McLaughlin defends the deep ecologist call for a gradual decrease in the human population and argues that it does not imply misanthropy or cruelty to presently existing humans (88). Instead, the claim is that to reverse the growth of human population is to find ways of providing a decent life for all.[28] In other words, an excessive human population interrupts the flourishing of human and non-human life. While the encroachment of human beings forms the main cause for the reduction in the richness and diversity of the non-human world, it has been shown that a substantial section of society itself prevents the flourishing of a larger group of people. Hence, by presenting data and evidence, deep ecologists establish that the human population should be strictly controlled in order to protect the value or rights of the non-human world, which deep ecologists claim to be inherent in the latter, as shown in the foregoing principles.

Grey argues that 'if the concerns for humanity and non-human species raised by advocates of deep ecology are expressed as concerns about the fate of the planet, then these concerns are misplaced' (1993: 468). For him, issues like extinction of species seem to be raised from a planetary perspective, and these are not initiated by humans; similarly, claims like human technology as disrupting the delicate fabric of the ecosphere, for instance, are only exaggerated. Hence, activities related to overpopulation are problematic only from an anthropocentric point of view (468). Grey seems to misplace, in the above arguments, the value orientation, which deep ecologists try to highlight throughout their philosophy. While advancing their principles and norms, deep ecologists do not seem to be bothered about naturally induced ecological processes or changes such as extinction, landslide, flood and other natural calamities that happen due to factors that lie outside the realm of human–environment interaction; rather, their concern is in regard to human-induced changes in the environment. Therefore, deep ecological enquiry is limited to the consequences of anthropogenic factors; any discussion beyond that level seems to have no relevance here. The eco-centric perspective deep ecologists adopt here is also proved by attributing intrinsic value or right to every living or non-living being in nature, which is an acknowledgement of nature's own order of life. Thus, it is derived that raising arguments in favour of planetary perspective does not weaken deep ecologists' value claims or indicate that it does not make any sense in this context.

According to Luke, even if the deep ecological principles are true, who will decide how to decrease human populations, where, when and why? (1988: 88–9). While the people of the developed world see overpopulation as the problem of the underdeveloped world, excessive consumerism in the developed world is seen by the underdeveloped world as extravagant, worsening and forcing nature to collapse. In the underdeveloped world, one cannot expect that people will voluntarily stop reproducing to protect the survival of nature. Even those who follow Earth Wisdom will define reproduction as natural by finding one form of Self-realization in new life. Hence, only a '"hard biocentrism" versus a "soft anthropocentrism" approach would be able to reduce the population' (89).

The fifth principle is derived from the fourth and is a warning about excessive human interference in the non-human world. Deep ecologists make clear that their slogan of 'non-interference' does not imply that humans should not modify some ecosystems, as do other species. What they problematise are the nature and extent of such interference (Naess, 1995a: 69). Two types of interference are emphasised (McLaughlin, 1995: 88). One is the destruction of existing areas of wilderness, and the other is based on particular forms of technology. The destruction of old growth forests is to be prevented, because this is irreparable within any moderate timescale. The per capita destruction of wild (ancient) forests and other wild ecosystems have been shown to be excessive in rich countries. The rationale for such preservation should focus mainly on the ecological functions of these areas (Devall and Sessions, 1985). This suggestion does not involve dispossessing indigenous peoples who exist within those ecosystems without destroying them (McLaughlin, 1995: 88). Deep ecologists refer to the ways of living of tribal peoples, who co-exist with nature rather than excessively interfering with it.

But many criticise deep ecologists' reference to indigenous people as caretakers of the forests. Trumbore alleges that a kind of wisdom is posited in these tribes that seems to have already lost (1996). Many primitive tribes were not and still are not particularly wise at being eco-centric. Luke sharply criticises deep ecology's appropriation of primal people. For him, 'deep ecologists lump the many primitive cultures into one cultural pile and then privilege these values and practices unquestioningly in their ecosophical thought' (1988: 74–5). Devall and Sessions claim that primal peoples are characterised by individuation, personalism, nominalism and existentialism.[29] Luke alleges that deep ecologists simply attribute these qualities to primal peoples without taking into account practices such as warring, slavery, tribalism, sexism, racism and so on that are followed in their society and the contradictions involved in them (1988: 75). He asks,

> Why define all Indian societies as truly "primal" or equally peaceful, nature regarding and respectful of the individual; in the larger picture of all primitive societies, do all primal cultures share these nature-regarding norms as ethical universals? Can the same rules, however, be followed today by ecologizing post-industrial peoples reinhabiting nature?
>
> *(73)*

Luke finds it to be part of the effort to establish the idea of 'reenchantment of Nature' (76–78), and part of the belief that the natural and supernatural worlds are inseparable and each intrinsically a part of the other (73). The myth, magic and rituals of primal societies form functional equivalents of enlightenment science and technology, which deep ecologists have treated reluctantly (Luke, 1988: 76). Luke accepts the view that ritual and myth can anticipate scientific domination, as Horkheimer and Adorno[30] argue, though deep ecologists conceive of these as the non-dominating science. According to Bronislaw Malinowsky,[31] primal myths and rituals are an operationalist mode of thinking, mediating primal people's efforts to control or influence nature.

Grey does not consider that all spiritual empathy with the non-human world is benign (1986: 214). Though other cultures can serve as an inspiration and function as an aid to develop a satisfactory critique of our own cultural vices by comparison with alternatives, 'we are certainly not obliged to accept such belief systems in toto' (214). For Martin,[32] 'it is misguided sentimentality to suppose that we can simply transplant the values and beliefs from other cultures to our own'.

In the second sort of interference, deep ecologists are critical of technologies that disrupt natural cycles. Modern agricultural practices involve large-scale monocropping, which requires many inputs, such as fertilisers, pesticides, irrigation and so on, which will harmfully affect the soil if applied unscientifically. However, practices such as multicropping, integrated pest management and a variety of organic farming techniques interfere less with natural cycles and can enhance the fertility of soils (McLaughlin, 1995: 88). But Trumbore criticises the anti-industrial and therefore anti-technological bias of deep ecologists (1996). According to him, one also has to take into account the benefits, like better food production, better healthcare, better methods of transportation and communication, which have improved human lives. Some realise that to return to a way of life that is totally tied to the rhythms of the Earth, as deep ecologists suggest, is not at all possible at this juncture (AtKisson, 1989). This is because Earth systems are very much disturbed, so adopting pre-technological methods would lead the former to destruction. Hence, what is now needed is to repair the damage. Zimmerman recommends developing efficiency and production methods in order to take some of the pressure off the environment and increasing wealth for highly populated countries to bring down their populations (AtKisson, 1989). It seems that deep ecologists are more concerned with the consumerist culture inherent in industrialism than with industrial technology (McLaughlin, 1995: 88). Industrial culture has lost sight of the distinction between vital and other needs. Deep ecologists see this as springing from an isolated ego, which is referred to as the modern Western self, striving primarily for hedonistic gratification or for a narrow sense of individual salvation in this life or the next (Devall and Sessions, 1985: 20).

> This socially programmed sense of the narrow self or social self dislocates and leaves us prey to whatever fad or fashion is prevalent in our society ... We are thus robbed of beginning the search for our unique spiritual/biological personhood.
>
> *(20)*

Deep ecologists do not cast off technology per se; rather, they are against the misuse of technology that is blind to the well-being of the non-human world. Naess is of the opinion that technology is more helpless than ever, because the technology being produced does not fulfil basic human needs, such as meaningful work in a meaningful environment (1987: 13). He finds fault with the trend of adopting technologies without recognising which are useful or applicable to their culture. Therefore, the result would be that culture is adjusted to the technology. Whatever kind of technology we use, deep ecologists insist that it must ensure the preservation of wilderness, of richness and diversity, which remain high values of the ecosystem that should be cherished (Trumbore, 1996). By valuing wilderness, we do not devalue people but rather elevate the value of the species, which cannot co-exist with us as neighbours (1996). To attain this level of wisdom, deep ecologists suggest that we must see beyond our narrow contemporary cultural assumptions and values and the conventional wisdom of our time and place, and that this is best achieved by the meditative 'deep questioning'[33] process (Devall and Sessions, 1985: 20). Only in this way can we hope to attain full, mature personhood and uniqueness. The arguments of deep ecologists point to the fact that discriminatory knowledge for the use of technology should come from a different value system, which one can adopt only by leaving behind what we now value the most.

Naess focuses on the incompatibility between ideal sustainable forms of economic growth and the present policies of industrial societies. 'Present ideology tends to value things because they are scarce and because they have a commodity value and the result is vast consumption and waste' (Naess, 1995a: 69–70). Though the sustainability concept is vague and controversial, McLaughlin recommends that any restructuring of economy should be founded on this notion; there needs to be clarity about 'what', precisely, is to be sustained (1995: 89). Deep ecology requires, at the least, sustaining the very conditions for the diversity of myriad forms of life, including the cultural diversity of human life (89). In certain important areas like agriculture, irrigation projects, landscape changes and others, one can adopt an approach that would least disturb the diversity of nature. The orientation of deep ecologists is to create awareness among people about the urgent need to change the present situation.

In the sixth principle, deep ecologists intend to carry out their alternative value system, which is based on a loving and caring attitude towards the non-human world, and that can be made possible via changing policies. They foresee that though these ideas may be voluntarily applied at an individual level, large-scale implementation will be possible by changing people's practices through policy changes. The fact is that the politics of current society is built upon the fundamental ideas of economic growth as conceived by industrial and consumerist ways of development. This principle is incompatible with other principles discussed from (1) to (5) (Devall and Sessions, 1985: 148).

Through seventh principle, deep ecologists claim that a way of living based on their philosophy of inherent value will result in an enhanced quality of life. However, present society, enmeshed within consumerism, is totally negligent of life quality. If people opt for the quality aspects of life, they would be able to realise that the existing patterns of labour and consumption are not satisfying but rather involve chronic dissatisfaction (McLaughlin, 1995: 89). Appreciating the quality of life instead of quantities of things leads to an increase in happiness, not a decrease (89). But the fact is that 'in shifting human satisfaction to appreciate the quality of life over higher quantitative standards of living, deep ecology has no program' (Luke, 1988: 89). This philosophical approach of deep ecology – that is, to change the self to change society with individual acts of will guided by 'correct' conscience/ consciousness – is labelled as moral anarchism by Luke, since it does not have a proper plan to save humanity (1988: 89).

Deep ecologists remind us again in principle eight of the importance of practicing their philosophy in order to make a change in the current situation. One should attempt to bring in necessary changes, keeping in mind the problems of economic growth and the emptiness of consumerism, though there are no clear indications of the priority areas that need change (McLaughlin, 1995: 89). In spite of the different opinions about what is most urgent now, he suggests that such differences should be respected in the light of the value of diversity (89). According to Luke, taking all the principles together, there is not a secure theory of the state, ideology, technology or economy (1988: 89). He calls deep ecology vision a 'utopian ecologism' in failing to outline practicable means for realising these ecologically moral visions; in effect, 'political action is displaced into the realm of ethical ideals, making it every individual's moral duty to change him or herself in advancing cultural change' (90).

2.2.1 Analysis

It is clear from the foregoing discussion that deep ecologists have a global or catholic vision not only about identifying problems in the domain of human ecology but also in tracing what they identify as the causes of these problems and in bringing forth a number of recommendations. Their point of reference obviously is the human–nature relationship. For the present purpose of the book, how they represent this relationship is of utmost importance. It is an ideal representation of the relationship between human and nature. It contrasts 'what is' of the relationship to 'what ought to be' of the relationship. It gets its ethical character from this representation. Thus, in their account of this relationship, deep ecologists emphasise values rather than facts. If the value system enters into the description of human agency in its relation to the environment, then it tells us about conditions under which certain environmental changes occur, although this will not amount to an explanation of such changes. Having scientifically explained the events that occur in the domain under discussion, we may understand more about the occurrences once we know what explains human actions in that domain. For deep ecologists, the question of value figures exactly here. Even when social scientific explanations supplement the ecological explanation in this domain, it still needs to make references to values that human agents hold in life. In this sense, the value aspect of the domain is irreducible to that of the factual. The facts could have been different, if the value system of the human agents, their attitude, were different. It is because of this perception that the deep ecologists found it more significant to provide a critique of the modern Western value system that allegedly distorted the relation between the human world and environment to the extent of bringing about disastrous consequences for all beings.

2.3 Ecofeminism

Ecofeminism[34] deals with the question of the underlying reasons for the twin oppression of women and nature. Ecofeminists recognise that there are also other forms of oppression based on sex, race, class, age and so on (known as sexism, racism, classism and ageism respectively) and that these systems of oppression are interconnected.[35] They identify an oppressive conceptual framework[36] – such as the patriarchal conceptual framework of society, which explains, justifies and maintains the subordination of women and nature by men – as the main reason for the oppression of women and nature. Different from deep ecologists, who argue for a non-human world, ecofeminists argue for both women and nature. The emphasis is not on 'intrinsic value'; rather, the focus is shifted to the independent material existence of women. In other words, ecofeminists attribute value to women's freedom to sustain on their own, but not under the power of men.

The main concern of ecofeminism is to make visible different sorts of women–nature connections and, where such connections are harmful to both women and nature, to dismantle them. Ecofeminists claim that there are historical (causal), conceptual, empirical and experiential, symbolic, epistemological, political (praxis), ethical and theoretical connections between feminism and environmentalism.[37] The historical and causal links between the domination of women and nature are located in the conceptual structures of domination[38] that construct women and nature in male-biased ways. A major part of the ecofeminist literature describes these conceptual links as emerging from patriarchal dualisms like reason/emotion, mind/body, culture/nature, human/nature and man/woman dichotomies and from the rationalist tradition. Some ecofeminists relate it to the scientific revolution of the sixteenth and seventeenth centuries, with a reductionistic, mechanistic view of nature and to the consequent Industrial Revolution, which intensified the exploitation of nature and the subordination of women.

The inferred sources of these oppressing or dominating trends, whether in the rationalistic or scientific periods, assume that the category of men is superior over women and nature. This kind of subjugation was made possible by first subjugating nature and thereby women by distancing the latter from the various roles they performed in close contact with nature, the best example being traditional agriculture. As part of the attempts to establish connections between the oppression of women and nature, various ideas and conceptions on the relationship between both are revived in ecofeminism. First is the organic theory that was prevalent in pre-modern Europe, which emphasised the identification of nature, especially the earth, with a nurturing mother, that is, a kindly beneficent female who provided for the needs of mankind in an ordered, planned universe (Merchant, 1993: 270). Another opposing image of nature was as wild and uncontrollable, that could render violence, storms, droughts and general chaos. According to Merchant, the change in controlling imagery was directly related to changes in human attitudes and behaviour towards the earth (1993: 270).

> Whereas the first image worked as a cultural constraint restricting the types of socially and morally sanctioned human actions allowable with respect to the earth, the new images of mastery and domination functioned as cultural sanctions for the denudation of nature.
>
> *(270)*

Both were identified with the female sex and were projections of human perceptions onto the external world.

In the first description, the woman–nature connection is made based on an imaginary view about the relation. The image of nurturing mother points towards one who will always take care of her children and who will in turn always be dependent on the latter. Hence, there is a mutual loving and caring attitude between them, which will ensure the protection of both, and there is no question of exploitation. Shiva refers to the traditional Indian cosmological view of nature, 'Nature both animate and inanimate, as an expression of Shakti (dynamic energy), the feminine and creative principle of the cosmos' (1988: 38). 'All the forms of nature and life in nature are the forms, the children, of the Mother of Nature who is nature itself borne of the creative play of her thought'.[39] 'The common yet multiple life of mountains, trees, rivers and animals are an expression of the diversity that Prakriti gives rise to' (Shiva, 1988: 39). All these quotes imply the nurturing relationship between human being and the Earth as mother.

Among recent ecofeminist theories,[40] radical ecofeminism holds that women are closer to nature than men. These radical feminists,[41] also known as cultural feminists, are sometimes termed 'nature feminists' (Warren, 1987: 14) or 'essentialists'

(Carlassare, 1996: 221)[42] since they argue for a pure femininity, a female essence, outside the boundaries of the social, which is identified with nature. They emphasise the physiological bond between women and nature through the capacity of women to carry, give birth to and nurse children.[43] It is through bodily processes, such as menstruation, that radical/cultural ecofeminists find the identification of women with nature. This group promotes their belief through a celebration of the feminine, particularly rituals of menarche and childbirth, and through the revival of goddess worship. For example, writings of Spretnak, Mies and Shiva focus on linking certain qualities of women and nature (Buckingham-Hatfield, 2000: 36). Spretnak, for example emphasises the powerful spirituality of ancient goddess traditions, which revered the Earth, through the myth of Gaia, Earth Mother. Likewise, Mies and Shiva refer to a spiritual ecofeminism, which taps into women's ancient wisdom such as knowledge of plants and their sensual energy. That is, 'in celebrating the naturalness of the body, human's connection to the Earth is reinforced' (36).

Radical feminists identify certain characters that form part of the cultural life of women, which they believe to be the reasons for women's oppression, and try to bring forth those same qualities to represent what constitutes 'woman' and to argue for equal position with men. By comparing women's bodily processes and nature's processes, these feminists treat nature as a different entity and try to free it from oppression. However, it has been pointed out that this can lead to the prejudice that women have specifically female or womanly interests in preventing pollution, nurturing animals or saving the planet (Warren, 1987: 14). Some radical feminists themselves allege that this kind of woman–nature connection can simply be a rationale for the continued subordination of women rather than their liberation.[44] But it may be the case that claiming independent existence of both women and nature may create a social space for discussing the problems of both, thereby forming a cause for the reduction of further destruction of nature. In this sense, instead of subordination, the women–nature connection may ensure the right of women to speak for themselves and for nature.

Lorde[45] points out that an essentialist notion of women leads to 'an erasure of difference between women and it allows women with race, class or national privileges to sidestep their obligation to take responsibility for their own power and also their participation in structures of domination'. It further assumes that certain experiences represent the experience of all women. Yet another problem of conceiving a unified, essentialised gender category of 'woman' is that it can ignore the diversity of women's lives and histories across the boundaries of race, class, nationality, age and sexuality (Lorde, 1984: 67–9). Lorde points towards the problems in categorising all women under a single title; that is, though women are under oppression, it may not be the case with all women. By participating in structures of domination, some women themselves become causative agents for the oppression of other women, along with men. In this sense, an essential notion of women may be an obstacle for understanding the different roles women perform as social agents, who also help in the production and reproduction of structures of domination. Yet Lorde's argument does not invalidate the intention of the feminists to argue for their freedom.

Social/ist ecofeminists criticise that cultural ecofeminists, as essentialists, are apolitical (Carlassare, 1996: 228), in the sense that they rely more on spiritual, psychological and intuitive explorations of the oppression of women, instead of on materialist analyses of institutions. Hence, they believe that the works of cultural ecofeminists do not spell out a path for political or social action, only a path for personal transformation. For example, the works of Daly (1978)[46] and Griffin (1978)[47] are marginalised as essentialistic. Biehl interpreted Griffin's text 'as regressively perpetuating the patriarchal essentialist associations of women with nature and men with culture that have been used to oppress women'.[48] Carlassare points out that an alternative interpretation of Griffin's text is possible, and this essentialist association can be interpreted as a tactic of resistance; the content of the text can be read to substantiate this interpretation (1996: 224). The criticism made by Jaggar is that both Daly and Griffin use essentialist language that is, invariably, 'poetic and allusive' rather than 'literal and exact'.[49] Thus, while Jaggar marginalises the discursive practices of some cultural ecofeminists on the basis that they are essentialist (Carlassare, 1996: 227), Biehl marginalises their epistemological practices as 'irrational' and hence essentialist.[50] Carlassare argues that for Daly and Griffin the essentialist language they use indicates that the politics of women's liberation includes revaluing that which has been associated with women and devalued. Carlassare opines that their texts can be viewed 'as strategically deploying and reconstructing the characteristics that have been traditionally associated with women for the sake of fostering social and psychological transformations and empowering women while working to liberate women from their gender construct' (1996: 228). Social/ist ecofeminists in general believe that changes in social, political and economic systems are required for the liberation of both women and nature, while cultural ecofeminists understand that changes in human consciousness and spirituality are inseparable from the changes in institutions that are required for the liberation of women and nature (Carlassare, 1996: 227). 'To them, oppression is a sign of spiritual crisis – political and cultural transformation will not occur without a concurrent shift in human consciousness' (227).

Radical and social ecofeminists are political in different ways. As they reveal through the slogan 'personal is political', radical ecofeminists give emphasis to the private or the personal matters of women and try to bring them forward as one dimension of being political. They are of the opinion that before expecting any changes in the institutional framework, a fundamental change in human nature is required. Social ecofeminists identify various institutions as the medium for the production and reproduction of social, political and economic systems. Hence, they try to be political by meaningfully intervening in institutional arrangements and by making necessary changes that will ensure the liberation of women. Thus, while social ecofeminists adopt a pragmatic approach, cultural ecofeminists take a philosophical position in their political outlook. The position of radical ecofeminists can be taken as a precondition for an understanding about the institutionalised oppression of women and nature. In both cases, the problems women face in life – i.e., radical ecofeminists in private space and social ecofeminists in public – are problematised in the public realm. Therefore, radical and social ecofeminists are political in expressing and dealing with the problems of the oppression of women and nature.

Carlassare notices that social/ist ecofeminists also take an essentialist position in two ways (1996: 230–1). Firstly, the female body and biological sex are considered part of material nature, in the sense that they are natural, not socially constructed. In other words, though women are made, not born, they are socially constructed out of naturally sexed, anatomical raw material. For Carlassare, 'basing gender on material nature or biological sex necessarily naturalizes and essentializes gender' (230). Some comment that it is questionable whether such fixed qualities can be attributed to individual bodies when it is difficult to say with any certainty that the body is a fixed and immobile concept.[51] Secondly, while social/ist ecofeminists deny that there is any immutable eternal essence that defines women, they do recognise that 'women' is a mobile construction that rests on spatially and temporally variable social relations; they often work with a historically continuous, simple, essentialised notion of 'woman'. Therefore, Carlassare asks 'if woman rests solely on variable social relations, how can the category be asserted without essentializing women?' (231). Thus, she asserts that it is possible to read constructionism as implied within essentialism, as is essentialism within constructionism (231).

Agarwal[52] and Mellor[53] argue that only a materialist interpretation will help us to see the underlying basis of women's relationships with the non-human world. Agarwal points out that the ecofeminist conception about women as 'constructed' is problematic on the following counts (1998: 195): (1) it posits 'women' as a unitary category without differentiating them by class, race, ethnicity and so on, (2) it locates the domination of women and of nature almost solely in ideology, neglecting the material source of this dominance (based on economic advantage and political power), (3) yet it says little about the social, economic and political structures even in the realm of ideological constructs within which these constructs are produced and transformed, (4) the ecofeminist argument does not take into account women's lived material relationships with nature and (5) the question of essentialism with regard to cultural feminism.

In order to challenge these constructs, Agarwal finds it necessary to have a theoretical understanding 'of the interplay between conflicting discourses, the groups promoting particular discourses and the means used to entrench views embodied in those discourses' (1998: 195), which she terms as 'the political economy of ideological construction', and to examine the underlying basis of women's relationships with the non-human world at levels other than ideology (196). She puts forward the idea of 'feminist environmentalism' (197–8), a perspective which would deal with conflicts over both resources and meanings in terms of action. On the feminist front, there would be a need to challenge and transform both notions about gender and the actual division of work and resources between the genders. On the environmental front, there would be a need to challenge and transform both notions about the relationship between people and nature and the actual methods of appropriation of nature's resources by a few (198). In such a conceptualisation of the interaction with nature, the link between women and the environment can be seen as structured by a given gender and class (caste/race) organisation of production, reproduction and distribution.

Mellor points out that the relationship between the subordination of women and the destruction of the environment reflects a deep and pervasive material relation (2000: 113). In other words, the material relationship between humanity and its natural context is gendered. The pervasive and material relation she refers to here is the fact that women's work and lives have historically been disproportionately concerned with the basic means of human existence, the production of food, people and society. Though Marx could unravel the class-exploitative activities of nineteenth-century capitalism and labour as the interaction of humanity with the natural world, he did not see the natural world as either limited or having its own 'needs' (2000: 109–10). Moreover, he viewed reproductive work in the narrow sense and assumed that there was a natural sexual division of labour, and the bearing and raising of children were unproblematically taken as women's work (2000: 10). The ecological political economy Mellor conceives firstly breaks down the distinction between production and reproduction, since reproducing and caring for children as well as growing food is certainly more important than producing weapons or cars. Secondly, it challenges the notion of the 'economic' that has failed to recognise the rationale for women's work and boundaries between paid, low-paid and unpaid work. Thirdly, it aims to thwart many of the current assumptions regarding man-oriented economic structures. Thus, it questions the idea that the primary motivation for production is money or profit and the impossibility of distinguishing between wants and needs. Fourthly, it envisages an economic framework that would enable human communities built upon destructive economic systems to provision themselves without exploitation of women, men, other species or the ecosystems of the planet (110).

Mellor emphasises the need to recognise women's unpaid domestic, communal and subsistence work (2000: 114). The issue is not about the formality of payment/non-payment of women's work, but about the way economic systems (capitalist and non-capitalist) have been gendered. Historically, economic activity has tended to be centred on men's activities like war, trade, construction and others – that is, the notion of the 'economic' was generally constructed within a world that represents male experience but does not reflect the world of women's experience. 'It is the work of human bodily existence that has generally been left to women. For example, care of the young, the old, the sick and the need for daily replenishment and cleanliness' (114). Therefore, she argues that the starting point of an effective ecological political economy would have to be based on the world of women's experience, not only of ecological sustainability, but also of the human life cycle, with priority given to work that is currently undervalued and marginalised (114).

Shiva notices how women's role in agriculture was marginalised in an economically dominant world. Historically, women possessed a supreme role in traditional agriculture (1992: 209). They were skilled in the production and preparation of plant foods, seed preparation, germination requirements, soil choice, plant requirements, weather conditions, micro-climatic factors, soil enrichment technologies, information about plant diseases, pruning, water supplies, predators, growing seasons, soil maintenance and so on. Women's participation in cultivation ensured the diversity of seeds and crops. Their knowledge was the mainstay of the indigenous dairy industry, forestry and others. Likewise, women have been the custodians of biodiversity in most cultures. But in the patriarchal worldview, man is the measure of all value, and instead of diversity there is hierarchy (205). Women, being different, are treated as unequal and inferior. Nature's diversity is not appreciated for its intrinsic value; value is assigned only when it is economically useful for commercial gain. In the patriarchal model of progress, the marginalisation of women and the destruction of biodiversity go together (205). That is, by introducing monocultures, uniformity and homogeneity, women are removed from all their traditional agricultural works. Shiva points out that while gender subordination and patriarchy are the oldest of oppressions, they have taken on new and more violent forms through the project of development.

Some ecofeminists focus on the study of the earlier form of patriarchy because they saw it as important, for understanding the problem of both gender and nature subordination, to identify to what kind of social practice this domination was first related. Lahar traces these connections to prototypical patterns of domination that begun with the invasion of Indo-European societies by nomadic tribes from Eurasia about 4500 BC.[54] Warren notes that Riane Eisler describes the time before these invasions as a matrifocal, matrilineal, peaceful agrarian era.[55] Mies attempts to make an idea of the earlier forms of patriarchy (women's oppression and exploitation) and traces its modifications up to capitalist accumulation and growth (1986: 49–71). She sketches women's close interaction with nature in the pre-historical period. According to this, among the group of hunters and gatherers, the first division of labour by sex – that is, between the gathering activities of women and the hunting activities of men – originated in the fact that women necessarily were responsible for the production of daily subsistence (54). Gathering of plants, roots, fruits, mushrooms, nuts, small animals and others was right from the beginning a collective activity of women.

> Women's production of new life, of new women and men was inseparably linked to the production of the means of subsistence for this new life. Mothers who give birth to children and suckle them necessarily have to provide food for themselves and for the children. Thus, the appropriation of their bodily nature, the fact that they produce children and milk, makes them also the first providers of the daily food, be it as gatherers, who simply collect what they find in nature, plants, small animals, fish etc. or as agriculturists.
>
> *(55)*

Historically, women have acquired a vast body of experiential knowledge about the functions of their bodies through observation and experience. This appropriation of her own body was closely related to the acquisition of knowledge about the generative forces of external nature, about plants, animals, the earth, water and air (54).

The necessity of providing the daily food could have led to the invention of regular cultivation of food plants such as grains and tubers. This signifies a new stage and an enormous increase in the productivity of female labour, which, it is assumed, made the production of a surplus possible for the first time in history (1986: 55). The technological precondition for the collection of a surplus was the invention of containers, baskets of leaves and plant fibres and jars. These first inventions, made by women, had connections to their subsistence production. Mies points out that critical research by feminist scholars proves that the survival of mankind has been due much more to 'woman-the-gatherer' than to 'man-the-hunter' (58), which she referred to as a 'predatory mode of production' (62). While the women experienced their whole body as productive, male bodily productivity cannot appear as such without the mediation of external means of tools. Women's technology, used for subsistence production and for gathering as well as for early agriculture, also remained productive, whereas the hunting technology of men was not productive. That is, hunting equipment proper cannot be used for another productive activity. The bow and arrow and spears are basically means of destruction (61). Mies points out that though there may have been inequality between men and women, hunters were not able to establish a full-fledged system of dominance (63).

D'Eaubonne observes that before 3000 BC women alone possessed a monopoly on agriculture, and men believed that the gods impregnated women (1996: 177–8). This changed when man discovered the possibilities at once, agricultural and procreational, the control of which he took over for his own benefit, resulting in the two perilous situations of overpopulation and the destruction of natural resources. Fischer also argues that a dominance relationship of men over women could be established only after men had discovered their own generative capacities.[56] Their discovery, according to her, went hand-in-hand with the domestication and particularly the breeding of animals as a new mode of production. Female animals were subjected to sexual coercion. This means that the free sexuality of wild animals was subjected to a coercive economy, based on breeding, with the object of increasing the herds. Likewise, women were also subjected to the same economic logic and became part of movable property. Unlike hunters, women no longer seemed important as producers or gatherers by pastoralists. They were needed as breeders of children (Mies, 1986: 63). Thus, the monopoly of men over arms and the long observation of the reproductive behaviour of animals made possible the new mode of production. This led to a change in their relation to nature as well as to a change in the sexual division of labour. Thus, the establishment of patriarchal lines of descent and inheritance could be seen among pastoralists (63). Thus, Mies attributes the asymmetric division of labour between women and men to this predatory mode of production, which is based on male monopoly over means of coercion and on direct violence, by means of which permanent relations of exploitation and dominance between the sexes were created and maintained (65).

As this account shows, in pastoralism, the changed economy demoted women to mere reproductive machines while men asserted superiority in economic matters.

Under feudalism and capitalism, the productive relations hold the same basic structure of being asymmetric and exploitative, while only the forms of dominance and appropriation changed (Mies, 1986: 66).

> The asymmetric division of labour by sex, . . . was then upheld by means of institutions like patriarchal family and the state and also by means of powerful ideological systems, above all by patriarchal religions, law, medicine, which have defined women as part of nature, which has to be controlled and dominated by man.
>
> *(67)*

In the capitalist structure, when capital accumulation became the dominant motor of productive activity, wage labour formed the dominant form of labour control (67); as a consequence, women's work and knowledge were ignored and they remained invisible in modern capitalist agriculture. Ecofeminists observe that along with the exclusion of women and nature from the 'productive' sphere, and by making them 'means of production', the reproductive sphere was also looked upon as unworthy.

Plumwood examines how this happened in the process of accumulation, exemplifying the case of the sealing industry in Australia (1996: 212–13). She cites this example in order to illustrate 'how the inferiorization of the sphere of nature and the feminine combines with the definition of oppressed groups as part of this sphere to yield both an ideology and a material practice of linked oppression' (212). The industrial export of seals started in 1798 in Bass Strait and Tasmania caused to reduce the number of seals to a point below the levels capable of commercial exploitation in eight years, which happened later in New Zealand also. Sealers typically killed all sizes and ages of seals. This was also repeated with whales. As this industry achieved growth, it needed numerous workers and this was made possible with the native people, including runaway convicts and soldiers. The industry involved the abduction and enslavement of large numbers of Aboriginal women, who were subjected to cruelty and rape, and the killing of other Aborigines, leading to the virtual annihilation of Aboriginal Tasmanians (213). Plumwood realises that it was the inferiority of the order of 'nature' – interpreted as barbaric, alien, animal and also passive and female, which contrasted with the truly human realm marked by patriarchal, Euro-centric and so on – that underlay all kinds of oppressions. 'Aborigines were seen as part of this inferior order, supposedly being "in a state of nature" and without culture' (213). Likewise, the motive for killing whales and seals might arise from contempt for the very processes of life. Both female and nature are ignored by undervaluing the process of reproduction, the result being that the category 'woman' was no longer considered an agent with any constructive role in the social or economic sphere.

Some ecofeminists point out that men's attitude of alienating themselves from life could have arisen from a painful sense of exclusion from the life process and the realisation that they can only appropriate life but cannot produce it (Salleh, 1996: 316). This argument takes support from the idea that the concept of 'labour' is usually reserved for men's work, work that is done with the hands or head. Hands and head are considered 'human' parts of the body, while the womb and breasts are described as 'natural' or 'animal' (Mies, 1986: 46), the result being that the above argument helps only to reinforce the superiority of men. D'Eaubonne explains that this unjust attitude of men towards reproduction by women and nature arises not only because it is men who hold world power but also because of the manifestation of a sort of power at the lower level allocated in such a way to be exercised by men over women (1996: 185). She notices a play of this power when debating the issue of overpopulation. Male society realises that there is a problem of exponential growth rate in population and somehow it must be controlled. Therefore, they accept the demand put forward by women for control over their future and procreation. At the same time, they fear that if the demands of freedom of access to contraception and abortion are met, this will be favourable to the latter and will negatively affect their controlling power over women (185). This dilemma works behind the contradicting positions male society takes on reproductive and population issues.

On the other hand, it is argued that overpopulation affects food production and economic growth, resulting in environmental depletion, and that women are responsible for this situation. Ecofeminists note that this kind of reasoning expects women to stop making new life and is a question of women's rights over her own body. While the patriarchal economy is the real culprit of environmental depletion, the responsibility is simply ascribed to women. Salleh points towards a study[57] which reveals that falling food production results from the formal economy itself which takes both land and men's labour away from family farming (1996: 317). Though overpopulation is a real issue, without considering woman's rights over her own body and other ethical issues related to this, targeting of Third World population control is unjust. Salleh calls our attention to the fact that while, in the Third World, children provide supplementary labour for overworked mothers, in the North each infant born will use about 15 times more global resources during his/her lifetime than a person born in the former.[58] Salleh argues that in the context of this kind of inequality, it is inappropriate to demand population control in the South (1996: 317).

The method of tackling the population issue reveals how women are deliberately kept in an inferior position that does not allow them to be a responsible human agent by participating in decision-making. While men control women, on the one hand, by taking away their privilege over their own bodies, on the other, overpopulation is shown as the problem of women that affects the economy. In both cases, the role of women is overturned by concealing the real situation. D'Euabonne points towards this contradiction in the double face of male power, which, at once, pushes women into production, while resisting the fact that their females could control their procreation, and through which men can ensure that their private interests will be satisfied (1996: 191).

The ecofeminist solution

Many suggestions have been put forward by ecofeminists for solving issues arising in the context of the oppression of women and nature. One suggests that the male system of domination and hierarchy be replaced by a system of female qualities. Warren recommends a feminist ethic, which provides a central place for values like care, love, friendship and appropriate trust.[59] Cultural feminists consider as essential an ethic of care to revalue the relationship between humanity and nature.

Gilligan opines that women and men have different conceptions of 'moralities'. She characterises the morality of men as 'the justice approach' and the 'rights conception' and that of women as an 'ethic of care' and 'responsibility conception' (Cheney, 1987: 120).

> Gilligan's two 'moralities' differ in their ways of representing moral dilemmas and resolving moral conflicts. Women see conflicts of responsibilities where men see conflicts of rights. Women resolve conflicts by the method of inclusion. Men use the method of fairness or balancing claims. Women think contextually, men think categorically. Men see aggression as the source of hurt. Women find it in failures of response. Women define the self through relationships of care and responsibility. Men define the self in terms of individual achievement. Women's images of relationship are web-like. Men's are hierarchical.[60]

D'Eaubonne points out that ecofeminists do not argue for superiority of women over men or even for the 'values' of the feminine, which exist on a cultural level and not a metaphysical one (1996: 192). For them, women's personal interests join those of the human community, whereas male's interests, on an individual basis, are separate from those of the general community as it is visible with the current male system. Ecofeminists highlight certain human qualities like care, love, responsibility and others that they value the most and attribute them to women. These women qualities are valued on the grounds that they do not divide human beings based on power, wealth, caste etc.; rather, they treat other people and nature equally and responsibly. But qualifying all women with such virtues is questioned at another level. In Rose's opinion, to argue that women have essential qualities like being nurturing and sympathetic means ignoring any differences between women, that is, between white women and women of colour, between those with children and those with none, between women in the North and women in the South and so on.[61] This criticism can be seen as politically motivated, since to generalise all women as embodied with certain virtues is to conceal the reality of many women who live under different social conditions.

Firstly, women's relationships with their environment needs to be understood within their varied social, economic, cultural, and political and class contexts since there are differences and diversity in their voices and experiences which cannot be ignored or overestimated.[62] Women in the developing world usually bear the ecological costs of various production processes, technological progress and maldevelopment (Shiva, 1988: 7–8); a considerable proportion of the daily lives of rural women in these countries are spent in the gathering, growing and harvesting of food and the collection of water and sources of fuel and energy (Elliott, 1998: 148). Even in countries where women are increasingly part of the formal economy, the situation is not different; women in developed countries are simply affected by environmental degradation in different and often less immediate ways than women in the developing world. Wherever energy, land and water are degraded, it is women's lives that are more likely to be adversely and directly affected (149).

The State of India's Environment reports that the specific difficulties that women have faced historically through to the present – for instance, their extraordinary work burden or lack of access to healthcare – are located more in social forces and do not arise out of ecological deterioration per se (1984–1985). These forces are marginalisation and powerlessness (Rodda, 1993: 91). The hardships they face include sexual division of labour, their double work burden (at home and outside) and the unequal distribution of resources like food within the household, which stem from women's inferior status in the household and from a lack of control over cash and productive resources like land. The fact is that while environmental destruction exacerbates women's already acute problems, men are affected only in a less serious manner.[63]

Secondly, the claim that women are more able to keep a loving and caring attitude towards nature, just because it is this group rather than men that works more closely with nature, especially in developing countries, is also refuted with the support of evidence. As various studies[64] have shown, among poor peasants and tribal households, women are responsible for fetching fuel and fodder, and in hill and tribal communities, they are often the main cultivators. In the course of their everyday interactions with nature, they have acquired a special knowledge of various species in forests and the processes of natural regeneration. The case of women who make a considerable contribution to agricultural production is similar. They are the repositories of knowledge about farming techniques, various seed varieties, seasonal variations and other farming practices. This knowledge is more a result of social requirement, which could be seen as a factor in arousing love and respect towards nature. One cannot deny the fact, of course, that men who form part of the cultivation process[65] also acquire such knowledge, which can work as a factor for their concern towards nature. Even in those countries, difficulties might arise for women from the social situation existing in that place. Another study reveals

> although women became aware of their common suffering, their experience itself did not always provide sufficient motivation for common action. Women did not question the fact that their responsibility for the domestic arena, which they saw as natural, made them the primary sufferers.[66]

64 Ethics

Thirdly, ecofeminists also ignore the environmental damage done by women as consumers (Rodda, 1993: 57). In the household, women are consumers of energy and water, either directly or through the use of cookers, washing machines, refrigerators and other domestic appliances (57). Women use a wide range of goods from forest products. Fashions related to women's clothing and ornamentation, in the past, were responsible for the exploitation of certain species. For example, animals were trapped for their furs, skins and products such as ivory and tortoise shell. In some cases, exploitation has almost led to animal extinction. Many products used in modern industry not only have environmental implications but are also known to be harmful to health. Environmental problems due to women consumers are seen mostly in developed, especially industrialised, countries. Thus, when men in developing countries can be harmfully affected, along with women in those places, women in industrialised countries along with men become agents contributing to environmental problems. Without considering such realities, the category of 'women' in totality cannot be described as possessing certain virtues (58).

All these concerns, raised in a political context, seem to bring forth certain value questions, all of which have implications in social life. The first case points towards the fact that it is the category of women, whether in Third or First World countries, that continues to suffer environmental degradation. It unravels the problem of social inequality among men and women in society. The second argument reveals that it is the social situation that decides whether men or women work as agents in close proximity to nature, rather than viewing women's closeness to the latter as a given condition. The last case analyses the role of women along with men in creating environmental havoc when both are part of the institutions that comprise the patriarchal social structure. It is also an indication of the current lifestyle, which is environmentally destructive, and points towards the fact that social practices need to be oriented towards nature.

According to some ecofeminists, environmental degradation is a gendered process of production and reproduction and thus experiences changes in the environment in different ways (Jackson, 1995: 116). Hence, the importance of understanding gender divisions of labour is related not only to gauging the amount of work done by men and women but also to recognising that men and women do different work. Moreover, an unequal allocation of resources reinforces a gender bias in the impact of environmental degradation and development policies on women and their lives (125). Salleh recommends a woman-based economy (ecofeminist economy) (1996: 316). There are both qualitative and quantitative differences between men's and women's productive contributions. Qualitatively, women's mediation of nature in all its labour forms is organised around a logic of reciprocity rather than mastery and control (316). According to Mies, this reciprocity is possible because women 'are not owners of their own bodies or of the earth, but they cooperate with their bodies and with the earth in order to let grow and make grow' (1986: 56). Salleh foresees that once the patriarchal connections between women and nature are exposed and the reciprocal relationship of women with nature is made visible, a fundamental change will be reflected in the relations of production (1996:

318). This recommendation is radically political in the sense that in order to have a woman-based economy, a restructuring of current social, political and economic structures of production and reproduction is required, since a feminist economy cannot be founded on male-oriented structures of domination. In other words, a reciprocal relationship does not presuppose the supremacy of the female agent as does the hierarchical model of the male-oriented system. Thus, activities on the earth will also be according to the feminine principle of love and care.

Another ecofeminist claim is that in a world in which women found themselves truly in power, the first act would be to limit and space out births.[67] They refer to the problem of overpopulation as a problem of men. Even before overpopulation became an issue, women were trying to reduce birth rates. They allege that man deigns to notice the issue of overpopulation on a planetary scale, whereas women notice the rabbit effect at the family level. Now women are about to acquire this power – that is, as the sole controller of procreation through massive availability of contraception and uninhibited access to abortion – and this is the exact area where women can most efficiently bring about the defeat of the male reign and women's ancient oppression (D'Eaubonne, 1996: 193). This is clearly a politically determined position, for ecofeminists hope to solve the two social issues if they get/acquire power. Firstly, this will be an occasion to show that overpopulation is more a problem of men than of women. This is because though women do not wish to have more children, this is decided by the class of men. When the former has the power to enact laws, they will be able to prevent 'untimely and unwanted pregnancy'. Secondly, women will get control over their own bodies, as they will have a major role as decision makers.

Ecofeminists attribute all these problems to the human–nature dualism that forms the basis of the androcentric viewpoint. Deep ecologists highlight the importance of viewing human beings and nature as two different entities and suggest a solution in terms of the 'identification' of the self with nature. But ecofeminists allege that deep ecologists only pretend to overcome the problem of human–nature separation by suggesting the idea of 'transpersonal' identification and the 'indistinguishability' thesis and in fact have never addressed and analysed the origin of this problem. The main allegation is that the 'indistinguishability' thesis does not allow deep ecologists to recognise the distinctness and independence of human beings from nature and the distinctness of the needs of things in nature from humans, which is a very important part of respect for nature (Plumwood, 1991: 295). In addition, the 'transpersonal' identification of deep ecology denies particular, emotional and kinship-based attachments, and thus it indirectly holds the superiority of reason (297).

Ecofeminists claim that human–nature dualism can be overcome by recognising 'excluded qualities – split off, denied or construed as alien or comprehended as the sphere of supposedly *inferior* humans such as women and blacks – as equally and fully human' (Plumwood, 1991: 299). They expect that this would provide a basis for the recognition of continuities with the natural world. Ecofeminists find value in ending dualistic trends, and categories like women and blacks are attributed value by considering them as 'human', like the class of men. Hence, so-called women qualities like reproductivity, sensuality and emotionality are taken to be as fully and authentically human qualities as the capacity for abstract planning and calculation (299). Thus, ecofeminists call for a reconceptualisation of the 'human' and 'nature' to free them from the legacy of rationalism. Warren tries to define what it is to be human, as informed by a non-patriarchal conception of the interconnections between human and non-human nature. She finds it possible in two ways: firstly, by a psychological restructuring of our attitudes and beliefs about 'ourselves' and 'our world' (including the non-human world), and secondly, a philosophical rethinking of the notion of the self that sees ourselves as both co-members of an ecological community and yet different from other members of it (1987: 19).

By redefining human, ecofeminists highlight the importance of human agents who are free from the patriarchal structure, as against the male and female agents. The non-human world stands different from human but not as one to be dominated. Against the instrumental view of the relation of self to others, which omits a significant dimension of the human experience, ecofeminists suggest a 'relational account of self' (Plumwood, 1991: 302) and prefer to see 'human beings and their interests as *essentially* related and interdependent' (301). They claim that it can allow for both continuity and difference, which are expressive of the rich, caring relationships of kinship and friendship rather than increasing abstraction and detachment from relationship. Warren observes, 'humans are who we are in large part by virtue of the historical and social contexts and the relationships we are in, including our relationships with non-human nature' (Warren, 1993a: 335). She is of the opinion that the relationships of humans with the non-human world are also constitutive of what it is to be human (335). Here ecofeminists emphasise the relationships of humans with nature and see it as important to understand the characteristics of each relation. Humans have been moulded by their experiences of interaction with nature for many years. Hence, they value the experiences of women also as human experiences and recommend understanding them as constructed entities. By using 'relational self', ecofeminists intend to treat the other with caring and respect, whatever the self comes to interact with as the 'other', whether a living entity or a non-living one. For example, they suggest that in climbing a mountain, the latter is to be treated as the case with any living entity.

Another point of difference is that compared to the holistic view of deep ecology, ecofeminism is concerned with preserving community; it does not make individuals subservient to the well-being of the whole (Cheney, 1987: 132). Our moral obligations to the biosphere may be best served by seeing ourselves as elements of a moral community rather than the deep ecology position of understanding the self as a functional part of a larger organic whole. This difference in approach is reflected in dealing with the issue of conflict resolution; that is, when deep ecology views conflict resolution as irresolvable, ecofeminists speak about consensual decision-making. The latter emphasises the context within which moral decisions are made, instead of abstract moral principles. Ecofeminists argue that what our responsibilities are is a function of where we happen to find ourselves in that web of relations that constitutes the community, the connections that define us and from which responsibilities are experienced as given rather than as freely contracted.[68] The kind of responsibility Gilligan is concerned with is not that which is correlated with rights but rather, the kind which is incurred through friendship.[69] The basis of responsibility is not the right of another but rather our particular connectedness to that other. Consideration of obligation, fairness and others grow out of an analysis of the nature of friendship, care and love.

2.3.1 Analysis

As ecofeminists bring the issue of man versus woman to the foreground in their analysis of environmental problems, it may appear that they sideline or reject the question of value and re-present the whole question as one of a predominantly political, that is, gender-based, relation of power. But it is taken here as an apparent sidelining. Ecofeminists would agree that the historically prevalent attitude to nature is distorted, and this distortion gives rise to environmental problems in the domain. The attitude in question is one of value-orientation. According to ecofeminists, when deep ecologists attribute the cause of environmental problems to an anthropocentric attitude, this tells only a partial story. What is called an anthropocentric attitude is in the final instance only an androcentric attitude. When we realise the full import of this identification, we naturally look for a redefinition of what is human. This means certain qualities that are continuous with nature are to be excluded from the definition of human. Anthropocentrism represented human as the image derived from male-dominated human practices. What is really valuable in human relations with nature are those qualities which are excluded yet manifested in categories like women, blacks and so on. Ecofeminists called for a change in attitudes towards nature and towards women. Besides rejecting the anthropocentric/androcentric attitude, this requires a redefinition of self as a co-member of the ecological community as well as outside it. What is needed is not identification with nature but rather, keeping the differences from nature intact, a redefinition of human agency in terms of a relational self, continuous with, yet different from, nature and other beings. Human beings should therefore be seen as elements of a moral community. Such an attitude could ensure an obligation towards the biosphere. The idea of a moral community and that of the relational self imply that moral decisions are context-sensitive, and for ecofeminists, there are no abstract moral principles on which human actions are based.

2.4 Social ecology

Murray Bookchin criticises the current trends of ecological movements for being either reductionistic or monistic and dualistic. He alleges that the common factor that these dualisms and monisms have in common is an acceptance of domination, either 'domination of nature by man' or 'domination of man by nature'. Instead of a nature–culture division, Bookchin puts forward concepts of 'first nature' and 'second nature' (1996a: 119), the latter derived from the former. By second nature, he means 'the development of uniquely human culture, with a wide variety of institutionalized human communities, effective human techniques, richly symbolic languages and carefully managed sources of nutriment' (119). Bookchin's main concern is to enquire into how second nature is derived from first nature; that is, how first nature, through highly graded and many phased evolution into second nature, gives rise to (1) social institutions, (2) forms of interactions between people and (3) interaction between first and second nature that sometimes complements each other, yielding a second nature that has an evolutionary development of its own (119–20).

Bookchin recognises that nearly all the present ecological problems arise from deep-seated social problems, which include economic, ethnic, cultural and gender conflicts and the rise of hierarchy, domination, patriarchy, classes and the State (1996a: 120). Social ecologists foresee that failing to link ecological problems with social problems will result in misinterpreting the sources of the growing environmental crisis. By highlighting the issue of social crisis, they put forward a value-loaded question and attribute the cause of this issue to the factors that characterise the 'social' sphere. They problematise hierarchy, dominance, patriarchy, classes, the State and others that maintain the social structure. As far as the social arena is shown to generate problems, they have taken an ethical position here.

According to Bookchin, as the very idea of dominating the natural world arises from the hierarchical mentality and class relationships that thoroughly permeate society, the way human beings deal with each other as social beings is crucial for addressing the ecological crisis. In the initial stages of the socialisation of biological facts of kinship, age and gender groups – their elaboration into early institutions – people existed in a complementary relationship with one another (Bookchin, 1993: 362). 'Each in effect was needed by the other to form a relatively stable whole', thus no one dominated the other (362). Later, the biological facts that underpin every human group were reworked into social institutions, and the latter were slowly reworked at various periods and in various degrees into hierarchical structures based on command and obedience. 'The *idea* of dominating nature has its primary source in the domination of human by human and the structuring of the natural world into a hierarchical Chain of Being' (365). Hence, social ecology tries to resolve the issue of the ecological deterioration of the natural world by enquiring into the structural as well as subjective sources of notions like the 'domination of nature' (369). That is, it challenges the entire system of domination that defined human relations and the relationship between human and non-human nature in terms of hierarchy and class structure. When social ecologists see that the issue of domination among society can be ended only by restructuring or reorganising existing structures of domination, they recommend some political change. They require the reorganisation of society to be accomplished along rational lines imbued with an ecological philosophy and sensibility. Neither an Eastern mystical view nor a Western mechanistic view would be able to derive second nature from first nature organically. That requires a mode of thought that distinguishes the phases of the evolutionary continuum from which second nature emerges while preserving first nature as part of the process (Bookchin, 1996a: 120).

Bookchin adopts the concept of 'dialectics',[70] put forward by Hegel,[71] which he developed as the basis of his ecological thinking. But differing from Hegel, Bookchin added an evolutionary perspective to dialectics and put forward the theory of dialectical naturalism, a dialectic that is 'ecologised' or given a naturalistic core. Dialectical naturalism is an attempt to grasp nature as a developmental phenomenon in both its organic and social realms.[72] That is, this idea approaches the world as a whole from a developmental perspective. 'Its various realms – inorganic, organic, and social – are distinct from each other, and yet they grade into one another. This approach above all focuses on the transitions of a developing phenomenon, which emerge from its potentiality to become fully developed and self-actualized' (Biehl, 1993: 381). 'This approach above all focuses on the transitions of a developing phenomenon, which emerge from its potentiality to become fully developed and self-actualized' (381). Bookchin tries to explain the emergence of organic life out of inorganic nature through such a transition. As a result of a developmental transition, each new potentiality in a development cumulatively contains all its previous phases, and when it is fully actualised it contains the potentiality to become a new actuality (382). The emergence of second nature from first nature – that is, the emergence of human society out of first nature – is in turn also such a transition. Though society contains the vast evolution of its biological heritage within itself, it goes beyond this evolution as such to become what is called social evolution, which is second nature.

The significance of dialectical naturalism is that it forms an objective framework for making ethical judgements. According to Bookchin, 'what-should-be' becomes an ethical criterion for judging the truth or validity of an objective 'what is' (1996a: 24). Thus, ethics is factually anchored in the world itself as an objective standard of self-realization rather than as a matter of subjective preferences. Consequently, goodness or badness (the question of moral or immoral) can be objectively determined by whether it has fulfilled its potentialities for rationality and morality. In other words, potentialities that are themselves actualisations of a dialectical continuum present the challenge of ethical self-fulfilment in the reality of the processual world. Therefore, for the social ecologist, truly ethical socialism or anarchism lies in this process and is more than a matter of personal opinion, values or taste (24).

2.4.1 Evolutionary perspective

The biological nature, what Bookchin refers to as 'first nature', is the cumulative evolution of ever-differentiating and increasingly complex life forms within a vibrant and interactive inorganic world (1996a: 29–30). It is first nature that leads to mammalian, primate and human life and exhibits a high degree of orderly continuity in the actualisation of potentialities that paved the way for more complex and self-aware or subjective life forms. The result of this continuity is reflected in the capacity of the life forms to conceptualise, understand and communicate with each other in increasingly symbolic terms (30).

Social ecologists claim that human subjectivity is 'the very history of natural subjectivity, not merely its product' (Bookchin, 1982: 235). They do not consider subjectivity as a characteristic unique to human beings; rather, it is taken to have a natural history of its own (Biehl, 1993: 380). The earliest form of this subjectivity can be found in unicellular organisms, as mere self-identity and sensitivity, which has expanded throughout natural history. In the evolution of life forms, nascent self-identity developed into more complex subjectivity and forms an ever-greater self-intentionality that emerged in maintaining themselves, in modifying their environment and in rendering that environment more habitable – an elaboration of the self-identity that distinguishes organic from inorganic development (383). Finally, 'mind derives as a form of a broad evolution of subjectivity, in the course of the cumulative development of increasingly complex forms' (380).

In this conception, the human being is represented as a highly evolved species derived from natural evolution; that is, they form a special category when they are in relation to other species by possessing more complex self-identity, subjectivity and self-intentionality than others. Likewise, the human species is said to have self-reflexive and communicative capacities like conceptual thought and language to an extent that is unprecedented in any other existing life form (Bookchin, 1996a: 30). These capacities that humans alone possess are manifested in the form of humanity's awareness of itself; its ability to generalise this awareness to the level of a highly systematic understanding of its environment in the form of philosophy, science, ethics and aesthetics; and finally its capacity to alter itself and its environment systematically by means of knowledge and technology; they place the human species beyond the realm of the subjectivity that exists in first nature (30).

Thus, social ecology explores the roots of the cultural in the natural, which occurs through the gradations of biological development that phase the natural into the social. It also tries to explore the important differences that distinguish the societal from the natural and to ascertain the gradations of social development that will yield a new humanistic ecological society (Bookchin, 1996a: 86). This position of social ecology, that is, to consider the social as deriving from the natural, seems to arise following the footsteps of evolutionary theory, which is the scientific explanation of the emergence of different species on earth. Though they present the human species as highly evolved with qualities such as self-identity, subjectivity and self-intentionality and the ability to comprehend knowledge, social ecologists seem to insist that the 'social' is to be viewed as an outcome of natural evolution. In this sense, though they attribute value to what is 'social', it seems to be conditional; that is, belief in the idea of evolution brings value to the acceptance of what they consider 'cultural' or 'social'. In other words, their solution to ecological problems rests on the idea that the social is an evolutionary consequence of the natural.

Bookchin suggests that the two lines of exploration, that is, both natural and social, should go together in producing a larger whole; only then one can transcend even the present capitalist society based on perpetual growth and profit (1996a: 86). Society's current trend is to view everything from the perspective of capitalism and hence to find an 'emancipatory movement' in it because it would free us from nature. But it results in ignoring the roots of society in nature and in promoting anti-humanist trends in ecological thinking (86). The problem with this view is that social ecologists hope to solve the issues in capitalist society by adopting the idea that the root of society is in the natural. This position blindly ignores the real causes of the problems in society as emerging out of certain social conditions. For social ecologists, when humanity fails to see that its self-consciousness and self-reflexivity are nature-rendered, they are away from nature morally and intellectually. The vacuum thus created would be filled only by market-oriented interests and an egoistic market place mentality. Bookchin reiterates that the way in which humans position themselves in the natural world is deeply entangled with the way they organise the social world. That is, the former derives from the latter and serves in turn to reinforce social ideology (86). Though social ecologists emphasise the 'natural' so much, they seem to take a political stand when they argue that in the current situation the biosphere can be rescued from destruction with 'technological fixes' and political reforms.

Social ecology challenges any idea about emergence of society unmediated by natural evolution, in which the human mind, society and even culture are *sui generis* (Bookchin, 1996a: 87). This is because, in such a case, they argue that non-human nature will be irretrievably separated from human nature. Social ecology emphasises the phased, graded and cumulative development of nature into society, which ultimately reaches the institutionalisation of the human community that distinguishes society from the non-human community (87). For social ecologists, the ecological principles that enter into biotic evolution do not disappear from social evolution; rather, the societal and cultural are ecologically derivative (Bookchin, 1996a: 88–9). The relationship between nature and society is a cumulative one, while each remains distinctive and creative in its own right. Thus, social ecology establishes an association between society and ecology, in which social is at least a fulfilment of the *latent* dimension of freedom in nature and the ecological is a major organising principle of social development (87).

Bookchin negates the positions of both biocentrists and anti-humanists when considering humans' position as moral agents (Bookchin, 1996a: 139–40). According to the former, human being as moral agent can practice an ecological stewardship of nature, while in the latter case, humans have a 'biospheric right' to use the biosphere to suit their own ends. But if we understand the moral responsibility of humans as moral agents as derived from natural evolution, an idea which social ecology advances, we cannot emphasise their unique attributes too strongly.

> For it is this unique ability to think conceptually and feel a deep empathy for the world of life that makes it possible for humanity, to reverse the devastation it has inflicted on the biosphere and create a rational society.
>
> *(140)*

For Bookchin, ultimately only a society that has become truly rational and ecological would be able to free us from the limits that oppressive and hierarchical societies impose on our understanding of nature (86–7).

2.4.2 Ecological outlook

In dealing with the social and natural relationship, social ecology while exposing and criticising the split between humanity and nature, puts forward its suggestions to heal them also. As a solution, social ecology advances a holistic approach; this means that 'in terms of their mutual interdependence, it seeks to unravel the *forms* and *patterns* of inter relationships that give intelligibility to a community, be it natural or social' (Bookchin, 1996b: 156). By adopting the concept of ecological wholeness, social ecology very much stresses the dynamic unity of diversity. Because in nature, balance and harmony are achieved by ever-changing differentiation, by ever-expanding diversity thus ecological stability being a function of complexity and variety. In other words, the capacity of an ecosystem to retain its integrity depends upon its diversity (157). Now, in order to consider an ecological outlook as uniquely liberatory, it needs to challenge conventional notions of hierarchy. This is possible by recognising every ecosystem as a food web, that is, as a circular, interlacing nexus of plant–animal relationships that include such wide varying creatures as microorganisms and large mammals, rather than a stratified pyramid with man at its apex (158). In Bookchin's opinion, natural ecosystems and human communities interact with each other in very existential ways (1996b: 159).

> Our animal nature is never so distant from our social nature that we can remove ourselves from the organic world outside us and from the one within us. We phase into society as individuals in the same way that society phasing out of nature, comes into itself.
>
> *(159)*

What makes social ecology so important is that it challenges the very function of hierarchy as a stabilising or 'ordering' principle in both realms of nature and society (160). For Bookchin, the fact that hierarchy is present in current society does not mean that it will persist there; rather, the fact that hierarchy is a threat for society itself reveals that it will not and cannot remain a social fact (160). The ecological outlook of social ecology reflects the value orientation this theory upholds. For these theorists, the question of value rests on aspects like diversity, interdependence, interrelationship and so on, found in nature. Hierarchy and domination are identified as factors that impede the harmony and balance in nature as well as in human communities. But according to social ecologists, evaluating a society as ecological is based on the condition that it emanates from their natural root, in the logic of differentiation of processes and patterns.

Social ecology advances an ethics of complementarity in which human beings must play a supportive role in perpetuating the integrity of the biosphere, since humans are considered the most conscious products of natural evolution (Bookchin, 1993: 369). Social ecology here stresses the need for social institutions to accommodate this ethics, through which humans can act as conscious and moral agents in the interplay of species and which will give active meaning to its goal of wholeness. Thus, it seeks the enrichment of the evolutionary process by diversification of various life forms (369–70). When the variety of life forms is greater in the ecosystems, the latter would be more stable (Bookchin, 1986: 11). Then these living forms themselves would participate in the evolutionary process, thus beginning to open alternative evolutionary pathways. Social ecologists conceive here that the responsibility of the human species is to actively participate in this process. Social institutions are meant here to help humans in fulfilling their duties as moral agents in this sense. The interaction of human beings in nature is seen as the interplay of various species rather than an identification of it as ways of intervening in various social processes for their production and reproduction.

Social ecologists go further to argue that humans must go beyond the natural and the social towards a new synthesis that contains the best of both (Bookchin, 1993: 370). The result of such a synthesis would be a creative, self-conscious and therefore 'free nature', in which human beings with their capacities of moral sense, conceptual thought and communication skills would be able to intervene in natural evolution. An ecological ethics of freedom would provide an objective directiveness to the human enterprise (Bookchin, 1996a: 90). Social ecologists observe that an ecological ethics of freedom cannot be divorced from technics that enhance our relationship with nature. Human beings must be active rational agents in the biosphere. The social ecologist discusses the practical aspects of organic ethics, which value a creative interaction with nature rather than a destructive intervention. For example, social ecologists observe that when doing cultivation, if humans take care of the well-being of the soil along with their own well-being, it will make a big difference in the existing situation. This is because in the former, human intentions are informed by an ecological sensibility, whereas the latter is led by economic considerations and also greed (90). Thus, social ecology insists on recovering the plasticity of the organic in the sense that every intervention in nature in terms of everyday practice must be infused with an ecological sensibility (Bookchin, 1996a: 90). In other words, the ethical dimension they put forward requires us to also take consumption as a creative process like production, originating in the soil and returning to it in a richer form all the components that make up the food cycle (90–1). Social ecologists expect to order all human activities in nature based on this principle. For example, if crafts people work with a respect for their materials, emphasising quality and artistry in production rather than mass-producing commodities, for human needs alone, it will have good implications. In the former, production and consumption go beyond the pure economic domain of the buyer–seller relationship, that is, beyond the domain of mere material substance, and enter into the ecological domain as a mode of enhancing the fecundity of an eco-community (91). An ecotechnology – for consumption no less than production – serves to enrich an

74 Ethics

ecosystem just as compost in food cultivation enriches the soil, rather than degrading and simplifying the natural fundament of life.

An ecotechnology, according to Bookchin, is thus a moral technology, a technology that stands in stark contrast with the kinds of interventions that a capitalistic form of technology does purely for profit (Bookchin, 1996a: 91). Social ecologists realise that the choice is only between an ecological alternative and a purely economic one, yet the necessity of meeting human needs cannot be ignored by a rational society. The technological advantage cannot be dismissed as such based on the damages per se that it has inflicted on both nature and society in the past few centuries (92). Therefore, scientific and technological knowledge are to be brought into the service of humanity and the biosphere alike. Social ecology highlights here the highly reciprocal and complementary relationship between humanity and nature instead of one structured around subordination and domination. In this conception, neither society nor nature dissolves into the other. 'Rather social ecology tries to recover the distinctive attributes of both in a continuum that give rise to a substantive ethics' (92). Though the ethical dimension of social ecology is built upon a value system that emphasises respect for natural cycles and processes, it seems that it also values the social needs of the people to the extent that these are clearly justifiable, as they are expected of a rational society.

2.4.3 Analysis

The identification of 'value' in the domain of interaction between human agents and the rest of the environment is made in a strikingly Hegelian or evolutionistic manner in social ecology. It locates the ethical attitude in the rational and objective features of the world as a process in which development proceeds diametrically. The question of value is a question of 'what-should-be-the-case'. What-is-the-case is judged from the point of view of 'what-should-be-the-case'. But 'what-should-be' is to be understood as that which is projected through human subjectivity, which is continuous with that of nature, and value should be sought in this connection. That is, to understand value is to understand how objective features of nature find expression in the form of human subjectivity. Value judgements should proceed from principles that identify the 'social' as an evolutionary consequence of the natural. Social ecologists, therefore, rediscover ecological principles in the societal, that is, the ethical, which is nature's own responsibility manifest in human subjectivity. These principles can be used to bring back the ecological in the societal and hence in nature. This envisages a rational reorganisation of society, informed by ecological philosophy and sensibility. Though according to social ecologists value is dialectically evolved through a natural process in the consciousness of the human agents and thus has an objective anchoring, it may confront the 'what-is' in order to transcend it. The ecosphere is thus value-laden not only because human subjectivity manifests ecological principles but also because from the rest of the biosphere to human, there is a movement of value realisation. In other words, human subjectivity recognises what is good for the ecosphere. Therefore, in the very relationship between human agency and the environment, value looms large as the most important dimension. Knowing what is the case is therefore distinct from what ought to be the case.

Notes

1 Refer to 'Conservation, Preservation and Environmental Activism: A Survey of the Historical Literature'. www.cr.nps.gov/history/hisnps/NPSThinking/nps-oah.htm-48k.
2 Light, A. 'Technology, Democracy and Environmentalism–On Feenberg's Questioning Technology'. www.abdn.ac.uk/philosophy/endsandmeans/vol4no2/ light.shtml.
3 Jeffreys, K. 1995, 'Progressive Environmentalism: Principles for Regulatory Reform', *NCPA Policy Report* No. 194, 2.
4 Donald Fleming pointed out that the idea of 'the appropriate ends and the appropriate technologies' came from scientific ecology, which was a science. See Fleming, D. 1972, 'Roots of the New Conservation Movement', *Perspectives in American History*, VI, 7–91, cited in White, 1985: 311.
5 Aurelia Peccei and Alexander King founded the Club of Rome in 1968. The first report by the Club of Rome, *Limits to Growth* by Meadows et al., was a pioneering attempt to highlight the dangers caused by the relentless pursuit of material growth by the West. Since 1972, the Club has published 18 reports on a wide variety of issues. See King, A. and Schneider, B. 1993, *The First Global Revolution: A Report by the Council of the Club of Rome*, New Delhi: Orient Longman, viii (foreword).
6 Governance refers to the institutions, set up for co-operation, co-ordination and common action between durable sovereign states.
7 Alfred North Whitehead (1861–1947) was a British philosopher, logician and mathematician.
8 The term 'deep ecology' was coined by Arne Naess, the distinguished Norwegian philosopher, in 1973. According to Naess, the conservation movements of the Progressive and New Deal eras, environmental pressure groups, the Club of Rome 'Limits to Growth' School and Animal Right Activists all come under shallow environmentalism. See Luke, T. 1988, 'The Dreams of Deep Ecology', *Telos*, 76, 66.
9 Naess refers to this view as 'shallow ecology', which is said to be anthropocentric in holding the idea that we ought to preserve the environment not for its own sake but because of its value to us. By separating humanity from nature, this view deadens the latter by seeing nature as inanimate while empowering humans to dominate it. See Fox, W. 1984, 'Deep Ecology: A New Philosophy of Our Time?' *The Ecologist*, 14(5–6), 194.
10 The basic assumptions of deep ecology are put forward by Naess and Sessions. See Naess, A. 1995a, 'The Deep Ecological Movement, Some Philosophical Aspects', in Sessions, G. (ed.), *Deep Ecology for the Twenty-First Century*, Boston, MA: Shambhala, 68.
11 The term 'life' is used here to include all living beings and also those which biologists classify as non-living, that is, rivers (watersheds), landscapes, ecosystems and others. See Naess, 1995a: 68.
12 According to Naess, this formulation referred to as ecocentrism takes individuals, species, populations and habitat as well as human and non-human cultures as constituting an ecosphere. See Naess, 1995a: 68.
13 Naess is not concerned with the philosophical debate about the distinctions among these words. However, he mentions that what he intends to express by the use of the term 'intrinsic value' in the eight principles is better conveyed by the term 'inherent value'. For him, inherent value and inherent worth are not different in sense. Refer Naess, A. 1995b, 'The Deep Ecology "Eight Points" Revisited', in Sessions, 1995: 216. The inherent value in a natural object is independent of any awareness, interest or appreciation of it by a conscious being. See Regan, T. 1981, 'The Nature and Possibility of an Environmental Ethics', *Environmental Ethics*, 3, 30, cited in Naess, 1995a: 69.

14 See Naess, A. 1998a, 'Ecosophy T: Deep Versus Shallow Ecology', in Pojman, L. (ed.), *Environmental Ethics: Readings in Theory and Application*, New York: Wadsworth, 142.
15 The view which sees all other living beings in nature in terms of 'usefulness' to them is called the 'instrumental' approach.
16 Birch, C. and Cobb, J. 1981, *The Liberation of Life: From the Cell to the Community*, Cambridge: Cambridge University Press, cited in Fox, 1984: 194.
17 Sessions, G. 1979, 'Spinoza, Perennial Philosophy and Deep Ecology', Paper presented to the first national 'Reminding' Conference (Philosophy, Where Are You?), Dominican College, San Raphael, California, 29 June–4 July, 18, cited in Fox, 1984: 198.
18 Term used by Fox to denote 'biospherical egalitarianism', similar in meaning.
19 This refers to the norm biospherical egalitarianism – in principle; the 'in principle' clause is inserted because 'any realistic praxis necessitates some killing, exploitation and suppression'. See Naess, A. 1998b, 'The Shallow and the Deep Long-Range Ecological Movement', in Pojman, L. (ed.), *Environmental Ethics: Readings in Theory and Application*, New York: Wadsworth, 134.
20 Gilligan, C. 1982, *In a Different Voice: Psychological Theory and Women's Development*, Cambridge, MA: Harvard University Press, 167, cited in Cheney, J. 1987, 'Eco-Feminism and Deep Ecology', *Environmental Ethics*, 9(Summer), 142.
21 Callicott, J. B. 1980, 'Animal Liberation: A Triangular Affair', *Environmental Ethics*, 2, 324–5 cited in Cheney, 1987: 142.
22 Gilligan, 1982: 30–2, cited in Cheney, 1987: 142–3.
23 Felt nearness largely determines our capacity to identify ourselves with a sort of being, to suffer when they suffer. See Naess, A. 1984, 'Intuition, Intrinsic Value and Deep Ecology', *The Ecologist*, 14(5–6), 202.
24 Naess cites that if it is difficult to avoid killing A because of its smallness, whereas killing B is easily avoided, we tend to protect B rather than A. See Naess, 1984: 202.
25 Naess finds in the system of Spinoza this idea called *Conatus in Suoesse perseverare*, meaning to strive to persevere in oneself of one's being (*in se, in suo esse*). It is not a mere urge to survive, but to increase the level of acting out (ex) one's own nature or essence and is not different from the urge towards higher levels of 'freedom' (*libertas*). Under favourable circumstances, this involves wide identification. Refer Naess, 1998b: 140.
26 Sadik, N. 1992, *The State of World Population*, New York: United Nations Population Fund, ii, cited in McLaughlin, A. 1995, 'The Heart of Deep Ecology', in Sessions, G. (ed.), *Deep Ecology for the Twenty-First Century*, Boston, MA: Shambhala, 87.
27 Wilson, E. O. 1992, *The Diversity of Life*, Cambridge, MA: Harvard University Press for discussion of the problem cited in McLaughlin, 1995: 87.
28 Sadik, 1992, cited in McLaughlin, 1995: 88.
29 Devall and Sessions, 1985b, *Deep Ecology*, Layton, UT: Peregrine Smith Books, 20–1, cited in Luke, 1988: 75.
30 Horkheimer, M. and Adorno, T. 1972, *Dialectic of Enlightenment*, New York: Seabury Press, 3, quoted in Luke, 1988: 72.
31 Malinowsky, B. 1955, *Magic, Sciences and Religion*, Garden City, NY: Anchor Books, 79–87, cited in Luke, 1988: 77.
32 Martin, C. 1986, 'The American Indian as Miscast Ecologist', in Schultz, R. C. and Hughes, J. D. (eds.), *Ecological Consciousness*, Washington, DC: University Press of America, 1986, cited in Grey, W. 1986, 'A Critique of Deep Ecology', *Journal of Applied Philosophy*, 3(2), 214.
33 This refers to the 'how' and 'why' questions, the fundamental questions regarding any social phenomena. See Devall and Sessions, 1985: 20.
34 Ecofeminism grew out of various social movements – the feminist, peace and the ecology movements – in the late 1970s and early 1980s, with an increasing consciousness of the connections between women and nature. The term was first used by Francoise D'Eaubonne. See Mies, M. and Shiva, V. 1993, *Ecofeminism*, New Delhi: Kali for Women.
35 Ecofeminist theory seeks to show the connections between all forms of domination, including the domination of non-human nature and ecofeminism is necessarily

anti-hierarchical. See King, Y. 1983, 'The Ecology of Feminism and the Feminism of Ecology', *The Journal of Social Ecology*, Harbinger, 17, cited in Cheney, 1987: 116.

36 Ecofeminists define a conceptual framework as a set of basic beliefs, values, attitudes and assumptions, which shape and reflect how one views oneself and one's world. Some conceptual frameworks are oppressive. An oppressive conceptual framework is one that explains, justifies and maintains relationships of domination and subordination. See Warren, K. J. 1993a, 'The Power and the Promise of Ecological Feminism', in Zimmerman, M. E. (eds.), *Environmental Philosophy: From Animal Rights to Radical Ecology*, NJ: Prentice-Hall, 322.

37 Warren, K. J. 1993b, 'Introduction', in Zimmerman, M. E. (ed.), *Environmental Philosophy: From Animal Rights to Radical Ecology*, NJ: Prentice-Hall, 256–62. Later she adds on socio-economic, linguistic, literary, spiritual and religious connections between oppression of women and nature. Refer Warren, K. J. 2000, *Ecofeminist Philosophy: A Western Perspective on What It Is and Why It Matters*, New York: Rowman & Littlefield, 180, cited in Glazebrook, T. 2002, 'Karen Warren's Ecofeminism', *Ethics and the Environment*, 7(2), 21.

38 Basically, three such conceptual links have been offered, that is, value hierarchical thinking, value dualisms and logic of domination.
    1 Value hierarchical thinking i.e., 'up–down' thinking, which places higher value, status or prestige on what is 'up' rather than on what is 'down'.
    2 Value dualism i.e., disjunctive pairs on which the disjuncts are seen as oppositional and exclusive and which places higher value on one disjunct rather than the other.
    3 Logic of domination i.e., a structure of argumentation, which leads to a justification of subordination. See Warren, 1993a: 322.

39 Beane, W. C. 1977, *Myth, Cult and Symbols in Sakta Hinduism: A Study of the Indian Mother Goddess*, Leiden: E. J. Brill, cited in Shiva, V. 1988, *Staying Alive: Women, Ecology and Survival in India*, New Delhi: Kali for Women, 39.

40 There are four leading versions of feminism and ecofeminism. They are liberal, traditional Marxist, radical and social/ist. Liberal and traditional Marxist versions are thought to have failed in making a reasonable connection between the oppression of women and the oppression of nature. Moreover, neither is effective in providing satisfactory, independent moral consideration to non-human nature. Socialist feminism attempts to integrate the insights of traditional Marxist feminism with those of radical feminism by making domination by class and sex–gender fundamental to women's oppression. The socialist feminist programme applies the historical materialist method of traditional Marxism to issues of sex and gender made visible by radical feminists. See Warren, K. J. 1987, 'Feminism and Ecology: Making Connections', *Environmental Ethics*, 9(1), 5, 8–13, 15–16.

41 Radical feminists argue that women's oppression is rooted in reproductive biology and a sex–gender system. By taking women's bodies and, in particular, women's reproductive biology as indispensable to women's nature, radical feminism brings child-bearing and child-rearing functions into the political arena. It makes women's sex politically significant. Thus, for the radical feminist, 'the personal is political'. Warren, 1987: 13–14.

42 Carlassare, E. 1996, 'Essentialism in Ecofeminist Discourse', in Merchant, C. (ed.), *Key Concepts in Critical Theory Ecology*, New Delhi: Rawat Publications, 224.

43 Daly, M. 1978, *Gyn/Ecology: The Metaethics of Radical Feminism*, Boston, MA: Beacon Press; Collard, A. and Contrucci, J., 1988, *Rape of the Wild: Man's Violence Against Animals and The Earth*, London: The Women's Press cited in Buckingham-Hatfield, 2000, *Gender and Environment*, London: Routledge, 36.

44 King, Y. 1996, 'Feminism and the Revolt of Nature', in Merchant, C. (ed.), *Key Concepts in Critical Theory Ecology*, New Delhi: Rawat Publications, 199.

45 Lorde, A. 1984, *Sister Outsider*, Freedom, CA: Crossing Press, 67–9, cited in Carlassare, 1996: 229.

46 Daly, 1978, cited in Carlassare, 1996: 224.

47 Griffin, 1978, *Woman and Nature: The Roaring Inside Her*, New York: Harper & Row, cited in Carlassare, 1996: 224.

78 Ethics

48 Biehl, J. 1991, *Rethinking Ecofeminist Politics*, Boston, MA: South End Press, 12–13, cited in Carlassare, 1996: 224.
49 Jaggar, A. 1983, *Feminist Politics and Human Nature*, Totowa, NJ: Rowman & Allanheld, 94, cited in Carlassare, 1996: 226.
50 Biehl, 1991: 2, 5, 11–17, 99–100, cited in Carlassare, 1996: 227.
51 See Susan Buckingham-Hatfield, 2000: 39. Judith Butler also questions the fixedness of sex. 'By asking how the definition of sex arose in the first place (i.e., anatomically, chromosomally or hormonally), what might at first be understood as a "natural fact" can also be seen as a product of political and social interests'. According to her, if one accepts that sex as well as gender is socially constructed, then any attempt to ascribe sex-specific attributes becomes impossible. See Butler, J. 1990, *Gender Trouble, Feminism and the Subversion of Identity*, London: Routledge, cited in Buckingham-Hatfield, 2000: 47.
52 Agarwal, B. 1998, 'The Gender and Environment Debate', in Keil et al. (ed.), *Political Ecology: Global and Local*, New York: Routledge.
53 Mellor, M. 2000, 'Nature, (Re) Production and Power: A Materialist Ecofeminist Perspective', in Gale, F. P. and M' Gonigle, R. M. (eds.), *Nature, Production and Power: Toward an Ecological Political Economy*, Edward Elgar.
54 Lahar, 1991, 'Ecofeminist Theory and Grass Roots Politics', *Hypatia*, 6(1), 28–45, cited in Warren, 'Introduction' 256.
55 Eisler, R. 1988., *The Chalice and the Blade: Our History, Our Future*, San Francisco, CA: Harper & Row, cited in Warren, 'Introduction', 256.
56 Fischer, E. 1979, *Women's Creation*, Garden City, NY: Anchor Press, Double Day 248ff, cited in Mies, M. 1986, *Patriarchy and Accumulation on a World Scale: Women in the International Division of Labour*, London: Zed Books, 63.
57 Debbie Taylor (ed.), 'Myth Conceptions', *New Internationalist* (October 1987), 8–9, cited in Salleh, 1993 in Zimmerman et al. (ed.), 317.
58 Trainer, F. E. 1985, *Abandon Affluence!* London: Zed Books, 1, cited in Salleh, 1993, in Zimmerman et al. (ed.), 317.
59 Warren, 1993a, in Zimmerman et al. (ed.), 333. For Baier, an ethics of love accommodates questions of justice and obligation by means of an understanding of appropriate trust, which itself can be understood only in the light of a satisfactory ethics of love. See Baier, A. 1985, 'What Do Women Want in a Moral Theory', *Nous*, 19, 55–6.
60 See Card, C. 1985, 'Virtues and Moral Luck', Unpublished paper read at the American Philosophical Association Meeting in Chicago, 1–2, cited in Cheney, 1987: 120.
61 Rose, G. 1993, *Feminism and Geography: The Limits of Geographical Knowledge*, Cambridge: Polity Press, cited in Buckingham-Hatfield, 2000: 39.
62 Asian and Pacific Women's Resource Collection Network, 1992, *Environment*, Kuala Lumpur: Asian and Pacific Development Centre, 2, cited in Elliot, L. 1998, *The Global Politics of the Environment*, London: Palgrave Macmillan, 148.
63 The State of India's Environment, 1984–85, The Second Citizen's Report, Centre for Science and Environment, New Delhi, India, cited in Rodda (prepared by)1993, *Women and the Environment*, London: Zed Books, 81; See also Jackson, C. 1995, 'Environmental Reproduction and Gender in the Third World', in Morse, S. and Stocking, M. (eds.), *People and Environment*, London: UGL Press, 118.
64 For an understanding of the role of women in Third World agriculture, refer Rodda, 1993: 81; Agarwal, 1998: 197; Elliot, 1998: 48.
65 In many Third World countries, both men and women contribute to agriculture. In Africa, generally men have the right to land and control farming activities. See Rodda, 1993: 59.
66 OECD, 1989, Seminar Report, *Focus on the Future: Women and The Environment*, London: International Institute for Environment and Development, cited in Rodda, 1993: 86.
67 Ecofeminists cite the performing of conjuration rites mentioned in anti-conceptual folklore, not only to avoid having a child but also to keep the husband away from the bed. See D'Eaubonne, 1996, 'The Time for Ecofeminism', in Merchant, C. (ed.), *Key Concepts in Critical Theory Ecology*. New Delhi: Rawat Publications, 188.

68 Gilligan, C. 1982, 172, cited in Cheney, 1987: 136.
69 Card, C. 1985, 23, cited in Cheney, 1987: 136.
70 As a form of reasoning, the most basic categories in dialectic, 'being' and 'nothing', are differentiated by their inner logic into fuller and more complex categories. Each category in turn is a potentiality that, by means of eductive thinking directed towards an exploration of its latent and implicit possibilities, yields logical expression in the form of self-realisation or what Hegel called 'actuality'. Dialectic explicates how processes occur in not only the natural world but also the social. A thing or phenomena in dialectical causality remains unsettled, unstable, in tension until it develops from 'what is' into what it 'should be' in all its wholeness and fullness. It must ripen into the fullness of its being. See Bookchin, M. 1996a, *The Philosophy of Social Ecology: Essays on Dialectical Naturalism*, New Delhi: Rawat Publications, 17–19.
71 Georg Wilhelm Friedrich Hegel (1770–1831) was a German philosopher and an important figure of German idealism.
72 Biehl, J. 1993, 'Dialectics in the Ethics of Social Ecology', in Zimmerman, M. (ed.), *Environmental Philosophy: From Animal Rights to Radical Ecology*, NJ: Prentice-Hall, 381–2.

PART III
Politics

The political dimension of environmental issues can be approached at three different levels, that is, conceptually, as lived experience and as part of the political process. Considerations of these three levels would enable us to represent the political dimensions with different and varied configurations. Part III intends to show by way of examples how the political has implicated the issues generated by human–environment interaction. At the conceptual level, systems of thoughts, such as reform environmentalism, deep ecology, ecofeminism and social ecology, are examined where there are implicit or explicit references to the political. These thought systems, which were already discussed in Chapter 2, are a response to the relentless pursuit of economic growth and the consequent damage done to nature. As lived experience, the political implications of environmental issues vary according to their contexts. Accordingly, the impacts of the human–environment interaction have immediate, recurring or anticipated repercussions in the social life of the people. This often results in social conflicts that call for urgent solutions, sometimes leading to the emergence of social or environmental movements that take up the issues. Here it seems very relevant to situate environmental conflicts in the larger context of the modern 'development' paradigm. They are the inevitable outcome of the 'development' activities that started in the second half of the twentieth century all over the world. Therefore, we need to have knowledge regarding how the capitalist mode of development deprived a large mass of people of their livelihood options, leaving their survival in trouble, which made them respond to the situation in the form of movements. The effort here is to understand the political dimension of these movements in the larger schema of the environment–development debate. Situating environmental conflicts in the economic growth-oriented 'development' paradigm has a bearing on the inquiry in Chapter 4 regarding what is political. Out of the two chapters (3 and 4) in this part, Chapter 3 tries to situate 'environment' in the 'development' context historically. This provides an account of the 'development' idea with an indication of how natural 'resources' were utilised in different periods.

In Chapter 4, after the conceptual level analysis, a random number of varying contexts of environmental struggles from different parts of the world are analysed. The case of Green parties, which are present in many countries, is also a kind of political response to the issues arising from 'development', and this is discussed in the third part. Formation of Green parties and their entry into political processes as a response to the experience of new social movements' politics in European countries are included in this part.

3
'ENVIRONMENT' IN THE 'DEVELOPMENT' CONTEXT
A historical inquiry

3.1 'Development' idea: the trajectory

A journey through the history of the 'development' idea leads us back to the notion of 'progress', which was in vogue until around 1940. The shift in the meaning of 'development' from 'progress' to one equivalent to indicators of economic growth like Gross National Product (GNP) has different connotations depending on the socio-economic contexts in which it emerged. 'Material progress' was the expression almost invariably used by mainstream economists from Adam Smith until the period of World War II, which later came to be known as the 'economic development of the West' (Arndt, 1981: 457). Arndt observed that as a policy objective, economic development was increasingly prominent during the nineteenth century, first in European countries and later in Japan, China and those places known as the 'Third World'. However, it was generally referred to as 'modernization', 'westernization' or 'industrialization' (458). It was Marx who gave the term 'development' a specifically economic connotation (459); all the mainstream economic writings before World War II used the word 'development' in the sense of 'development or exploitation of natural resources',[1] even through the interwar period (463). However, in the immediate post-war years, 'economic development' became virtually synonymous with 'growth in per capita income' in the less developed countries (465).

According to Du Pisani, from pre-modern times thinking about 'progress', the precursor of the 'development' idea, slowly started surfacing (2006: 84). He traces the development of the idea of 'progress' until modern times.

> In the medieval period, the Christian conception of progress encompassed millennialism, utopian ideas and a sense of the importance of improving upon this world in preparation for life in the next. By the thirteenth century,

two crucial strands of the European conception of human progress had been established: awareness of the cumulative advancement of culture and a belief in a future golden age of morality on this earth.[2]

The Renaissance period propagated ideas of cyclical recurrence, while Reformation thinkers emphasised the linear progress of humanity (Nisbet, 1980: 103, 117–19; see also Smelser and Baltes, 2001: 12173). In 1683, French scientist Fontenelle first articulated the Great Idea of Progress based on new science and improved technology that would lead to unlimited progress.[3] However, the role of providence was still visible in the eighteenth century, though it was understood to work through nature (Smelser and Baltes, 2001: 12173). Several major theories of progress emerged in this period, especially those of Adam Smith and Adam Ferguson, which focused on economic mode of production (12173). During the Enlightenment and its aftermath (1750–1900), the idea of progress reached its zenith in Western civilisation and became the dominant idea of the period (Nisbet, 1980: 171). At this time, the link between progress and modern, empirical and exact science was consolidated and the realisation that humankind can master nature grew stronger (Nisbet, 1980: 208; Von Wright, 1997: 3, 4). In the context of the eighteenth-century Industrial Revolution, human progress was also linked to economic growth and material advancement (Du Pisani, 2006: 84). This period witnessed the rise of competitive capitalism undermining feudal relations of production, of Western thought emphasising rational knowledge, of science and technology and dichotomies such as backward–advanced, black–white and so on (Lewis, 2005: 3).

Cowen and Shenton (1996)[4] put forward a different interpretation of 'development'; that is, in nineteenth-century England it referred to remedies for the shortcomings and maladies of progress. This involved questions like population (according to Malthus), job loss (for the Luddites), the social question (according to Marx and others) and urban squalor. Nederveen Pieterse remarks that in this argument, progress and development are contrasted and development differs from and complements progress (2001: 5). Therefore, twentieth-century development thinking took different positions and policies that in effect were reactions to nineteenth-century progress and policy failures, for instance, the dismantling of existing social relations and issues of job loss and the like, an aftermath of industrialisation (5).

By the colonial era, the colonisers had constructed themselves as rational agents of progress, while local people were portrayed as backward (Lewis, 2005: 3). In this period, development took the form of

> colonial resource management, first to make the colonies cost-effective and later to build up economic resources with a view to national independence. Industrialization was not part of colonial economics because the comparative advantage of the colonies was held to be the export of raw materials for the industries in the metropolitan countries.
>
> *(Nederveen Pieterse, 2001: 5)*

The introduction of European-style religion, education and administrative systems went together with the quest for economic gain.

> By the early twentieth century, the relationship between colonial administration and ideas of planned change had become more explicit and responsibility for economic development came to be complemented by the incorporation of welfare objectives and responsibility for minimum levels of health, education and nutrition for colonial subjects.
>
> *(Lewis, 2005: 3)*

After 1945, in Europe and North America, development was increasingly presented in terms of economic growth and modernity (Lewis, 2005: 3). The belief was that the benefits of economic growth would 'trickle down' to the poor, while the transfer of new technology would bring material benefits. Modernisation theory, which held these ideas, was exemplified by the approach of US economist W. W. Rostow. 'When development thinking broadened to encompass modernization, economic growth was combined with political modernization, that is, nation building and social modernization' (Nederveen Pieterse, 2001: 6). Modernisation theorists were of the opinion that the advanced industrial countries of Western Europe and North America represented the logical end-point towards which the former colonies of Africa, Asia and Latin America have to advance.[5] However, neither expansion of industry nor rapid urbanisation helped erase the economic and political inequalities of post-colonial period; rather, these often grew worse in conjunction with the very processes of modernisation (Smelser and Baltes, 2001: 3594). Those dependency theorists who succeeded rejected the modernisation paradigm and focused instead on the unequal relationship between North and South in relation to terms of trade, arguing that an active process of 'underdevelopment' had taken place as peripheral economics were integrated into the capitalist system on unequal terms, primarily as providers of cheap raw materials for export to rich industrialised countries. The dependency approach was popularised by the work of A. G. Frank during the 1960s but became less influential later (Lewis, 2005: 4).

By the mid-1970s, in the context of the impact of oil shocks, declining faith in the capacity of economic growth to reach the majority of the world's poor and debates about ecological limits to growth, there occurred a shift in development circles away from large-scale, state-oriented modernisation efforts towards localised strategies for meeting the needs of the world's poor:[6] that is, a shift in focus away from growth towards issues of redistribution and equity (Smelser and Baltes, 2001: 3594). In other words, new understandings of development came to the fore, focusing on social and community development, with the onset of alternative development thinking (Nederveen Pieterse, 2001: 6). These development strategies, whether labelled 'farmer-first', 'bottom-up' or 'grass roots', laid emphasis on decentralisation, localisation and the satisfaction of basic human needs for food, shelter, health and security (Smelser and Baltes, 2001: 3595). In the mid-1980s, following

Amartya Sen's work on capabilities and entitlements, the idea of 'human development' brought forth the understandings of 'development' as capacitation; the point of 'development' in this view is that it is 'enabling' (Nederveen Pieterse, 2001: 6). Realisation of the limited nature of commonly used economic measures of development led the United Nations Development Programme (UNDP) to devise the Human Development Index (HDI) in the late 1980s, which incorporated three dimensions of development in relation to human well-being: a long and healthy life, education and knowledge and a decent standard of living (Willis, 2005: 7). The core definition of 'development' in the Human Development Report of UNDP is 'the enlargement of people's choices' (Nederveen Pieterse, 2001: 6; Behera, 2006: 14). Behera points out that even in the era of globalisation, rural 'development' has acquired a central role in international development discourse (14). This bottom-up approach to 'development' is put into practice within the theoretical and empirical frame of good governance, decentralised and micro-level planning and for 'participatory development', which obviously happens in the context of rural development as policy and practices and also as a process vis-à-vis globalisation (14).

During the 1950s and 1960s in countries ranging from India to Brazil, import substituting industrialisation and the state involvement that went with it resulted in impressive rates of economic growth. However, by the end of the 1970s, development strategies in Africa, Latin America and South Asia were in disarray (Smelser and Baltes, 2001: 3558). Imports were growing faster than exports, creating balance of payments problems, and state expenditures were increasing more rapidly than revenues, creating fiscal problems (3558). Thus, during the 1970s, the role of the State in managing hardships in Third World countries was increasingly questioned. It was alleged that the widespread involvement of the State in economic activities was leading to inefficiency and slower rates of economic growth than would be achieved if the market were left to its own devices (Willis, 2005: 52). Accordingly, since the late 1970s in Asian, African and Latin American countries, statist development programmes have increasingly been replaced by market-oriented policies; by the late 1980s, State-led developmentalism had suffered a major blow. This period, which was directed by neo-liberalism, eliminated the foundation of development economics (Nederveen Pieterse, 2001: 6). According to this view, what matters is getting the prices right and letting market forces do their work; that is, the central objective of economic growth is to be achieved through structural reform, deregulation, liberalisation and privatisation (6). As a development ideology, neo-liberalism most resembles the well-known modernisation paradigm, but in fact has less to offer because the role of the State has been minimalised (Schuurman, 1993: 12).

Socio-economic practices founded on market-oriented policies during the 1980s caused the emergence of several environmental problems, including pollution, deforestation, soil erosion and global warming, on an unlimited scale. Hence, a kind of developmental concern gradually emerged that emphasised linkages between the welfare of communities and their access to natural resources (Smelser and Baltes, 2001: 3595). By the end of the 1980s, understanding of these linkages along with growing scientific and public concern over processes of global environmental change (such as ozone depletion) led to the formation of an idea called 'sustainable development' (3595). This combined to foster greater emphasis on development strategies that could accommodate the needs of the present generation without jeopardising the availability of resources for future generations. This period also witnessed emerging diverse views that emphasised equity, local control over resources and empowerment of subordinate groups, ranging from indigenous people to women to subsistence farmers, who became victims to the singular focus on economic growth (3595).

The post-1980 period (some refer to the 1990s) critically looked at the established conceptions of development that already had much popularity, especially in the context of greater awareness of environmental concerns, gender equality and grass root approaches (Willis, 2005: 29). This shift, which came to be represented as 'post-development' thinking, put forth an anti-development position. That is, post-development thinking advocated a radical thinking of the assumptions and goals of development, as it created issues of global poverty, exploitation and inequality and so on. This critique questioned the 'Western cultural mind-set which imposed homogenizing materialist values, idealized rational-scientific power and created unprecedented levels of environmental destruction' (Lewis, 2005: 4). Nederveen Pieterse, though, agrees with the positive claims made by post-development and the affirmative counterpoints it raises against development, such as indigenous knowledge and cultural diversity, Gandhian frugality, conviviality, grass roots movements and local struggles; however, he nonetheless argues that these are not specific to the post-development idea and do not result in rejecting 'development' (Nederveen Pieterse, 2001: 107). Post-development theorists approach the discourse of 'development' in the sense that they examine how 'development' is defined and discussed over the years. Instead of being neutral, 'these theorists argue that understandings of "development" reflect prevailing power relations and enable some ideas of "development" to be presented as correct, while others are dismissed' (Willis, 2005: 32).

Escobar identifies the history of 'development' in the post–World War period as the history of the institutionalisation and employment of planning ideas (Escobar, 1997: 183). He argues that the process was facilitated in each period by successive development 'strategies'. A rough periodisation of development initiatives can be presented in the following way: an emphasis on growth and national planning in the 1950s, to the Green Revolution and sectoral and regional planning of the 1960s and 1970s, including 'basic needs' and local level planning in the 1970s and 1980s, to environmental planning for 'sustainable development' and planning to 'incorporate' women and grass roots into development in the 1990s and continuing the planning process into the new millennium (Escobar, 1997: 183; See also Willis, 2005: 28).

As the above account reveals, the lineages of 'development' seem to elicit different dimensions, such as economic, political, cultural, human, social, rural, community, environment and so on. It includes the application of science and technology to collective organisation but also manages the changes that arise from the application of technology (Nederveen Pieterse, 2001: 6). These techno-economic developments can include infrastructure works such as roads, railways, irrigation dams, canals, ports and others that are meant to promote improvements, ranging from indirectly in relatively economically underdeveloped regions to industrialisation for bringing economic growth directly. These are usually implemented in the form of 'development projects'.[7] The category of 'green projects' also comes under 'development projects', which though green nevertheless promise to bring out economic growth – for instance, modern amusement parks and eco-tourism development projects through the development of national parks (Bapat, 2005: 9). Under neo-liberalism, 'development projects' were a major phenomenon from the 1980s, especially in Third World countries. Of these, some projects demanded additional human effort and more convenient socio-political environments than others. For example, 'some projects require technical innovation while others could not hope to succeed without lessening at least within their own confines, racial, religious or other hostilities among various sections of the community' (Hirschman, 1967: 14). In practice, two main trends are followed for implementing these projects, the difference arising from the changing perception of the 'development' idea itself (Meyer and Singh, 2006: 240). When the 'top-down' approach was in vogue, 'development' started with the outsider providing some good or service, which a community may or may not need. But it was alleged that in this approach people were treated as objects and that 'development projects' failed to achieve their goals. Because of such debates, the emphasis moved towards a 'people-centred' or 'bottom-up' approach. This focuses on the needs and wants of the people. The people define the goals of development in this approach and from the beginning participate in 'development projects'.[8] In this case, the degree of participation varies, and these are three kinds (Meyer and Singh, 2006: 240). Some development projects involve an outsider coming in with an agenda and then harnessing the community's knowledge, people and so on. Others involve an outsider offering services to a community, which sets the research agenda itself. A third kind involves development taking place within a community without the help of outsiders. Despite the differences, however, there are certain underlying principles common to all of them (240).

3.2 'Development' interventions in nature and human life

As mentioned at the beginning of Part II, the author's interest in understanding the meanings of 'development' over time is to examine against this backdrop the mode of human engagements with 'nature'. In other words, to understand the changes in the mode of appropriation of natural resources based on the shift in 'development' conceptions. Though a concern towards environmental issues was generated worldwide in the 1990s through the idea of 'sustainable development',[9] there was no such concern during any other period in the history of development thinking. Mainstream theories and models of development thinking reveal that none of the classical, neoclassical, Keynesian or post-Keynesian theories of economic growth and radical theories of progress devoted serious attention to problems related to environment and sustainability (Haque, 1999: 198). Similarly, developmental theories and models, including various reformist economic-growth theories (such as the theory of dualism, big-push theory, vicious-circle theory and stages of growth theory and different versions of modernisation framework), that emerged in relation to development in Asian, African and Latin American countries, the dependency theory and other reformist developmental approaches like the 'basic needs' approach, were less concerned about the issues related to environmental degradation and resource depletion (198).

Though discussion on the destruction of natural resources on a wider scale often starts with the first phase of development – that is, during the British colonial invasion – some argue that what we identify today as 'consequences of development' stems from a long history of 500 years, affected by 'the miseries of colonialism ranging from those of politico-economic and cultural dispossession to genocide'.[10] Gurukkal refers to the ruthless demographic takeover by West European whites all over the North and South temperate zones as the first major catastrophe by which the gradual formation of the imperialist world order began perturbing both humanity and nature (1994: 75). For Shiva, the first radical change in resource control and the emergence of major conflicts over natural resources induced by non-local factors is associated with colonial domination of the Southern part of the world (1991: 14). A major intervention that occurred in the colonial period was the forceful shift from food crops to cash crops using two strategies. The first was by forcing the local people in the colonies to grow cash crops instead of food on their own plots, and the second was the direct taking over of the land by large-scale plantations growing crops for export.[11] In Third World societies before colonial rule and the infusion of Western systems, people lived in relatively self-sufficient communities that planted rice and other staple crops, fished and hunted for other food and were supplied housing, clothing and other needs through small-scale industries which made use of local resources and indigenous skills (Peng, 1992: 16; also see Shiva, 1992). Besides turning the best land to the cultivation of cash crops, colonialism forced the most able-bodied workers to leave the village fields to work as slaves or for very low wages on plantations. Moreover, the colonisers encouraged a dependence on imported food and blocked native peasant cash crop production from competing with cash crops produced by settlers or foreign firms (Harle, 1978: 48–9). In Shiva's words, 'colonial domination systematically transformed the common vital resources into commodities for generating profits and growth of revenues' (1991: 14).[12] This transformation of common resources into commodities supported the first Industrial Revolution in a major way, permitting European industries access to the resources of South Asia (14). An astonishing fact is that after achieving independence, the newly formed Third World governments not only never abandoned these colonialist policies, seeking ways to repair the social and ecological destruction that they had caused, but also followed in the footprints of their colonialist predecessors (Goldsmith, 1992: 49).

The next stage of intervention in nature for the utilisation of natural resources occurred in the Third World countries, by bringing the latter within the orbit of international trade. This could have started since the famous speech by Harry S.

Truman[13] in 1949, in which he declared the Southern hemisphere as 'underdeveloped areas', for the first time in history (Sachs, 1997: 2). He used 'development' in the sense that Third World countries should 'develop' and that development should be in their own interests, as opposed to those of the First World.[14] In 1944 at the Bretton Wood Conference held under US leadership, 'aid' was institutionalised as the Industrial World's principal tool of economic colonialism (Goldsmith, 1992: 52). Three international institutions – the International Monetary Fund (IMF), World Bank (IBRD) and the General Agreement on Tariffs and Trade (GATT) – were set up as the medium for introducing and implementing development schemes in Third World countries (52). At first, the World Bank was involved in activities to develop these countries by building roads, harbours, ports and so on: the infrastructure required to make possible the import of manufactured products and the export of raw materials and agricultural produce. It then invested heavily in energy generation, particularly in hydropower. Since the 1970s, it has played a leading role in financing the commercialisation of agriculture in the Third World and, especially, the substitution of export-oriented plantations and livestock rearing schemes for traditional subsistence farming designed to feed local people (52). The amount of capital pumped into Third World countries to finance such policies has considerably increased in these years (53). However, the adoption of neo-liberalisation policies worldwide has led to the opening up of Third World countries to multinational corporations in the late 1980s and the early 1990s and a push for an economic reform agenda that facilitates the flow of foreign capital into these countries. The planning and implementation of large-scale projects in the name of development was the fashion of the time and was soon normalised. Infrastructure funding for the different development projects[15] became available through multilateral donors in the form of economic aid and technology transfer (Bapat, 2005: 26). The 'development projects' undertaken from the late 1980s on included large engineering infrastructure projects aimed at the rapid economic growth of a region in particular and of the country as a whole. Such infrastructure development projects included irrigation and water supply projects, involving dams; transport projects like highways, airports, railways and ports; energy projects including mining and power projects; industrial development parks; and, more recently, tourism development projects, including eco-tourism following the creation of national parks and wildlife sanctuaries (26). These specific interventions or strategies in the form of international organisations to achieve 'development', set up as part of an international development endeavour, are what Gillian Hart (2001) terms 'big D' development, in contrast to 'little d' development, which she saw as the general progress of capitalism.[16]

Escobar explores how 'development' functions as a discourse, especially in Third World countries (1992: 413). For him, this is to understand why many countries in the Third World conceived of themselves as 'underdeveloped' in the early post–World War period. It was made possible through the systematic elaboration of fields of knowledge and institutions, which established different forms of power that act through individuals, government officials and communities themselves and made them think of an underdeveloped state. The situation is so pervasive that one cannot get away from this discourse, since 'development' itself has become the social reality (414). 'Development' is omnipresent in different forms, for example, through various kinds of development plans designed and implemented by governments, institutions carrying out development programmes in cities and rural areas, experts studying underdevelopment and producing theories extensively, introduction of pilot projects, presence of foreign experts and multinational corporations and so on (414).

The development strategy of economic 'aid' was severely criticised by many scholars. The term 'aid' itself has been severely questioned by Bauer (2002). According to him, the term has enabled aid supporters to claim a monopoly of compassion while critics dismissed it as lacking in understanding and sympathy (359). Foreign aid is alleged to have encouraged the 'notion of the West (or North) as a single economic decision-making entity, a homogeneous aggregate with identical interests capable of imposing its will on the Third World' (362). Bauer questions even the rationale of 'aid' strategy. He cites the case of Third World regions like Southeast Asia, West Africa, and Latin America, which had progressed rapidly long before aid. Conversely, he points to the fact that Third World societies that have not progressed much over the last hundred years reflect factors that cannot be overcome by aid and are indeed likely to be reinforced by it (Bauer, 2002: 363). The argument raised in support of 'aid' was that it served to legitimise foreign domination in colonies, since the poor and 'backward' needed organised and professional assistance to survive (Rahnema, 1988: 133). But in the later stage of the 'aid' programme, which is the result of 'international cooperation', the alliance was between ex-colonial powers and emerging nation–states, both committed to the economisation of their societies. Rahnema alleges that while some aid and development strategies have served to increase certain forms of economic wealth, it is grass roots populations worldwide that heavily suffered from them (126). Moreover, aid is often provided as part of 'macro-development strategies', and the populations concerned are seldom consulted; rather, they only serve as legitimising factors (134). Thus, projects that aim at 'eradicating' poverty resulted in the impoverishing of huge masses of people who had never been poor (125). Likewise, in many fields such as education, health, food and others, the implementation of projects has only created new problems in developing countries.

Many have examined the reasons for the failure of such projects. Exemplifying the case of Lesotho, Ferguson makes significant observations regarding 'development projects'. He raised severe criticism against such projects, arguing that they totally failed to help poor people and only contributed to the deprived state of people through its side effects (Ferguson, 2008: 328). He refuses the argument that the real purpose of development projects is to aid capitalist penetration into Third World countries, as put forward by leftist-political economists. This is because such projects brought neither modernisation nor significant economic transformation in Lesotho. Here, the development apparatus is not a machine for eliminating poverty; rather, it functions as a machine 'for reinforcing and expanding the exercise of bureaucratic state power, which incidentally takes "poverty" as its point of entry and justification launching an intervention that may have no effect on the poverty but does have other concrete effects' (329). Some scholars enquire as to why progress continues to be fragile in many developing countries despite unprecedented expansion in the quantity of 'development' research and the number of projects undertaken (Edwards, 2008: 306). Edwards ascribes it to the absence of strong links between *understanding* and *action*. In addition, he finds the following problems with the conventional approach to development. Firstly, people are treated as objects to be studied rather than as subjects of their own development, which therefore creates a separation between the researcher and the object of research, and between understanding and action. Secondly, the idea is that development consists of the transfer of skills or information from the expert to others, with the assumption that the expert is the only person capable of mediating the transfer of these skills to society. Usually, the attitude of experts prevents people from thinking for themselves (307). Thirdly, the devaluation of indigenous knowledge, which grows out of the direct experience of poor people, can be used as the basis of a successful development policy of a region (308). Fourthly, there is a refusal to accept the role of 'emotion' in understanding the problems of development in the technocratic approach. Generally, in this kind of study, any hint of 'subjectivity' is seized upon immediately as 'unscientific' and therefore not worthy of inclusion in a 'serious' study of development. In Edward's opinion, it is impossible to understand real-life problems fully unless one grasps the multitude of constraints, imperfections and emotions that shape the actions and decisions of real, living people (308). Following Hope et al., he suggests that all education and development projects should start by identifying the issues that local people speak about with excitement, hope, fear, anxiety or anger.[17] Lastly, the values and attitudes adopted in conventional research are essentially selfish; this prevents the researcher from having a serious understanding of the situation under inquiry (Edwards, 2008: 308–9).

Rahnema attributes the failure of the 'development' model in developing countries to the following reasons: (1) while it took a couple of centuries to realise the development model that succeeded in the Northern Hemisphere, the presently 'developing' countries are urged to reach the same goals in a much shorter period and with means and resources far beyond their reach, (2) economic development took place in the North under very different historical circumstances; in the colonised world, additional constraints imposed by ruthless colonial exploitation are present that were absent in the Northern world and (3) the achievements in the North were, in a way, the result of an endogenous process, whereas both the process and nature of the present 'development' designs in the South are basically exogenous, alien and often imposed from above (1988: 131). According to Scott, such high modernist schemes depended not only on bracketing contingency but also on standardising the subjects of development (2008: 300). The great majority of them were strongly committed to a more egalitarian society, to meeting the basic needs of its citizens and to making the amenities of a modern society available to all. The kind of human subject for whom all these benefits were being provided was singularly abstract. Such 'subjects' were conceived as devoid of gender, tastes, history, values, opinions or original ideas, traditions and distinctive personalities to contribute to their enterprise. The lack of context and particularity were the necessary first premise of any large-scale planning exercise. The power of resolution of this exercise is assumed to be enhanced, depending on the degree to which these subjects were treated as standardised units. Scott noticed that such projects treated the natural world in the same manner, i.e., yield was given priority over quality. Another criticism is against the little confidence such schemes repose in the skills, intelligence and experience of ordinary people (300).

The process of 'development', whether colonial or in a modified form under capitalism, is understood as involving objectification and subjectivation processes, which are most influential in the case of 'development projects'. That is, by participating within the development discourse, individuals are made objects/ are objectified as labouring subjects; at the same time they happened to become an agent of it by being a bearer/subject of it and will in turn objectify others and make them participate in the unfolding of the project of development (Raju, 2003: 58–9). Under capitalism there are various modes and umpteen sites of operation of objectification through which people are reconstituted as consumer subjects (Gurukkal, 1994: 72).[18] But Raju finds this conceptualisation inadequate since this is a kind of non-self-reflexive belief /confidence in the claims and promises of the project and discourse of 'development' (59). He argues that something more is involved in this process of development, that is, in the act of mastering or conquering nature, which might be better explained by a concept called 'Developmental Modernity' (59). He explains that before the advent of modernity, the situation was such that there was only a differentiation between man and nature; they were not separated at that time. But with the unfolding of modernity, they were separated until man recognised that there is nature in him as well. It is with this separation that nature becomes a 'resource'. In other words, nature was earlier there in distinction to him and he could see nature out there, but not in order to master or internalise it as a resource lying out there subsumable by his will. But Developmental Modernity authenticates any operation of human beings on nature in two ways: first, as they are treated as already separated from the latter and second, conceiving themselves as free-willed humans, with respect to the controls and disciplinary power upon nature out there as well as inside one's self (Raju, personal communication).

The 'development' paradigm that followed capitalist and neo-liberal economic policies has been criticised severely by many authors on account of various impacts it has on diverse fields of life. Gurukkal argues that it is internationalisation of natural resources that is realised through numerous institutional devices and agencies (1994: 76). He continues,

> it is a sequential process of shifting control over natural resources from local power-structure to supra-local, national and international in the ascending order. Nationalization of natural resources divested local communities of

their natural rights and internationalization is now divesting the nation of its sovereign rights.

(76)

Shiva characterises 'development' as a post-colonial project, a choice for accepting a model of progress in which the entire world remade itself on the model of the colonising modern West without having to undergo the subjugation and exploitation that colonialism entailed (1996: 272). 'Development' means heavy industrialisation and market-oriented high productivity; it is a process of squandering natural resources through chemical-intensive agriculture, including unscientific use of fertilisers, pesticides, water for irrigation and so on, and energy intensive technological production, including careless maintenance of industries, unscientific management of forests, poor conservation of ecological systems and others (Gurukkal, 1994: 71, 73–4). Thus, within the modern development paradigm, technology has acquired totally free access to natural resources, which has set a pattern of their over-exploitation (74). 'Development' that is based merely on capital accumulation and commercialisation of the economy and that aims only at surplus and profit results in the creation of wealth, often accompanied by the problems of poverty and dispossession of a vast majority of the world's population (Shiva, 1996: 272; Foster, 2003: 10). This craving for quick growth often resulted in rapid absorption of energy and materials and in the dumping of more and more wastes into the environment, aggravating environmental degradation (Foster, 2003: 10).

The adoption of neo-liberalisation policies to expand market forces, to enhance open competition, mass production and foreign competition and to maximise consumption along with a reduction in state anti-poverty programmes has resulted in a number of environmental problems, such as pollution, the greenhouse effect leading to global warming, ozone layer depletion, over-exploitation of natural resources resulting in depletion of non-renewable resources, clearing more forests, creation of more slums and so on in Third World countries (Haque, 1999: 199).

Studies reveal that along with the adverse consequences of capitalist development in nature, there are similar repercussions in the lives of women (an extensive discussion of this is included in Chapter 2, under 'Ecofeminism') and other marginalised sections of society. Shiva alleges that economic biases and values against nature, women and indigenous people are very much evident in the fundamental assumptions of this mode of development, which can be summarised as (1) nature is unproductive and, hence, organic agriculture based on nature's cycles of renewability creates only poverty and (2) women, tribal and peasant societies embedded in nature are similarly unproductive, just because it is assumed that 'production' takes place only when mediated by technologies for commodity production; this is the case even when such technologies destroy life and not because in co-operation they are capable of producing only *less* goods and services for needs (Shiva, 1996: 274). According to this view, a clean river cannot be considered a productive resource until it is 'developed' into a dam. Shiva characterised this form of development as equivalent to 'maldevelopment', a development that is deprived of the feminine, conservation and the ecological principle (274). Modern, efficient technologies are founded on resource and energy intensive production processes, which demand ever-increasing resource withdrawals from the ecosystem that can disrupt essential ecological processes, thus converting renewable resources into non-renewable ones (277). Shiva exemplifies this process with the case of a forest that is a rich source of biomass. The industrial and commercial need for wood commonly is so demanding that it requires the continuous over-felling of trees, which exceeds the regenerative capacity of the forest ecosystem and eventually converts forests into non-renewable resources. Thus, essential ecological processes are disrupted, resulting in additional problems like pollution of air, water and soil. In addition, the destruction of forests exacerbates the burden of women's work and makes the collection of water, fodder and fuel more energy- and time-consuming processes (277). Mies and Shiva realise that under a capitalist–patriarchal system, nature and women undergo the same pattern of exploitation and oppression; they connect these two kinds of oppression to tackle the issues that arise from this situation (1993: 2–3). According to them, such issues arise from the dichotomy that subordinates nature to man, women to man, consumption to production, local to global and so on (5).

3.3 Emergence of environmental movements

As shown above, the drastic resource use that started in the second phase of 'development', and that has been initiated to meet the international requirements and demands of the elites in the Third World, has threatened the interest of the politically weak and socially disorganised group of people whose survival is primarily directly dependent on the products of nature outside the market system (Shiva, 1991: 14). The massive expansion of energy and resource-intensive industrial activity and major development projects like large dams, exploitation of forests, mining and energy-intensive agriculture has led to the narrowing of the natural resource base for the survival of the economically poor and powerless. This occurred either by direct transfer of resources away from basic needs or by destruction of the essential ecological process that ensured renewability of life-supporting natural resources. Shiva argues that ecology movements emerged as the people's response to this threat to their survival and as a demand for the ecological conservation of vital life-support systems (19).

In addition to the inaccessibility of natural resources, another important consequence of the 'development' process is the displacement of a large mass of people without proper rehabilitation programmes. Though dislocation of life could be found as a consequence of dam construction[19] even during the Ancient and Medieval periods and also in the pre-independence era, it was minimal due to the abundance of land and the small population of those times; however, it seemed to be a significant problem during the colonial period, and with the onset of globalisation, it has assumed larger proportions (Murickan et al., 2003: 26). Studies show that policy makers are responsible to a certain extent for the situation of displacement remaining a necessary evil of development, especially in the light of clear identification of 'forced eviction' as a 'gross violation of human rights' by the United Nations in June 1993 (27). It is alleged that policy makers and international financial institutions conceal the trauma that displacement causes to the affected people by using the phrase, 'involuntary relocation', though in reality it is nothing but 'forced eviction'. Another claim by policy makers that displaced people are beneficiaries of a compensation and rehabilitation package is also severely questioned. It is pointed out that this is ironical since the individuals who suffer the most from the project are called beneficiaries. Moreover, the justification for displacement, according to policy makers, is that some people have to suffer for the nation to prosper; it is usually the tribals and dalits who are sacrificed again and again for the development cause (27). Due to this same reason, Mies and Shiva argued that 'development projects' are 'undemocratic' in nature (1993: 10). They usually operate based on a false notion of 'national interest',[20] and every local interest feels morally compelled to make sacrifices for what seems to be the larger interest. The number of cases is increasing where there are conflicts between national interests and the interest of the people adversely affected by development (Mathur, 1995a: 2). Mies and Shiva find that this is how each community made way for large dams in post-independent India (1993: 10). They allege that what was being projected as 'national interest' were the electoral and economic interests of a handful of politicians, financed by a handful of contractors and industrialists who benefited from the 'development projects'. The collective struggle of communities engaged in resistance against large dams, such as Tehri and Narmada in India, formed the real but subjugated common interest against the narrow and selfish interest that had been elevated to the status of 'national interest' (10).

The process of emergence of environmental movements all over the world by the end of the 1980s can be situated against the backdrop of the intricacies that arose from the development activities discussed earlier. The situation is such that though people in Third World countries struggle to extricate themselves from situations created by aid and development, governments were/are reluctant to help them, which has made them dependent on ultimately self-destructive processes; in effect, 'these governments simply "aid" themselves and their supporters, to remain in power' (Rahnema, 1988: 134). Rahnema characterises the uniting of the grass root population in the form of non-cooperative, non-violent movements as immune defence systems aimed at rejecting their modern attackers (135). According to Shiva, the impact of ecology movements cannot be assessed merely in terms of the impact of the particular development project from which they originated; rather, it requires analysis of the very fundamental categories of politics, economics, science and technology that together have created a classical paradigm of development and resource use (1991: 23). The next part will analyse some case studies that will expose the 'political' dimension involved in the power relations employed in such development projects.

Notes

1 The idea of 'resource' has been given different meanings in different periods. According to Rees, these ideas generally took shape in response to increased knowledge, technical improvements and cultural developments, as 'perceived needs' take various forms in each of these cases. See Rees, J. 1990 (1985), *Natural Resources: Allocation, Economics and Policy*, London: Routledge, 12. Zimmerman points out that to consider an element in nature as a 'resource', it should satisfy two preconditions: firstly, the knowledge and technical skills must exist to allow its extraction and utilisation, and secondly, there must be a demand for the materials or services produced. Refer Zimmerman, E. W. 1951 (revised edition), *World Resources and Industries*, New York: Harper & Row cited in Rees, 1990: 12.
2 Nisbet, R. 1980, *History of the Idea of Progress*, London: Heinemann, 77, 100, cited in Du Pisani, J. A. 2006, 'Sustainable Development – Historical Roots of the Concept', *Environmental Sciences*, 3(2), June, 84.
3 Von Wright, G. H. 1997, 'Progress: Fact and Fiction', in Burgen, A. et al. (eds.), *The Idea of Progress*, Berlin: Walter de Gruyter, 3, cited in Du Pisani, 2006: 84.
4 Cowen, M. P. and Shenton, R. W. 1996, *Doctrines of Development*, London: Routledge, 130, cited in Nederveen Pieterse, J. 2001, *Development Theory: Deconstructions/Reconstructions*, New Delhi: Vistaar Publications, 5.
5 Leys, C. 1996, *The Rise and Fall of Development Theory,* Bloomington, IN: Indiana University Press, 4–5, cited in Smelser, N. J. and Baltes, P. B. (eds.), 2001, *International Encyclopedia of Social and Behavioral Sciences*, Vol. 6, New York: Elsevier, 3594.
6 Sutton, F. X. 1989, 'Development Ideology: Its Emergence and Decline', *Daedalus,* 118(1), 35–58, cited in Smelser, N. J. and Baltes, P. B. (eds.), 2001: 3594.
7 Simon reveals his dissent in using the word 'development project' for diverse programmes, agendas and even principles espoused by very different donor and recipient governments, non-governmental organisations and international financial institutions, by post- or anti-developmental critics. He argues that there neither is nor was such a monolithic or singular construction, even during the heyday of modernisation in the 1960s and early 1970s. See Simon, D. 1997, 'Development Reconsidered: New Directions in Development Thinking', *Geografiska Annaler*, 79B(4),186.
8 Goulet, D. 1995, 'Authentic Development: Is It Sustainable'? in Trzyna, T. C. and Osborn, J. K. (eds.), *A Sustainable World: Defining and Measuring Sustainable Development*, Sacramento, CA: International Centre for the Environment and Public Policy, California Institute of Public Affairs, cited in Meyer, M. and Singh, N. 2006, 'Two Approaches to Evaluating the Outcomes of Development Projects', in Rowlands, J. (introduced by), Eade, D. (series ed.), *Development Methods and Approaches: Critical Reflections*, New Delhi: Rawat Publications, 240.
9 According to the World Commission on Environment and Development WCED, sustainable development is development that meets the needs of the present without compromising the ability of future generations to meet their own needs. (1987: 43).
10 Crosby, A. 1988, 'Ecological Imperialism: The Overseas Migration of Western Europeans as a Biological Phenomenon', in Worster, D. (ed.), *The Ends of the Earth: Perspectives on Modern Environmental History*, Cambridge: Cambridge University Press, 103 ff, cited in Gurukkal, R. 1994, 'Ecological Perspective of Development', in Joy, K. P. (ed.), *Eco-Development and Nature Conservation*, New Delhi: AIACHE, 75. See also White, R. 1985, 'American Environmental History: The Development of a New Historical Field', *Pacific Historical Review*, 54(3), 322.
11 Harle, V. 1978, *The Political Economy of Food*, Hants: Saxon House, cited in Goldsmith, E. 1992, 'Economic Development: A False God', in Bahuguna, S., Shiva, V. and Buch, M. N. (contributed authors), *Environment Crisis and Sustainable Development*, Dehra Dun: Natraj Publishers, 16.
12 Shiva cites a number of cases from India. Forced cultivation of indigo in Bengal and Bihar and cultivation of cotton in Gujarat and the Deccan led to large-scale commitment

of land for the supply of raw materials for the British textile industry, the harbinger of the Industrial Revolution. Forests in the sensitive mountain ecosystems of the Western Ghats and the Himalayas were felled to build battleships or to meet the requirements of the expanding railway network. Forests of the Bengal–Bihar–Orissa region were used for running wood fuel locomotives in the early stages of railway expansion. The latter stages of colonial resource utilisation and control included the monopolisation of water rights as in the Sambar Lake of Rajasthan or the Damodar Canal in Bengal. See Shiva, V. 1991, *Ecology and the Politics of Survival: Conflicts over Natural Resources in India*, New Delhi: Sage Publications, 16.

13 Raju argues that the 'inventions' of development began to appear in Kerala (in the Princely state of Travancore, under British administration in India) long before the turn of the nineteenth century. He points out that the project of progress through 'industry' was identified, equated with development and placed within representations in which nature stands separated from man. Hence, to make Truman's declaration a cut-off point is like arguing for essentialism and treating 'developing' nations as a given universe. Similarly, representation of contemporary development projects as post-war phenomena is equal to creating a 'Truman effect' capable of making changes in the 'developing' world. See Raju, 2003, 'Developmental Modernity: Man and Nature in the Discourse of Wealth and Labour', *Contemporary India*, 2(1), 46–7; 62–3.

The Travancore state was referred to as an 'undeveloped' state of the country even before the nineteenth century, and there is a call for change through increasing the area of cultivation by reclaiming lands, enhancing the yield of existing lands by deep ploughing, proper manuring, judiciously selecting the best and most prolific varieties of indigenous of exotic seeds, irrigating where it is needful and practicable and carefully harvesting the crops. See Varma, R. 1874, *Our Industrial Status*, Trevandrum Debating Society, CMS Press, Cottayam, Trivandrum, 11 cited in Raju, 2003: 54.

14 Nandy, A. 1986, *Introduction: Science, Hegemony and Violence*, United Nations University, Unpublished manuscript, cited in Goldsmith, 1992: 50.

15 Development projects are a special type of investment. There are two kinds of investment by both government and private firms. Private firms make investments and develop or select corresponding investment projects, mostly in order to enhance their own projects. Government and international financial institutions like the World Bank do it, in principle, in order to enhance their favourable influence in the welfare and development of the target countries. See Hirschman, A. O. 1967, *Development Projects Observed*, Washington, DC: Brooking Institution, 14.

16 Hart, G. 2001. 'Development Critiques in the 1990s: *culs de sac* and Promising Paths', *Progress in Human Geography*, 24(4), 649–58, cited in Willis, K. 2005, *Theories and Practices of Development*, London: Routledge, 29.

17 Hope, A., Timmel, S. and Hodzi, C. 1984, *Training for Transformation: A Handbook for Community Workers*, Gweru: Mambo Press, 8, cited in Edwards, M. 2008, 'The Irrelevance of Development Studies', in Chari, S. and Corbridge, S. (eds.), *The Development Reader*, New York: Routledge, 308.

18 Both Raju and Gurukkal take these concepts from Michel Foucault. See Foucault, M. 1972, *The Archaeology of Knowledge and the Discourse on Language*, New York: Pantheon Books.

19 The problem of displacement is not a consequence of dam construction alone; it can result from other 'development' activities such as construction of transportation corridors like railways, highways, airports, transmission lines, irrigation canal networks and others that require right-of-way; construction of new ports and towns; construction or improvement of urban infrastructure (e.g., sewerage systems, subways, intra-city roads); inception of mining operations, particularly strip mining; and the protection of grazing areas and transhuman routes. See Asian Development Bank, 1991, Guidelines for Social Analysis of Development Projects', Manila: ADB, 47, cited in Mathur, H. M. 1995b. 'The Resettlement of People Displaced by Development Projects: Issues and Approaches', in

Mathur, H. M. (ed.), *Development, Displacement and Resettlement: Focus on Asian Experiences*, New Delhi: Vikas, 16–17.
20 The idea of national interest emanates from an earlier period, when the precursor of the 'development' idea, that is, progress, was the fashion. In the nineteenth century, the progress of the nation was equated with the progress of the people, and personal preference was to be set aside for the social and national priorities of the progressive industry. See Raju, 2003: 50.

4

THE QUESTION OF 'POLITICAL' IN ENVIRONMENTAL THOUGHT SYSTEMS, MOVEMENTS AND AS A POLITICAL PROCESS[1]

4.1 Conceptual-level engagement

4.1.1 Reform environmentalism

Reform environmentalism mainly aims at reform through legislation. It does not challenge existing social, economic and political structures but rather tries to modify structural arrangements according to the consequences of the actions of humans as social agents or to the newly rising needs of the people. Thus, for example, when pollution was recognised as a problem affecting humans, new laws like the Air Act, Water Act and other acts were introduced. Environmentalist organisations that recommend reform are in agreement with the centralised power structure of the government in policy making activities. Thus, these groups try to influence authority through lobbying or advocacy groups. What makes one group different from another is the way in which they influence the government, while direct-action groups differ in the method of protest they choose. Reform environmentalist groups are pragmatic, in the sense that they look for immediate remedies at action level when conceiving any environmental problem. Usually these do not function as permanent remedies, only as temporary solutions. Moreover, they try to bring in necessary changes in the form of social policies, which have a bearing on the social practices of human beings.

4.1.2 Deep ecology

Deep ecology is generally viewed as an apolitical[2] doctrine, in the sense that it does not provide us with a model for a renewed political system or recommendations for any reform in government policies or any institutional changes to deal with environmental issues (Doyle and McEachern, 1998: 36). Rather, it finds problems with human subjectivity. It seeks to change values from within the individual. The argument is that individuals must change their inward relationships to nature (69). For the deep ecologist, the values, interests and worldviews of humans determine their behaviours or attitudes towards other humans and towards non-human nature. They require humans to shift their lifestyles from market-oriented to nature-centred culture. Deep ecologists are radical in their social philosophy since they question the existing paradigm by bringing forth a new set of key values and principles. For example, the intrinsic value argument radically challenges the prevailing notion that 'nature is a resource', an essential and hitherto unquestioned axiom of Western history (38).

Therefore, the theory of deep ecology looks forward to a radical change in the individual, which they spell out only as an ideology, not as a political programme. They fail to give suggestions as to how an individual's outlook can be influenced by translating their ideas into social policies. However, deep ecology is radically political in the sense by which it brings in fundamentals such as the concept of the 'human' and the latter's approach to nature as the factors determining any favourable change in environmental matters.

The deep ecology movement called Earth First! conceives itself of as an ideology, a way of life. It was created as 'a tribe of eco-warriors' rather than as a corporation with by-laws governed by the United States. Activists do not call themselves 'members of Earth First!'; rather, they are 'Earth First!ers', which suggests a much closer relationship to the movement. They feel a strong, almost spiritual relationship with their organisation. They have a strong relation to indigenous religions and the use of symbols.[3] Earth First!, a direct-action NGO, can be said to be political since it engages in protest activities against the American political system for not addressing their concerns. As a result, Earth First! people tried to reject the system and fight against it. They conducted nationwide demonstrations and rallies, as well as Earth First! road shows. In addition, they adopted many political tactics, including civil disobedience activities[4] such as tree-sitting, monkey wrenching, chaining themselves to earthmoving equipment, sabotaging bulldozers, pulling out survey stakes, cutting down billboards and blocking roads for logging or other development operations. Tree spiking, or inserting either metal or ceramic spikes into trees (without harming the tree) to destroy mill saws, was another popular tactic (Wehr, 2011: 114). Dave Foreman, one of the founders of Earth First! and the most important leader, always promoted ridicule as a political tactic; this is also evident in many of Earth First!ers' essays, songs and debates. Strong commitment and attachment enabled the group to build a close web of grass root chapters all over the country.

Though the Earth First! movement emerged by criticising the American political system, they did not offer recommendations for any reform in government policies, any institutional change or any alternative programmes. Due to this, their position is often represented as apolitical in the conventional political sense. Their radical deep ecological position of bringing change at the individual level is clearly reflected in the millenarian group of Earth First! activists rather than the apocalyptic[5] group. The former believed in the importance of Earth First!ers in the creation of a post-apocalyptic, environmentally aware society and therefore advocated the education of the public as well as their own children. Their focus lies on the 're-wild(ing of) humanity' by reconnecting the people with their natural roots and nature itself. They claim that there is no solution without educating the public, social justice and co-operation with other movements.[6] The millenarian group's position is more in tune with deep ecology theory, in that both take a philosophical position that emphasises rethinking the 'human' aspect and its relation to nature as important in tackling environmental issues, whereas the other group points towards social and economic causes. Thus, Earth First! are radically political in the way they view ecological problems and deal with them on a practical level.

4.1.3 Ecofeminism

Ecofeminists are radically political in the sense that they unravel hitherto unnoticed problems of patriarchy by extending the issue of the domination of women by men to the domination of nature as well. Under man's reign, the exploitation of both women and nature occurs at various steps in the process of production and reproduction. Patriarchy pervades all fields of social structure and social practices, through various institutions, and influences every aspect of the lives of women, including labour, health (physical and mental), education, nutrition, sexuality and their interaction with nature. Male-dominated institutions include family, religion, those that come under legal, economic, political and knowledge systems and so on. Ecofeminists disclose many life instances in which practices that oppress or subordinate women and nature are reproduced through these institutions, reiterating the necessity of correcting them; hence, they challenge these institutional structures. In addition, they highlight the question of power at work in the interactions between man and woman, between man (women are also included, though indirectly, by becoming part of the institutions created by man) and nature. According to them, it is male power that controls all the institutions. This is again problematic when the State makes decisions regarding the functioning of these institutions, favouring hierarchy and domination by men. Here the State also acts as a part of the social structure that reinforces patriarchal value; hence, ecofeminists identify State 'power' as corresponding to male 'power'.

Though all the strands of ecofeminism seem radically political in their effort to problematise the realm of human–environment interaction, they differ among themselves in suggesting solutions to overcome the status quo. For example, liberal ecofeminists do not question the structural arrangements of the State's policy making authority but suggest a reform of human affairs with nature by implementing new laws and regulations from within existing structures of governance. Their political position is thus an adherence to a State-oriented ideology and practice. For cultural ecofeminists, change at the individual level – that is, change in human consciousness – assumes importance before implementing any change at the institutional level and hence is radically political in their approach. Social ecofeminists, who are critical of the existing state of affairs, demand changes in socio-political and economic structures, which only can liberate women and nature. This strand of ecofeminism can be considered as taking a conventionally political stand, though they have not formulated any definite programme for implementing these changes, either in the form of social policy or for adoption at the level of government. Though some social ecofeminists have come up with the recommendation that male power should be replaced by female power, the concept of 'power' itself is not challenged; rather, it is only shifted from one social agent to another while remaining within existing socio-economic and political structures. However, ecofeminists in general try to bring forth behavioural qualities like love, care, friendship and so on (identified as attributes of women's character) to interpersonal levels and also to the sphere of human–nature interaction and, in this sense, take a radical political position in their environmental approach.

4.1.4 Social ecology

Social ecologists recommend a total replacement of the existing political system, including the political parties and related structures, boundaries like nation-states and its bureaucratic structures and economic institutions based on capitalism. According to them, by retaining the current systems of production and reproduction based on hierarchy and power, we can never overcome the problem of exploitation of people and of nature. Thus, they find problems with human–human affairs, which also have implications for nature. The alternative they suggest is an ecological politics structured around an organic ethics that is rooted in organic relationships between people as well as between people and nature. The social ecologist rejects the Centre–State as the authority and identifies communities, towns, villages and others as the arena of decision-making processes. Here the emphasis is on grass roots power that is located and confederated, rather than centralised power. According to social ecologists, an ecological movement should never compromise on its principles to enter into the parliamentary system; rather, they should follow the idea of libertarian municipalism as the political alternative.

Though social ecologists highlight the problems of power, domination and hierarchy, they differ from ecofeminists in the sense that they conceive of these as pervading all human relations, whereas for ecofeminists these are problems concerning the relation between men and women only. In addition, unlike deep ecologists, social ecologists do not recommend a change at the individual level, since the problems are assumed to have arisen only from the structural arrangements.

4.2 'Political' in the case of environmental movements

The contexts of social conflicts are usually varied in character and have bearings on different fields of human life. These issues generally arise when (1) governments or other external forces deny people the right to use forests and other natural resources on which they depend for their daily subsistence, (2) multinational companies exploit water and other resources of a region, putting the lives of local people in trouble or denying the people their right to a hygienic environment, (3) government displaces local or indigenous people in the name of development activities and (4) there is a perceived threat to biodiversity and endangered species of plants and animals. When the issues that require immediate solutions are delayed indefinitely or defeated by using power, people join against injustice in their day-to-day affairs. This generally takes the form of movements (environmental and social) with both social and political consequences.

The distinctive feature of this perspective is the presence of a 'power factor' that controls relations between people in a specific manner. A situation of social conflict becomes complex when the number of dominant agents involved in it are many and the relations between them take multifarious dimensions based on power. Those who are more powerful, that is, with access to wealth or political lobbying, influence the decision-making activity of governments; this usually has an adverse effect on those who are the real claimants to locally available natural resources in the existing socio-economic and political system. Thus, the question (politics) of power often overshadows other concerns of vital importance, including the question of survival, for a larger group of people. Similarly, the approach to nature or environment is often influenced by the ways in which people are related among themselves politically, and this will have a bearing on the tactics adopted to tackle environmental (and social) problems. That is, many environmental conflicts are driven by dominant power relations over the environment, which often benefits a few while threatening the survival of the majority. Generally, questions of survival or displacement that are, at a glance, 'social' issues, also have environmentally significant dimensions. Likewise, activities employed in nature that are motivated by commercial interests or as part of 'development' plans are more harmful to the environment than local activities. For example, when regions of natural importance are destroyed for construction activities or other purposes of profit or self-interest, they may undergo modification in quick and manifold ways, whereas the activities of local people may have comparably less or nominal impact in their natural surroundings. Thus, unlawful power relations may result in irreparable consequences to both the people's lives and the natural environment.

Thus, the movements that emerge from this crisis demand political solutions, which are supposed to ensure the protection of the rights of individuals, as assured by the Constitution of the country. As a result, the governments are forced to intervene in the issues in order to resolve them, in which sometimes governments themselves form a party in generating them and often they resort to strategies including rearrangements in the existing institutional structures, modification of policy framework, enactment of laws and so on. Thus, the political dimension of environmental issues, which these movements address, forms a distinguishing feature of the sphere of human–environment interaction, since it has global and long-term impacts. The nature of each movement varies depending on political complexity, which is determined by the number and kind of agents that surround the issue in question.

In this part, an attempt is made to analyse the different contexts in which various environmental movements emerged, with the purpose of exposing the patterns of power relations in each case and their influence on the decision-making processes. The case studies examined here for analysis are classified on the basis of the nature of agents involved in each case, as often the affected people have to confront these agents for justice. This study relies on various accounts of environmental movements that emerged from the 1970s onward, in and around India and other parts of the world, as reported by different authors. These works are mainly descriptive in nature and provide us with the details of the political context, such as judicial intervention, policy formulation, the role of the political parties and the involvement of media and activist groups of the movements under scrutiny.

4.2.1 People versus State

(a) Concern for biodiversity

(i) Movement against Silent Valley project

The proposal for the Silent Valley Hydroelectric project in India was the first case that attracted public attention worldwide (for details, see Khagram, 2005: 42–9). It was initiated by British rulers during the colonial period in 1929 and was considered ideal for the generation of hydropower. Silent Valley is one of the few tropical rain forest areas[7] that remained relatively undisturbed by anthropogenic activities for at least 50 million years. It occupies an area of approximately 8,950 hectares in southwest India, primarily in the state of Kerala. Combined with the Nilgiri and Nilambur forests to the north and the Attappadi forests to the east, the Silent Valley comprises part of 40,000 hectares of forest in the broader ecosystem known as India's Western Ghats. Kunthipuzha, the stream which flows along the Silent Valley, originates at a height of more than 7,000 feet in the outer run of the Nilgiri forests, descends rapidly to approximately 3,500 feet on the northern edge of the plateau, and then pursues a southward course before cascading down to the Mannarghat plains through a gorge at an elevation of over 3,000 feet. This gorge was the site selected for the Silent Valley project (Khagram, 2005: 41).

The first stage of the Silent Valley hydroelectric project initially envisaged the construction of two power units and ultimately four units of 240 MW (For details see Report of the Joint Committee, 1997: 53–62). The scheme, on completion, was expected to contribute 522 MU of electrical energy per annum to the Kerala grid in addition to the 240 MW of energy (75). Furthermore, the water released from the powerhouse was expected to irrigate about 10,000 ha of land lower down in Palghat and Malappuram districts. The Kerala State Electricity Board (KSEB) published a legally required notification in the *Gazette of India* in June 1973 regarding the commencement of the more than 390-foot high, 120-megawatt Silent Valley hydropower dam. The Planning Commission sanctioned the first phase of the project in 1973, but it could not be taken up until 1976 owing to financial constraints. In 1976, the National Committee on Environmental Planning and Coordination (NCEPC) set up a task force to study ecological problems in the Western Ghats region, including the Silent Valley area. The Task Force recommended that the hydel power project should be abandoned and the area be declared a Biosphere Reserve. The Task Force suggested some safeguards in case the project could not be abandoned for any reason. The Kerala government opted for the inclusion of safeguards as suggested by the Task Force and the Kerala state legislature unanimously favoured going ahead with the project.

However, criticism of the project began at local, national and international levels immediately after the project was reinitiated. Arguments and counterarguments were raised for several years. At a conference of the Switzerland-based International Union of the Conservation of Nature (IUCN), one of the oldest transnational environmental organisations in the world, a resolution was passed appealing to the government of India to preserve the Silent Valley area more effectively (Khagram, 2005: 45). The IUCN, along with the World Wildlife Fund (WWF) and other non-governmental organisations, highlighted internationally the issue of the Silent Valley project as part of a growing transnational campaign to save rain forests around the world. This generated considerable political pressure on the Indian authorities. In addition, these actors provided some critical information, such as aerial photography and satellite imagery of the Silent Valley forests, which Zafar Futehally (Vice President of the Indian Chapter of the WWF) and other critics put to strategic use domestically in India. The Kerala Forest Research Institute (KFRI) also recommended that the Silent Valley–Attappadi area should be kept undisturbed and be declared a Biosphere Reserve. Organisations including *Kerala Sastra Sahitya Parishad* (KSSP; Kerala Forum for Science Literature), the Kerala Natural History Society, the Bombay Natural History Society, the Indian Science Congress and others strongly urged the government to abandon the project on ecological grounds. Moreover, other organisations, such as *Parisara Asoothrana Samrakshana Samiti* (PASS; Committee for Planning and Protecting the Environment) and Silent Valley Scheme Protection Committee (SVSPC), expressed anti-dam opinions. However, KSEB, the Kerala government and other political parties in the State opposed this view on the grounds that the backwardness of the northern region in particular and the State as a whole was because of the absence of industries and the generation of electricity would help to establish factories. The KSSP was able through its many activities to rouse public opinion on the need to save Silent Valley (D'monte, 1991: 9–10). It sent many science groups to different villages, published journals, enacted street plays and conducted book exhibitions, and gained an impressive membership of 7,000 socially concerned people. It conducted its own study to show why the valley should not be destroyed and how the same amount of electricity could be obtained in other ways. They also argued that the destruction of the Silent Valley could not be justified because 40% of Kerala's power was already being exported to other states. They recommended the introduction of lift-irrigation programmes at the earliest opportunity. In addition, scientific groups of botanists, zoologists and geologists officially set up by the Central government lent their support to the KSSP. The organisation also collected the signatures of around 600 teachers, prominent citizens and students and sent a memorandum to the Kerala government protesting construction of the dam. As a result of the KSSP's activities, even people who had little interest in environmental issues up to that point were moved to act.[8]

Two writ petitions by a group of voluntary agencies seeking to forbid the state from proceeding with the project were filed with the Kerala High Court, which issued an interim stay against the project.[9] In January 1979, the President of the Indian Wildlife Board, who was also the Finance Minister of the Government of India, urged Kerala state officials to halt the project (Khagram, 2005: 45). In May, 30 ministers of India's federal parliament sent a similar appeal. By the summer, individuals and organisations outside Kerala, particularly well-known conservationists from Bombay, formed the Save Silent Valley (SSV) Committee (45). The members of this Committee proved to be critical actors in coordinating the anti-dam campaign. In October 1979, Dr M. S. Swaminathan, Secretary of Agriculture, Government of India, visited the project area and recommended that the hydroelectric project be abandoned and the entire area developed into a rain forest Biosphere Reserve (Report of the Joint Committee, 1997: 57). The different ministries of the Indian government were at opposite poles regarding the issue. For example, the Department of Science and Technology and the Ministries of Irrigation and Power supported the project, while NCEPC and the Ministry of Agriculture opposed it. During the interim period between the collapse of the Janata-coalition government in July 1979 and parliamentary elections in January 1980, the members of the SSV Committee lobbied the interim Prime Minister to take personal action against the project. A study conducted by the Ministry of Agriculture reported that the Silent Valley forest needed to be preserved, and an alternative project was to be formulated to meet the irrigation and power needs of Kerala (Khagram, 2005: 46). As a result, the interim Prime Minister asked the Chief Minister of Kerala to drop the project because of the growing controversy. In January 1980, the Kerala High Court dismissed the two writ petitions against the project and lifted the stay on construction (Report of the Joint Committee, 1997: 57). Thus, having received sanction from the Court, the Kerala government, led by the Communist Party Marxist (CPM), decided to implement the project, and the KSEB tried to complete the construction work at the earliest opportunity.

The Kerala government also used many tactics to prevent the people's movement against the project. Thus, in October 1979, arguing that any public opposition would be sub-judice while the High Court hearing on the original petition was still being conducted, Kerala officials obtained an injunction preventing an open meeting that had been organised by the SSV Committee in the state capital, Trivandrum (Khagram, 2005: 47). The *Hindu* newspaper played a major role in supporting the anti-dam campaign and greatly contributed to its gaining nationwide attention. Numerous critical editorials, full-page features and letters were published on the Silent Valley project in the *Hindu*, as well as in other regional and national papers. In January 1980, after the elections, Indira Gandhi was sworn in as the Prime Minister of India and the anti-dam proponents tried to lobby the Central government to halt the project. Members of the SSV Committee sent letters and cable to the Prime Minister after the elections. The IUCN Director General also sent a letter from Switzerland asking her to take steps to stop the project, coordinating his international plea with the activities of the domestic SSV Committee in India. When the CPM came back to power in the state elections, they tried to get permission from the Central government to implement the project. Finally, a joint committee, consisting of four members nominated by the federal government and four appointed by Kerala state authorities, was constituted to assess the project. In addition, the Department of Environment, created from the NCEPC by Indira Gandhi in November 1980, announced a long-term study to investigate the environmental impacts of the three river basin projects in Kerala, including the Silent Valley. In December 1980, the Kerala government declared the Silent Valley Reserve Forest a national park, excluding the project area. In the summer of 1983, the joint federal–state committee report on the Silent Valley was completed, recommending that it was in the public interest to conserve the Silent Valley Forest. In November, the Kerala state authorities announced their decision to stop the project, and by 1984, the areas to be submerged by the dam were incorporated into the Silent Valley National Park ((Khagram, 2005: 49).

The Silent Valley project is the first case in independent India that focused on an issue of nature and garnered the attention of the public by emphasising the need to protect biodiversity. The peculiarity of the case is that though most of the studies made by different agencies regarding the viability of the project suggested that Silent Valley must be protected due to its natural importance, the Kerala government remained adamant in their decision to implement the project owing to their political interests. It was the intervention of various NGOs and activists at the local, national and international levels that provided a favourable political context in which to discuss the issue. Specifically, the activities of organisations like KSSP, at both the local and national levels, greatly contributed to creating awareness of the reality of the project, in opposition to the claims of the KSEB, and of the importance of protecting the Silent Valley forests and its benefits to humans. Their studies raised critical questions regarding the necessity of the project, the state of the real energy requirements and the existing levels of energy consumption. The study reports and campaigning programmes by the members of this organisation worked as responsible political agents, disseminating knowledge among the citizens and mobilising them against government policies regarding environmental matters. The intervention of the court in issuing a stay order to the State government helped inform the public about the seriousness of the issue. The court also revealed its dissatisfaction regarding the government's irresponsibility in understanding the situation while planning and processing the project and regarding the policy decision and the assessment of the conditions taken thereafter. The political lobbying undertaken by many individuals in various NGOs, at both national and international levels, of high authorities like the Prime Minister, and the latter's communication with the state authority on this basis, helped to politically pressure the State government to make a decision against implementing the project. Another important aspect is the role played by the newspapers in exposing the real situation regarding the Silent Valley issue and the political play of the government in tackling the issue. Thus, it seems that the joint political effort made by the NGOs, various state institutions and agencies, activists, the press, the court and people like teachers, students and laymen helped to put pressure on the State government to rethink the project and finally to withdraw it by declaring Silent Valley a national park.

(b) Deforestation and livelihood issues

Deforestation and its impact on the livelihood of people dependent on the resources at the fringes of the forest became an important issue that motivated many a struggle in different parts of the world. The issues vary widely depending on the socio-economic and political circumstances existing in each place. The nature of the struggle and the tactics used also differ depending upon (1) the agents who accept leadership in mobilising the affected people and (2) the political context of the regions, including the policies taken by governments with regard to the forests. In spite of the differences between the social situations prevailing in different countries, the general trend is that those who are in and close to 'power' tend to deprive large masses of people of their means of survival. In what follows, we consider a few cases from India and Japan.

India

The conflict between people and the State over forest resources in India is the direct result of the situation created in the contexts of the government taking over the forests during the colonial period and after independence. The forests were under the control of local village communities until the second half of the nineteenth century, and there was little state intervention. But the situation changed after the inception of the forest department in 1864 (Gadgil and Guha, 1995: 85). The Indian Forest Act was passed in 1878, according to which the forests were divided into reserved, protected and village forests (40). Large areas of forests were taken over by the colonial government as 'reserved forests' between 1860 and 1890, and only a few were retained as village forests.[10] Even in those forests retained for the use of the communities, they were denied all rights to regulate the use of resources. Instead, these were treated as open access lands where anybody could come and harvest produce, without the sanction of the local communities. This resulted in the overuse of these tracts of land, which was used in turn to justify the progressive conversion of community lands into reserved forests. Thus, the extent of such lands was reduced from 7,185.9 sq km to 353.3 sq km between 1890 and 1920 (Gadgil and Guha, 1995: 40–1). Even after independence there was not much change in the policies, and the state of tension continued until the latter half of the twentieth century. It is in these circumstances that the local population, including hunter–gatherers, shifting cultivators, peasants, peasant nomads, artisans and others who could not withstand the loss of traditional rights of access and use, started to protest against the imposition of State control on forests in various parts of the country.

(i) Chipko movement

The earliest form of people's organised protests, known as 'Chipko' movements,[11] began in the 1970s and were held against the State governments. In 1970, a major flood occurred in the Alakananda valley in the Himalaya region that inundated several villages and fields and made the villagers aware of the connection between deforestation, landslides and floods (for details, see Sheth, 1997: 218–19). In 1971, a demonstration was organised by the *Dashauli Gram Swarajya Sangh* (DGSS), a co-operative organisation based in Chamoli district, highlighting socio-economic problems such as ending liquor sale, untouchability and so on, and for giving priority to local use of forests. They also demanded the replacement of the contractor system with forest labour co-operatives (FLCs) and the setting up of small-scale industries.[12] This kind of 'Chipko' (to hug) protest was planned in 1973, when the villagers of Mandal requested and were refused an allotment of ash trees to make agricultural implements by the forest department. Instead of ash trees, they were asked to use chir trees, which were totally unsuitable for the purpose. The villagers faced utter injustice when the government allotted ash trees to the Symonds Co., a sporting goods firm. The UP government tried to compromise with the people by allotting the DGSS ash trees on condition that the company would be allowed to take its quota. But resistance by the villagers forced the company to flee Mandal without felling even a single tree. However, the government went ahead with its plan for the yearly auction of forests despite the warning of protests by the villagers.

Another site of felling was the Reni forest (Guha, 1989: 158–61), a locality affected in that period by landslides. Reni was a village inhabited by members of the Bhotiya community, who had abandoned nomadic pastoralism in favour of settled agriculture. Meetings were conducted and decisions were made to adopt the Chipko technique. Fearing opposition to the felling operations, the forest department resorted to subterfuge. By keeping the men of the village away for a lost cause, the forest department officials planned to fell the trees. But the women of the village took direct action by hugging the trees, which forced the authority to withdraw from their decision. Following this, the government agreed to set up a committee to investigate the incident, and based on the understanding that the 1970 floods were the result of widespread deforestation, commercial felling was banned for a period of ten years in the upper catchment of the river and its tributaries. The committee also noticed the difficulties that had arisen due to resin tapping and put a restriction on the practice of tapping, insisting that it should be according to the rules. The constitution of a forest corporation, or Van Nigam, was another step taken to examine all forms of forest exploitation. But these conditions were not properly maintained in later years, and the forest auction was continued in different parts of Garhwal. On many occasions, Chipko activists intervened and helped the local people to respond to the injustices of the forest department. Protests were held in many places, including Dehradun, Uttarkashi and other places in Garhwal and Nainital of Kumaun, challenging the department's decision to continue either resin tapping or commercial felling. A protest mainly led by women[13] occurred in the Pindar Valley, near the village of Dungri-Paintoli. Here the men of the village wanted to sell their oak forest to the horticulture department, which intended to establish a potato farm on the land. But the women understood that if the forests were cut, they would have to walk a long distance to collect fuel and fodder.[14] The intervention of Chipko activists, helped by the district administration, ensured the protection of the remaining forests.

The Chipko movement that emerged as the predecessor of the people's organised protest seems to have arisen as a result of the State's (especially the forest department) unjustifiable political attitude towards the village people.[15] The State government, which is obliged to take care of its people, has either neglected them or failed to perceive them as socio-political agents who also have certain roles in performing State functions. When the concerned authority of the State decided to manage the forests on commercial lines by selling the products to private companies and denied the original inhabitants of the region their rights to use the forests, the former actually kept the latter out of the political realm. In addition, the forest officials often misused their official power by aiding private contractors in making profits. All these instances of State malpractice made the people unite for their right to use the forests as the source of their household needs. The increasing participation of women in protest activities is an indication of the political awareness created among the people as a result of the political intervention of the activists of various organisations. This awareness made them recognise forests as the socio-economic foundation of their lives and argue for their rights to use forests primarily, instead of outsiders. In many instances, the protest that emerged from this outlook of the people forced the forest department and the State government to make decisions in favour of the villagers. The decision of the State government to manage the forests scientifically seemed to be a one-sided approach and flawed for three reasons. The government failed (1) to take into account in policy making the village people's way of living and their customary usage of forests, (2) to ensure the participation of these people while making any decisions regarding forests and thus ensuring the protection of the rights of this group and (3) to foresee the role of the forests in keeping the natural processes in order and controlling the ecological damage that had resulted due to forest destruction. Though the 'Chipko' movement is the outcome of a political struggle in a localised context, this kind of resistance against the ruling authority was adopted in other states of the country as well, for example in the Appikko Chalewali movement that took place in the Western Ghats in the Uttara Kannada region of Karnataka in the 1980s (Sheth, 1997: 219–23), and the protest by women in the Asna village of Bastar district in Madhya Pradesh (MP) in 1987 (Sundar, 1998: 227–49), where similar political situations prevailed.

Japan

Japan is the largest buyer and user of tropical hardwood (timber) and timber products such as woodchips, pulp, plywood and others in the world (for details, see Wong, 1998: 131–50). Until World War II, Japan's domestic forestry production satisfied its demands for wood, but demand quickly outgrew domestic output after 1955. The timber was mainly used for industrial purposes and housing construction; fully grown natural forests in various parts of Japan were cut for commercial use and replaced by artificial forests. Rising costs and a shortage of domestic timber supply ultimately compelled the Japanese government to lift all controls on timber imports in 1961. Japan has a history of importing timber for more than 70 years, and Southeast Asia formed the major supplier of timber resources to this country. Japanese logging began in the southern Philippines in the pre–World War II years by small- and medium-sized companies, and in the post-War period the forestry investment returned first to the Philippines, during which time the timber trade was mainly undertaken by large general trading companies (GTCs).[16] By the 1960s, the GTCs had moved to the forests in Kalimantan and southern Sumatra in Indonesia, often with the Japanese government's assistance and loans. Throughout the 1960s and 1970s, the Philippines and Indonesia were the major suppliers of timber to Japan. When Indonesia banned log exports in 1985, Japanese forestry investment turned to non-peninsular Malaysia: Sabah and Sarawak. In 1987, 96% of its tropical hardwood came from only three places: Sarawak, Sabah and Papua New Guinea. Increasing log export restrictions in producer countries in Southeast Asia, rising prices and declining supply have prompted many Japanese companies to turn to the import of softwood from North America and to diversify their sources of tropical timber imports. Between 1960 and 1963, Japan's total log imports more than doubled, and those from Southeast Asia increased by 70%. By 1973, the peak year of Japan's tropical log imports, consumption increased by nearly six-fold to 27 million cu m from 4.5 million cu m in 1960. The manipulation of Japanese forests for the purpose of fuel wood and timber has for many years created different kinds of socio-political responses on the part of the people.

(i) The anti-tropical timber campaign

Until 1986, there was no serious move against Japan's tropical deforestation processes. It was in 1987 that Japan Tropical Forest Action Network (JATAN), the Japanese anti-tropical deforestation NGO, emerged in the first council of the meeting of the International Tropical Timber Organization (ITTO); it became the principal Japanese NGO to concentrate on the tropical deforestation problem. JATAN conducted a series of lectures to raise public awareness and organised an international conference to bring together Japanese and foreign activists and researchers concerned about the problem. Petition campaigns were also launched to protest the Malaysian government's actions against tribal peoples in Sarawak and to appeal to the Japanese government to reduce the country's massive consumption of tropical timber. A comprehensive study report, 'Timber from the South Seas', was undertaken in Japanese on the tropical timber trade in Southeast Asia and was completed in 1988. Environmental activists and forest peoples from Sarawak, Papua New Guinea and other places were invited to Japan to speak in public forums in order to publicise tropical forest destruction and related issues. Japan took the initiative in publishing the report by WWF in English, and it was launched with substantial media coverage in Japan. In addition, JATAN organised intensive campaigns and demonstrations targeted at Japanese GTCs for their role in tropical deforestation in Southeast Asia. Dramas were staged in front of GTC offices; the 'Destruction Award', in the shape of a chain saw, was given to these companies, catching the attention of national and international media due to the novelty of the demonstration techniques. JATAN was also effective in influencing a GTC, Obayashi, to decide to reduce tropical timber use to 35% in 1990. Another effort was made by JATAN to request that the country's local governments end the use of tropical timber imports, as a result of which 66 local governments agreed not to use tropical timber in public projects, by August 1995. The acceptance of NGOs in Western democracies and international organisations worldwide put pressure on the Japanese government to act in the same manner. Also, in the face of severe international criticisms, the Ministry of Foreign Affairs and the Forestry Agency in particular became more receptive to dialogues with NGOs. After making both the public and the government aware of the situation and acquiring credibility, JATAN shifted its attention to research on tropical deforestation and related problems, building organisational membership, forging ties and exchanges with environmental NGOs in the producer countries and continuing public education in Japan.

The report points out that JATAN could succeed in their efforts to make the Japanese people more responsible for their nature by using certain strategies (Wong, 1998: 144–5). Firstly, instead of blaming them for their greed and insensitivity in consuming tropical timber, JATAN targeted the GTCs. This was made possible by urging the Japanese public to reduce their consumption of tropical timber and to support the domestic campaign based on their sympathy and empathy for the damage to nature and human lives. Secondly, the NGO was careful to use Japanese communication styles, culture and norms, due to which the movement did not appear as a mere extension of white environmentalism and foreign pressure. Thirdly, along with academic and research interest in tropical forestry and its associated issues and problems, the domestic campaign also stimulated interest in the broader subject of Japan's role in international development and the global environment. In addition, it raised popular consciousness about the connection between Japanese domestic consumption and the external environment.

This campaign in Japan is the result of the awareness of a few citizens regarding their political responsibility. The government of Japan seems to be engaged in highly irresponsible activities regarding the timber trade without being conscious of either the country's natural environment or the people's sustenance related to it, both of which are presumed to be their duties. The activities of NGOs like JATAN have contributed largely to making changes in the political sphere of Japan at four levels. Firstly, it helped to politicise the issue of deforestation, which satisfied the commercial interests of those who are in power in the government. Secondly, it opened the way for common people's participation in national politics through its entry to politics. Thirdly, it exposed the role of NGOs in making the public aware of such national issues. Fourthly, it brought forth the need to develop public debates over such politically important matters at both personal and institutional levels. The NGOs thus succeeded in influencing many local governments to act politically by ending the use of tropical timber.

(ii) The forest grant movement

Another movement of political significance under the initiative of the forest-dependent people of the country was the Forest Grant Movement in Japan. In Japanese culture, the mountains are said to be the source of village prosperity in both upland and lowland areas. Here the ancient people depended on the timber value of the forests for survival, which is already lost. This made the mountain village people to start a movement in upland areas that called on the government to provide them with new resources for forest protection (Knight, 1998: 110–30). The history of the Japanese forests reveals that they have long been manipulated for the supply of fuel wood and timber, with preferred patterns of growth varying from one period to another; that is, sometimes firewood forests were grown and at other times these were replaced by timber or conifers. By the 1970s, foreign timber had displaced domestic timber, resulting in the collapse of domestic forestry; as a result, forestry as a source of employment became greatly diminished in upland Japan. In addition to this, rapid economic growth in the cities, along with a failure to establish alternative industries to provide local employment, caused large-scale out-migratory depopulation and the economic decline of mountain villages in later decades. Hongu, an upland municipality, is an example; it has undergone large-scale depopulation in the post-war period, with a population of 10,276 in 1955 declining to 4,345 in 1994. In 1965, there were 861 employed forest labourers; by 1994, this had fallen to less than 150. The Hongu population decreased steadily as the employment base contracted and other attempts to generate occupation like local industry did not succeed.

In these circumstances, the Forest Grant Establishment Promotion League was founded by 36 municipalities in 1992. It held its first conference in February 1993 in Hongu; more than 600 people gathered, representing over 100 municipalities. This was followed by a second, larger conference held the following year in Sapporo City, Hokkaido, attended by some 1,200 people representing 326 municipalities. By November 1994, the league had a membership of 431 municipalities, representing one-third of depopulated municipalities, and 13% of all Japanese municipalities. The demand of these conferences was for a 'forest grant' to be paid to upland areas in recognition of the vital role they play in maintaining the nation's forests. The subsidy would be allocated in proportion to the area of forest in each municipality. That is, this grant represents a *return* that the government should make to mountain villages in recognition of the public benefits derived from the forests over which the villagers exercise stewardship. Thus, it is not a subsidy but a proper compensation for their environmental care-taking. Therefore, remote upland districts like Hongu, which is almost entirely covered by forests, deserve the grant – that is, the mountain villagers are asking the authorities for their rights.

The emergence of the idea of the forest grant movement can be situated in three contexts (Knight, 1998: 116–25). Firstly, it is the result of the need for developed countries like Japan to protect their national forests in order to get rid of the pressure to reduce carbon dioxide emissions, which, as the Rio Summit emphasised, result in global warming. The Climate Change Convention also requires nations 'to prepare national inventories of GHG (greenhouse gas) emissions and sinks'. Therefore, this situation can be taken as permitting Japanese forests – and their mountain village custodians – in effect to come to the defence of Japanese industry by subtracting their absorptive capacity from the total emissions of industry. The author points out that while they may claim a global role as a site of carbon-fixing, in practice they can be seen as playing a national role in protecting Japanese industry from international pressure to reduce carbon emissions. Thus, international carbon politics presents Japanese upland municipalities with a new opportunity for domestic leverage. Secondly, it is argued that urban people should be responsible for the mountain villagers because of the close relationship between Japanese forests and Japanese culture. Japanese culture is based on and predominantly shaped by the livelihood long provided by the forests. The contemporary abandonment of the mountain villages resulting from the modernisation processes of the downstream villages is tantamount to breaking the last link with the forests, the foundation of Japanese culture. That is, it points towards the importance of mountain villages as sites of traditional culture, which supported the downstream village people. Moreover, the regional unity that was enjoyed between the upstream (rural) and downstream (urban) villages has been affected adversely, as mountain village life has suffered a 'loss of autonomy'. A third aspect is the acknowledgement of the ancestral people of the mountains who had planted the trees and grown them into forests, due to which the environmental well-being of the nation has been maintained. Hence, the present generation is arguing for the grant in the name of the past generations.

This case is an example of the utilisation of a global political cause for local political support. Local livelihood problems arise from the different forest policies adopted by various rulers in different periods. The priority was not the sustenance of the village people but rather the industrial market demands that determined the future of the forests. The degradation of the upstream–downstream domestic resource transfer practice is also a factor that made the economy of the mountain village people problematic, forcing them to think of some economic alternatives. Rural-urban life very much depended on the mutual co-operation between the two, and this traditional informal arrangement of resource transfer between the two regions was disturbed by the influence of politics of the market-oriented economy of the latter, which in turn affected the self-reliance of the former. Thus, it seems that the mountain people were 'politically' motivated to make use of national and international political contexts as the background against which they raise their claim of rights for the forest grant, the politics of which cannot be denied by the government or the larger public.

(c) Development and displacement issues

India

(i) Save Narmada movement

The Narmada river project forms the most important case study and pictures how short-term, current development policies of various State governments and the politics encompassing them can result in the pauperisation of a large mass of people and their continuing struggle for the 'right of living'. The Narmada river valley project consists of Sardar Sarovar Project (SSP) at Vadgam on the Gujarat–Maharashtra border and Narmada Sagar Project (NSP), later renamed as Indira Sagar at Punasa in MP, further upstream. SSP is an interstate multipurpose project comprising the four major states of Western India, that is, MP, Gujarat, Maharashtra and Rajasthan, with a terminal major dam in Gujarat. The specialty of this dam project is that the command area of major beneficiaries lies in one state, Gujarat, while the major displacement problem affects MP, though Maharashtra and Gujarat are not exceptions. The Narmada river valley project is a scheme that envisages the construction of 30 major dams, its tributaries, 135 medium and 3,000 minor dams on the Narmada. The focus of popular opposition has been the Sardar Sarovar reservoir, the largest of the project's individual schemes, which called into question the policy behind it. In order to get an idea about the complexity of the issue, it seems relevant to contextualise its emergence historically.

The proposal for constructing a dam harnessing Narmada waters has a history beginning as early as the 1950s (Sangvi, 2002). The thrust for a large project on the Narmada came as part of the development policy adopted in the country after independence. From the beginning, the height of the dam was a focal point of issue. In August 1960, the Planning Commission cleared the Broach Irrigation Project, the precursor to SSP, in Gujarat, with a height of 162 feet, for irrigating 9.97 lakh hectares of land; in the second stage, the height of the dam was decided to be 300 feet, to which Planning Commission did not agree. Gujarat and the Centre proposed a dam of 425 feet at the SSP site, but the MP government contested the claims of Gujarat on Narmada waters by reinforcing their ownership of it. The Narmada Water Resources Development committee, appointed by the Union government, proposed a dam of over 500 feet near Navgam in Baruch district of Gujarat in 1965. In July 1968, the Gujarat government submitted a formal complaint under the Inter-State Water Disputes Act, 1956. The government of India decided to constitute the Narmada Water Dispute Tribunal (NWDT) in November 1969. In this, Gujarat claimed a larger share of water on the basis of the projected needs of its 'drought prone area' in the far-off Kutch region. In this effort,

Gujarat also made Rajasthan a party to the dispute, though the latter has nothing to do with Narmada. The state of Rajasthan was brought in through political doors in a meeting with the Prime Minister on 12 April 1974. Rajasthan was included to strengthen Gujarat's demand for an increased height of the canal and the dam, disregarding the objections of MP and Maharashtra.

The *Nimad Bachao–Narmada Bachao Samiti*, that is, Save Nimad–Save Narmada Committee, was formed in the mid-1970s and presented its case before the NWDT. In this representation, the samiti pointed out the possible harmful impacts of such a large reservoir, such as the displacement of people including tribals, farmers, backward castes and classes, leading to their unemployment and destitution; they also pointed out the harm of the submergence of the fertile lands of Nimad region, along with issues like earthquakes, increased silting and so on. The samiti also submitted a memorandum to the then-Prime Minister, Mrs Indira Gandhi. The NWDT rejected the claims of Gujarat to provide irrigation for 11 lakh hectares in Kutch and water for Rajasthan and finally declared its award. According to this decision, the height of the SSP was decided to be 455 feet and that of NSP[17] 860 feet from the mean sea level. Madhya Pradesh was allotted 18.25 MAF (million-acre feet) of water, Gujarat 9 MAF, Rajasthan 0.50 MAF and Maharashtra 0.25 MAF of the Narmada waters. Though SSP, with a height of 436 feet and dead storage level of 307 feet, was adequate for the irrigation needs of Gujarat and Rajasthan, it was raised to 453 feet to compensate for the power loss to MP and Maharashtra. Without any reason, the height was again raised to 455 feet, which in effect would cause submergence.

The award of NWDT generated widespread agitation in the plains of western Nimad area, as it would cause the submergence of its fertile land. Due to the lack of political unions and organisational leadership, and the absence of appropriate process, demands and strategies, it soon dissipated. But when the political situation changed in MP (Arjun Singh was sworn in as Chief Minister), the government signed a 'confidential' agreement with the Gujarat government, on 25 August 1981, for exploring the possibilities of resolving the problems of the displaced people as much as possible. In the meantime, the World Bank entered the scene with loans for the purpose of resettlement and lobbied the Gujarat government to accept the Bank's conditions regarding settlement. The Indian NGOs also accepted the World Bank intervention. Tata Economic Consultancy Services (TECs) was appointed for economic appraisal. In 1980, the Central government created a new Ministry of Environment and Forests (MoEF); in 1983, it formulated guidelines for River Valley Development Projects for the Union and State governments. Until 1987, MoEF did not accord clearance to the Sardar Sarovar and Narmada Sagar projects due to incomplete plans for rehabilitation, catchment area treatment, compensatory afforestation and command area development. Due to political pressure by the Gujarat government, the then-PM, Mr Rajeev Gandhi, took necessary steps to sanction conditional clearance by the MoEF for the dams in June 1987. However, the MoEF laid down conditions that the following eight important studies were to be completed before December 1989: resettlement and rehabilitation, catchment area treatment, command area treatment, flora and fauna, carrying capacity, compensatory afforestation, seismicity and health impacts. On 5 October 1988, the Planning Commission gave conditional clearance, retaining the conditions laid down by the MoEF.

People's resistance

From the outset of the proposed construction of the dam, there was confusion regarding its aftermath. People in the valley organised in groups to oppose such a move from the government and started to question development projects. In the 1980s, people's environmental awareness was increasing in light of the experiences of some of the earlier projects in different parts of the country. In MP, protestors – including prominent social activists, legislators and local leaders – opposed the High Dam at Navagam (SSP), as it would submerge the fertile lands in the Nimad region. *Narmada Bachao Samiti*–Save Narmada Committee raised vital issues ranging from the submergence of fertile land and displacement to the loss of cultural heritage and natural resources from 1972 to 1975. In 1983, 'Kalpavriksha', a group of activist–researchers from a Delhi-based organisation, published a report, exposing the environmental and human costs involved in the Narmada valley projects. In 1986, SETU (Center for Social Knowledge and Action), an NGO in Ahmedabad, problematised the resettlement project of the World Bank. On 16 February 1986, *Narmada Dharmagrastha Samiti* (NDS; Narmada Displaced People's Organisation) shared people's anxiety about the fundamental questions regarding their right to know, to participate in the decision-making process, their own displacement, the evaluation of their own lives and resources, proof of the government's ability to restore these and so on. They also doubted the availability of land for resettling all 33 adivasi villages. In several memoranda of 1986–1988 and during district level meetings with the government, the samiti demanded full information regarding the dam, the likely displacement and the proposed resettlement. They tried to discover whether all those who were affected directly or indirectly by the dam would be included as 'project affected'. And, considering the nature and magnitude of displacement, they questioned the authorities' claim of 'public purpose'. The resistance strengthened when the people understood that the government could not respond to these issues; they held padayatras (journey on foot), village level meetings and magni parishad (demand conferences) in Dhadgaon in November 1986. In 1987, the samiti also conducted a people's survey of the number of oustees and an assessment of their natural resources to counter the government's inadequate assessment and disinformation. In their dealings with government authorities, NDS tried to present issues such as the tribals' right to information, the right to decisive participation, cost–benefits of the project and the spiritual, social and aesthetic aspects of their lives, along with issues of non-availability of land and the consequent impossibility of resettlement.

NDS made contact with the *Khedut Mazdoor Chetna Sangath* (KMCS; Farmer Labourer Organisation), an organisation fighting on the issues of land and other resource rights, livelihood and self-respect of the adivasis from the early 1980s. *Narmada Ghati Navnirman Samiti* (NGNS; Narmada Valley Reconstruction Committee) was established in Nimad in 1986 with the participation of many veteran

Sarvodayi leaders, totally opposing the dam. They took out a *Narmada Jan-Jagaran Yatra* (Narmada People-Awareness Journey) in 1986 with the purpose of raising awareness about the adverse impacts of large dams in the valley and stressed the need for decentralised, sustainable development, planned by the villagers themselves, for agriculture, water and energy. In Bhopal, the 'Campaign Against Indira Sagar Project' (CAISA) started in 1988. Thus, the attempts of the *Narmada Bachao–Nimad Bachao Andolan* in the 1970s were strengthened with the connections to various organisations and their support, which led to a mass-based and comprehensive struggle that emerged towards the end of the 1980s. Medha Patkar contacted the NGNS around mid-1987, along with many other activists, and launched campaigns to organise, mobilise and link up the people of the entire Nimad stretch. In 1987, a 'Meeting Against Large Dams' was convened at Anandvan by the social activist Baba Amte with the participation of activists from the Narmada valley, and a 'Declaration Against Large Dams' was published that linked several issues such as displacement, environmental destruction, adverse cost-benefit, overestimation of benefits and others.

People of the six villages, who were affected by the earlier projects, were organised as the *Narmada Asargrasta Sangharsha Samiti* (NASS; Narmada Affected People's Struggle Society), Gujarat, in early 1988, with the help of NDS activists. NASS worked in close coordination with organisations in Maharashtra and MP. The villagers and the representatives of these organisations contacted the officials of the 'Rehabilitation and Resettlement Sub-group' of Narmada Control Authority (NCA) in order to get clarification of their basic concerns regarding the number and definition of oustees, land availability, community resettlement, cost–benefit of the dam and to provide any additional information and documents. However, they could not get any answers, which made the organisations in Maharashtra, MP and Gujarat to oppose the dam. A major rally held in Kevadia colony on 30 January 1998, which was the first signal that a united struggle of people from all three states (including people from Dhule, Ahmedabad, Baroda, Indore, Mumbai and Delhi) was evolving. Support groups for the struggle in the Narmada valley also evolved over this time, starting in 1987 in Dhule, followed by Mumbai, Delhi, Pune, Indore, Bhopal, Ahmedabad, Baroda and, later in the 1990s, in Bengal, Karnataka, Kerala, Tamil Nadu, Bihar, Rajasthan and other states. The emerging collective was recognised as *Narmada Bachao Andolan* (NBA; Save Narmada Movement) from 1988 onwards.

In 1988, over 25 organisations and a number of social activists and experts gathered in Ahmedabad to deliberate over the SSP. Trade unions, organisations of tribals, dalits and others formed the *Narmada Yojana Vichar Samiti* (Narmada Project Deliberation Committee) to work in Gujarat on the issue of the dam. The *Lok Adhikar Sangh* (LAS; Association for People's Power) and other organisations pointed out that the Narmada project would aggravate already existing inequities and exploitation in Gujarat. At that time, NBA became more active against forced displacement and destructive development. A detailed and nation-wide action plan for the Narmada struggle was charted out on 5–6 May 1989 at a major meeting of NBA supporters in Mumbai. The Andolan took responsibility for mobilising the people's organisations for the 'Convention Against Destructive Development' at Harsud on 28 September 1989. Over 50,000 people from 300 organisations throughout India participated. Meanwhile, the State governments tried many times to weaken the struggle in Gujarat and MP using police force. The agitation was also intensified against the World Bank in 1990–1991. The NBA highlighted the Bank's errors in its analysis and evaluation of data and understanding of the issue.

Another important event was *Jan Vikas Sangarsh Yatrai* (People's Struggle for Development), in which men, women, tribals, peasants and others from all over the country were united in the border village between MP and Gujarat. They demanded a review of the dam in a time-bound manner and with independent experts, for which the leaders started an indefinite fast on 7 January 1990 – an occasion in which hundreds of people and organisations from every corner of India expressed solidarity with the struggle. It was called off after 22 days, on 30 January, only after the World Bank announced an independent review of the project. The review was made by Bradford Morse, the former Chairman of United Nations Development Programme (UNDP), and concluded that resettlement according to laws and regulations was impossible, that environmental stipulations had been violated and that the expected benefits would not accrue. Thus, the Indian government withdrew from the loan agreement, forming an important step in the struggle. During the monsoon of 1991, the village Manibeli in Maharashtra was threatened by submergence, as the height of the dam was close to 32 metres. By that time villagers had become bold enough to make the decision to die in water. On 11 July 1993, a house at Vadgam, the first village near the dam, was submerged. Following this, the Andolan declared its *Jal samarpan* (sacrifice in water) on 6 August 1993. The Union government was under pressure for a comprehensive review of the case due to appeals from all over India and the international community, and on 5 August, the government declared the review. The review committee report was incomplete and the Supreme Court asked the committee to complete it, providing recommendations.

By 1994, the dam had reached a height between 56 and 57 metres, and in May NBA filed a comprehensive petition in the Supreme Court against the dam and displacement. However, the dam work was allowed to proceed, despite the report by the Five Member Committee (FMG), that is, the review committee. An eight-day warning dharna, followed by an indefinite dharna and fast, was held at Bhopal between October and December 1994. On 13 December, the Supreme Court made the FMG report public, saying that the Central government and the three state governments must provide their written responses within four weeks and the discussions in the NCA must start immediately. The MP government also promised to put the demand for the reduction of the height of the dam before the Court, and the 22-day long fast ended. In December 1994, NCA decided to suspend riverbed construction on the dam. It was another victory for the people. During the suspension of dam work according to the court order, the government continued other dam-related works and efforts to relocate the people to show 'progress in resettlement' by presenting false affidavits in the court. However, a major change occurred in the court's approach during the four years of the interim period with the retirement of the Chief Justice, which had a serious impact on this case. On 18 February 1999, the court, with the new Chief Justice, gave an interim order allowing the Gujarat government to go ahead with the construction of the dam, to a total height of 85 metres. It also approved an in-house 'Grievance Redressal Authority' appointed by the Gujarat government, limited to the oustees to be resettled in Gujarat. The Gujarat government had filed false affidavits in the court regarding resettlement and the availability of land. Though the MP government submitted affidavits for the reduction of dam height from 455 feet to 384 feet, it helped the Gujarat government by falsely submitting that land for oustees was available in MP, when in fact it was not. On 1 April 1999, 2,000 men and women launched *Manav Adhikar Yatra* (Human Rights March), traversing the villages and towns of MP and Maharashtra and culminating in Delhi at the Social Welfare Ministry. The Yatra aimed to reassert the right to life and to oppose displacement under threat of submergence. Various organisations of tribals, dalits, backward classes, minorities, fish workers, industrial labourers, mill workers and other victims of displacement and destructive development joined the march. A *satyagraha* (i.e., seeking truth), a non-violent method of political protest and resistance, against the unjust submergence was also launched on 20 June 1999 in Domkhedi (Maharashtra) and in Jalsindhi (MP). The Supreme Court gave its verdict on 18 October 2000. It sanctioned construction of the dam up to 90 metres and thereafter, at each subsequent stage, by the consent of the NCA, which was contrary to the NWDT provisions.

The Review Committee of NCA decided on 18 August 2001 to raise the height of the dam up to 100 metres after resettling all oustees below it by December, despite the fact that there was no land for resettlement. The MP government, in the 50th meeting of the R and R Sub-group of the NCA held on 29 August 2001 at Bhopal, proposed an amendment to the NWDT Award (NWDTA) to facilitate cash compensation instead of land for land. NBA pointed out that the government so far had taken a position that the NWDT is inviolable, but when they found it difficult to provide the land for oustees, this law was open for 'amendment'. Hence, NBA argued that such a move is in violation of the NWDTA, Supreme Court Order and International Conventions, to which India is a party. They opined that it also tampered with the basic values and premises of the Constitution of India, which confers on all citizens the right to life and equality. As a reaction to the State government's anti-people stance, activists launched an indefinite fast from 17 September, due to which the Maharashtra government promised to verify the number of oustees, land availability and the lapses in rehabilitation through a Task Force with the participation of NBA and to ask the NCA not to increase the height of the dam above 90 metres. It also agreed to prepare a master plan for resettlement with NBA participation in the Planning Group and Overview group. On 24 January 2002, the Chief Ministers of Gujarat, Narendra Modi and Digvijay Singh of MP, in the presence of Prime Minister Mr. Vajpayee, decided to take the height of SSP from 90 metres up to 100 metres by June 2002.

By 2006, the dam height had reached 400 feet (121.92 metres), in violation of the NWDTA as well as the Supreme Court order. As per those, rehabilitation of families up to that height should have been completed before taking the dam walls that high. The NBA filed further cases in 2002 and in 2005, challenging the construction of the dam without completing rehabilitation.[18] In 2006, when the dam height was cleared to 400 feet, it was clearly at the expense of the constitutional rights of the affected people. Due to vociferous protest at all levels, including a 21-day fast by three affected people and Medha Patkar in New Delhi, the Prime Minister directly intervened and appointed the Oversight Group (OSG) headed by Shri V. K. Shunglu. Though facing many drawbacks, the Shunglu committee report clearly showed that rehabilitation was incomplete at 121.92 metres, thus justifying the issues raised by the NBA. The gates of the Sardar Sarovar Dam were not installed at that time since permission had not been received, as the Rehabilitation and Resettlement Sub-group had not cleared the request from Gujarat government. The Environmental Sub-group had already given permission for the full height of 138.68 metres, despite obvious evidence that environmental measures stipulated by NWDTA were far from complete. However, NCA gave clearance for the completion of the dam wall in June 2014, with the installation of the 55-foot (17 metres) high gates. Nonetheless, the dam construction has been stopped at 400 feet (121.92 metres) since 2006. In the rest of the dams on the Narmada, like Omkareshwar, Maheshwar and Narmada Sagar, the cases are continuing and the rehabilitation measures are far from satisfactory. 'Land for land rehabilitation' is not implemented, and what the MP government has offered is 'cash-based rehabilitation', which is not only inadequate but also does not fulfil the purpose of rehabilitation, that is, to ensure alternative livelihood. In 2008, the Jabalpur High Court appointed the Justice Jha Commission to look into matters regarding cash-based compensation and corruption involved in this business. Based on the report of this Commission, the Jabalpur High Court, following the Supreme Court Judgement of 2009, issued an order on 6 January 2015, directing a stop (stay) to the cash-based rehabilitation immediately.

The Narmada river struggle forms the most important case of how states can misappropriate their political power throughout a long period for such a short-sighted project in the name of 'development'. From the outset of the project, it has been clear that the governments remained insensitive to the poor and the underprivileged communities and disregarded them as a class not qualified for a secure life like other citizens. It seemed that both the governments and the court tried to step back from their responsibilities towards the people, the former from ensuring the fundamental rights of people in a democratic society and the latter from granting justice to those who became the victims of 'development'. The project was implemented through several faulty promises, such as assurances of rehabilitation programmes, when in fact there was no proper plan or availability of land and other facilities of life.

The development plan itself rested on false and unfounded assumptions. First of all, the projects were conceived of without the consent of the affected people.

Construction work on the dam started without the basic studies on it being completed. The criteria put forward for deciding who was to be considered project-affected persons were not justifiable. The Central and State governments betrayed the courts and the people many times by submitting totally false data regarding the rehabilitation of the oustees and compliance with environmental conditions. The approach of the court also seemed unjustifiable, since most of the time its instructions were not helpful for the affected people because the verdicts were not based on evidences and true arguments. The claims of the affected people and the NGOs, especially those of NBA, were neglected. The court seemed to rely on the government alone, acknowledging it as the final authority on matters regarding the number of the displaced, programmes for rehabilitation and other claims of the benefits of the project. Moreover, the court seemed to be interested in the completion of the project rather than the resettlement issues. There are also indications that the power structures in the government influenced the court. The Supreme Court earlier took a sympathetic stance with regard to the affected people by putting a limit on the height of the dam. However, this consideration was taken away on 18 February 1999 by the Chief Justice, and thereafter the height of the dam increased to the maximum and the construction works were continued without objection. Therefore, the complexity of the situation persuaded the poor people of the affected states to come forth fighting for their rights for survival and justice. This situation, in which there was intense opposition to the project, can be viewed as an outcome of a pre-planned political game on the part of the governments. While on the one hand the government totally failed to acknowledge the affected people's natural right to living and the ways in which their lives were enmeshed with nature's cycles, on the other it persuaded the people of various States to sacrifice their lives in the name of 'national interest' for the 'development' cause.

In this case, the most significant political development was the participation of the NGOs, especially NBA. It has done a great job of politically mobilising the affected people and of making them aware of their fundamental rights, such as the right to information, right to life, land and other natural resources and also the right to participate in decision-making processes. They made people conscious of the illegal ties between the governments and other power structures. The people were also politically empowered to question the illegal practices and aggressive and unlawful behaviour towards them. NBA tried to communicate with people by participating in both conventional and non-conventional political processes, and thereby compelled the parties and conventional political forces to take notice of issues that emerged as basic to people's lives (Sangvi, 2002: 158). NBA's approach towards the village people was radically political in the sense that they tried an integrated strategy of making relations with people from village to national and international levels. It was also careful to not fall prey to the political play of the rulers. Despite all the resistance efforts, the dam works completed, which was possible only by denying justice and rights to people by the government, the activities that are extremely undemocratic and unconstitutional.

Victory of the oustees in Narmada

During the 1970s and 1980s, oustees of the dams started asserting their rights and confronted the government on issues of cost–benefit, social and environmental destruction. While Tawa, Bargi, Barna and Sukta dams in MP were completed during the 1970s and 1980s, work has started on Narmada Sagar, Maheswar, Man, Goi and Veda. The oustees started organising and demanding their rights and just resettlement in Tawa, Bargi and other completed dams. In the proposed and ongoing claims, the people's organisations started to question the dam builders about the propriety of the dam and displacement.

The oustees of the various early dam projects started protests to get sanctions for their rights over the natural resources of their local region from 1992. The oustees of the Bargi dam started protests for their rights over water, land, forest employment and other resources in the resettlement area. They conducted *satyagraha* at Bijasen in 1992, and conducted a 55-day *satyagraha* during the monsoon of 1993 against the filling of the reservoir beyond 418 metres. They also conducted a boat rally of hundreds of fishing boats to proclaim the fishing rights of the oustees over the reservoir. The rallies, long marches, confrontations with police and politicians and so on made the MP government declare their exclusive right over reservoir fishing on 11 May 1994. This opened a way out in the life of the resettled people. The organisation of the oustees and people affected by Bargi dam, *Bargi Bandh Visthapitevam Prabhavit Sangha*, organised 54 primary fishing co-operatives of over 2,000 oustees in the three districts, capped by the Oustees' Fishing and Marketing federation. The federation, despite stiff opposition from the fish mafia, ice-mafia, contractors, politicians, State Fisheries Cooperation and bureaucrats, succeeded in increasing food production and rates to the fisher people and repaid a government loan of Rs. 5 lakhs. These successes of the people in Bargi prompted other claim-affected people in the valley to fight for their rights. The Bargi people then protested for their right to cultivate the draw-down land for the winter cropping season. Again, they resorted to *satyagraha* in submergence water at the dam at a level of 418 metres for 36 hours, resisted police repression in the monsoon of 1995 and finally withdrew when the government granted their requirements. Nonetheless, the government broke its promise in 1997 and 1998; each time, the oustees held dharna and indefinite fasts. People wanted the draw-down lands to be opened up immediately, even if the gates of the dam had to be opened. Though the administrators and engineers opposed this, in December 1998, the government opened the gates of the dam and made assurances that the reservoir level would be kept at 418 metres. However, against the MP government's order for a fresh lease to the Bargi oustees for fishing, the bureaucrats and vested interests filed a petition through the MP State Fisheries Corporation in June 2000 and stayed the lease. The *Sangha* had equitably distributed about 8,000 hectares of land by 2001 and got ready for the winter agriculture. Through these experiences, the oustees became aware that full and just rehabilitation was nearly impossible and that they have to struggle a lot to get the government to implement its assurances. The oustees of Tawa dam, who had been fighting for their rights from the early 1980s, also secured their rights over the reservoir by 1996. They organised themselves into co-operative societies and handled the production and marketing of the fisheries. Their success turned out to be a model of management and development of reservoirs by people for themselves.

The oustees' struggle points towards the insincere and irresponsible attitude of the MP government in keeping their promises to displaced people. The oustees were to be rehabilitated without making proper arrangements for their livelihood. This situation forced them to protest for their rights over natural resources. However, due to the pressure of the protest movements the government decided to grant them rights over land and water resources. Here the 'power' structures of the region also tried to defeat the people's movement, yet government support led them to succeed in their struggles.

Indonesia

(i) Movement against Bali projects

In Indonesia, concern over the environment began in connection with the exponential growth of tourism industry in Bali (for details see Warren, 1998: 179–204). In the late 1980s, the regional economic development based on agricultural intensification, small-scale tourism and handicraft export and so on assumed a very different character, when deregulation of the banking system fed a boom in tourism investment. Official figures show a ten-fold increase in foreign and domestic investment in major projects in Bali between 1987 and 1988, from US$ 17 million to 170 million, almost doubling again in 1989–1990. From the early 1990s, luxury tourism developments affected Bali adversely, causing socio-economic and environmental impacts. People started feeling discontented about this kind of development, and their reactions gradually found their way into the public domain with projects like the Garuda Wisnu monument and Bali Nirwana Resort (BNR). While the former included the plan to build an enormous golden statue of Garuda Wisnu, the latter was to be set on the cliff facing the ancient and beautiful temple of Tanah Lot. A major change was the conversion of agricultural land at the staggering rate of more than 1,000 ha per year, primarily for large-scale resort and residential developments, along with infrastructure projects to provide the already insufficient electricity, water and roads to serve them. Immigration from other parts of Indonesia, initially attracted by employment in the booming construction industry, reached levels of 60,000–80,000 in 1992–1993, resulting in serious ethnic and religious tensions. Replacement of small local hotels, displacing land and labour, formed another area of change. Increasing traffic seemed an added burden to the overloaded road system and caused rising levels of air pollution. The waste problem had become 'an epidemic'. Huge new tourist facilities like the high-class hotels (e.g., the Nusa Dua area) were areas that placed further demands on water reserves in other parts of the island already showing signs of crisis. Land expropriation and the displacement of farmers were another issue that reflected political disaffection with a pattern of capital-intensive development on a grand scale that caused social unrest throughout Indonesia. The environmental problems connected with these developments began to be noticed from the 1990s onwards, including unregulated mining of limestone and coral for hotel construction and extension to the airport; the incursion of high-class hotels into the remotest parts of the island against the provisions of the 1971 master plan for tourism; the erosion of beaches; increasing levels of plastic, sewage and air pollution; salination of underground aquifers; and the diversion of water from farms to hotels, golf courses and so on.

In the period between 1990 and 1994, the press played a critical role in promoting consciousness of environmental issues and in defining the relationship between these issues and broader questions of politics and culture. The regional press played a pivotal role in mobilising resistance to the Garuda Wisnu monument and BNR projects. The regional newspaper *Bali Post* tried to expose the environmental degradation that these projects introduced. It made front-page announcements of both projects, which created public controversies, and followed these with several by-line articles, editorials and letters to the editor. Several innovations in the media presentation of these issues were deployed to arouse and maintain public interest. The paper organised seminars through which the opinions and positions of the government officials and public figures could be made regarding the projects, supported by arguments and information. Another novel feature, which functioned to mobilise public opinion and maintain momentum, was the special comment column 'Your Turn' in the *Bali Post*. The column invited responses on topical themes of serious import and gave space to about 100 contributors to express their opinions. Along with playing a key role in bringing these projects under public scrutiny, the paper self-consciously set out the terms of discourse. From the outset, the connection between environmental and cultural integrity framed the debate. This is the link that captured the public imagination and contributed to a significant shift in attitude among the Balinese towards large-scale tourism development, which was entering a new phase in the 1990s.

The proponents of the projects put forward plans to solve the environmental and other issues with technology. They claimed that the project would rehabilitate the barren and eroded land of the Bukit site, making it productive by conversion to an alternative use. Local people who had only been able to scrape a meagre existence from dry farming would now be able to find employment in the more lucrative tourist sector.[19] In the case of local water supply, the landscape manager points to plans for establishing a three-stage wastewater treatment facility, the first of its kind in Indonesia, for garden and golf course maintenance. When environmental exploitation became tied to the appropriation of important cultural symbols, it generated various public opinions, and hence opposition to the Tanah Lot development was more intensive than that of the Garuda Monument. Though in the latter, appropriation of religious symbols for outside interests formed the cause of opposition, in the former, there was an additional factor at play: the development was to be physically located at one of the most important sacred sites in Bali. Thus, a more organised response to the BNR development, co-ordinated by a coalition of student groups and scholars, culminated in the first major political demonstration on the island. The power of religious symbols in the debate was such that questions of environmental protection were ultimately subordinated to those of cultural preservation, very intimately bound up with social and economic tension between centre and periphery. There were many indications of cultural or religious anxieties among those who participated in the opposition struggles. For example, most of the groups that joined the struggle bore religious or cultural names like Society for Balinese Studies, Forum of Hindu Students, Balinese Youth and Student Alliance and others, including Hindu, Muslim and Catholic student groups from outside Bali. The metaphor of erosion was overtaken by images of invasion and the question of environmental discourse became one of cultural appropriation and physical dispossession. This anxiety, that Balinese were losing control over both environmental and cultural resources, came through very strongly in *Bali Post* reporting as well as in readers' comments in letters to the editor and the 'Your Turn' column. Powerful front-page colour images of earthmoving equipment traversing the flattened landscape, maps indicating the layout of the BNR complex and the adjacent location of nine other projects to follow suit in the Tanah Lot tourism zone and the BNR's own sketch of golfers playing at hole 3 in view of Tanah Lot Temple reinforced the conflated sense of physical dispossession and cultural displacement. Press publicity for the activist campaign of protest demonstrations and marches to the regional parliament (DPRD) and Governor's office, sit-ins, poetry readings and prayer meetings at Tanah Lot Temple eventually had an impact. Through strongly worded headlines, newspapers induced groups like the *Parisada Hindu Dharma*, the Hindu religious organisation of Indonesia, and the regional parliament, to take a public position. The *Parisada* issued a religious pronouncement (*Bhisama*) interpreting traditional religious texts on the sacred space at temple sites, which effectively prohibited any development that might pollute the 'zone of sanctity' within a 2-kilometre radius around Tanah Lot Temple. Hereafter, the controversy seemed to concentrate entirely on this question. As religious faith and tolerance are key principles in the ideological constellation that underpins the Indonesian nation–state, such a declaration could not be ignored. The President also issued a statement through the State Secretariat, indicating that the *Parisada* decree should be the basis for resolution of the conflict. The regional parliament suspended the project until the environmental impact assessment report, (AMDAL) could be reviewed by the regional AMDAL Commission, which was explicitly given the directive to take account of the *Parisada* decree.

At this point, two political interventions constrained the opponents of the project. First was the replacement of the early military commander who had permitted the demonstrations to continue thus far with another, who tried to crack down the demonstration; this resulted in attacking students and hospitalising them, after which large public demonstrations as a form of resistance ended in short period. The second event was the closure of three national weeklies – *Tempo*, *Editor* and *DeTIK*. The critical coverage of the issue was earlier stopped in *Bali Post*. On 9 August, it was announced that the Garuda Wisnu Kencana (GWK) monument proposal had been approved. And on 12 September, after an eight-month suspension, the AMDAL Commission presented its report, announcing that the Tanah Lot project would also proceed. However, the Environmental Impact Assessment Commission allowed the projects with certain concessions. It required that the 'essence' of the *Bhisama* ruling must be observed and that the project be redesigned, eliminating condominiums, relocating all dwellings away from the temple and planting a green strip to screen the project from view. But after the banning, the press was not open to the issue as earlier and the gaps in newspaper coverage and their silence made the public to a reverse reading of the issue, that is, as a manipulative strategy of the authority. However, at the end of 1994, opposition to the project was very strong, and the depth of antagonism to the BNR project in particular and to the government in general deepened. Students and academics who organised the protests were committed to upholding the letter of the religious ruling. A group of farmers who had sold the land to the project joined them, but due to different reasons later disagreed with the arrangements. This was a better development in this case, since up to that point the weak link in the opposition movement had been the fact that proponents could claim that the majority of landholders had sold out willingly for reasonable compensation. The landholders had been given little information about the project and were under considerable pressure to sell from regional government officials in order to satisfy the latter's profit motive. By the end of 1994, the religious factor and the experiences of the former landholders finally led to outright opposition of the project. On 20 October, a petition signed by 96 villagers affected by the BNR development was presented to the head of the regional parliament. This asserted that the land had been resumed through threats and deception. They demanded the return of the project site so that they could manage it with care and thus be free from blame for the wrong and improper use of ancestral lands. The concern about ancestral displeasure was a major factor in the farmers' changed position. The destruction of a small shrine belonging to one of the former landholders, despite guarantees of protection of these sites by the Bakrie group, exacerbated the discontent and turned the landholders to political action, which again intensified at the developers' offer of financial compensation for the desecrated shrine. The later resistance made by the combined alliance of students and farmers succeeded in (1) halting the project for eight months at considerable cost to the Bakrie group, (2) forcing some redesign of the project to distance the dwelling from the temple and (3) signalling a significantly changed attitude among the general public to the new direction of development.

This case is an example of social protest by the people against the destructive impact of development in a political context. The government, which is supposed to protect the natural and cultural wealth of a region, seemed to be politically insensitive to the social life of the region, including its environmental and human resources. In such circumstances, it was the intervention of the press that took the responsibility of exposing the intricacies of these two development projects and making the people aware of the extent of the destruction this kind of development might bring in terms of environmental degradation and survival issues. The activists and editors of the newspapers and others who took the lead in mobilising the people to protest against the governments' development policies, strategically made use of the cultural symbols of Wisnu and Bali, the Hindu deities of the local people. They made people conscious of their right to protect their cultural values, which formed the pillars of their life. It seemed that the cultural dimension rather than the environmental factors made them politically active, even though the loss of the latter would affect them seriously. In other words, the people were mobilised for the protection of their rights to livelihood and a hygienic atmosphere by placing these needs within the cultural context. The involvement of the student groups also provided support for their resistance struggles. Though there is no intimation of outright withdrawal from the project by the government, they were politically put under pressure to re-examine some of the decisions that led to intense resistance from the people.

Africa

The emergence of environmental movements in Africa has a history that can be traced and connected to the context of growing social struggles for power, space and resources (for details see Obi, 2005: 1–18). Environmental movements in Africa are embedded in the continent's history and the daily struggles of its people to make a living from their lands and waters. The African people had a rich knowledge of their environment before the colonial invasion. Natural resources like land, water and forests were held in sacred trust and symbolically insured against abuse, in many African cultures. It was the forceful integration of the African environment into the world market through the instrumentality of the colonial State that laid it open to predatory extraction, disease, pollution and degradation by external hegemonic forces. However, African nationalist movements had strong environmental components, especially in rural, anti-colonial movements and rebellions.[20] African environmental history has provided evidence of the dialectic of state intervention (in the environment) versus local resistance (to the appropriation of natural resources). It has also underscored the role of environmental considerations in the logic of anti-colonial movements and its social constituents. However, with independence, the 'social' dimension was de-linked from the 'political' realm, which implied the subordination of popular as well as environmental movements. That is, after independence, political parties flourished whereas social movements wilted.[21] Anti-colonial, anti-nationalist movements were a coalition of social movements – peasants, workers, students, the elite and political parties. After independence this coalition disintegrated, with the ruling elite abandoning popular and rival forces.

By the late 1960s, as the contradictions within the post-colonial ruling elite in Africa deepened, the party in power crushed the opposition and suppressed social movements, leading to one-party rule that resulted in military rule. Within this context of authoritarianism, social movements were suppressed. By the 1980s, only the single-party and military regimes were challenged by democratic forces in the internal contradictions and crises of legitimacy within the former. Social movements re-emerged to organise struggle for the liberation of the country from the elite group.

Apart from internal contradictions arising from long years of dictatorship, corruption and misrule, the refraction of the global recession into the dependent monocultural African economies led to severe crises with far-reaching and adverse social and political consequences. As a result, rural areas were more affected by the deregulation of the economy, the further commodification of Africa's natural resources – like forests, water and minerals – and intense exploitation by multinationals, the logging industry and state monopolies, in order to extract more profit, surplus or revenues. Likewise, the poor people living off the land (in cases where they were not dispossessed) exerted more pressure on the environment to survive in the face of the rising costs of essentials and social services. It was in this context of the sharpening of social contradictions, partly as a result of the conditionalities and impacts of structural adjustment, that the legitimacy of the State was increasingly eroded and subjected to growing challenges by popular forces. In this dire struggle of survival, the ongoing exploitation of environmental resources was overlooked, leading to further degradation of the environment in the process. This also suggested the intensification of struggles over shrinking or relatively scarce resources. It was in this context that the excluded groups organised themselves into environmental movements. This enabled them to protest their exclusion, stake claims and defend the right to gain access to environmental resources critical to their survival and reproduction.

(i) The movement for the survival of the Ogoni people

The Ogoni are the group of people found on the plains of the Niger Delta, east of Port Harcourt, the capital city of the Rivers State. With a population estimated at approximately 500,000 occupying an area of 404 square miles, the Ogoni are an ethnic minority group in a region of many (and mostly larger) ethnic minority groups. These people had been in the quest for self-determination from the British colonial period and thereafter under the regime of the elite group of the country. In 1908, they protested against inclusion in the Opobo division and by 1947 were granted their own Ogoni Native Authority under the then-Rivers Province. In the late 1950s they were a part of the struggle for a state for minorities, which was only realised seven years after independence in 1967, when the Rivers State (an administrative region in the Nigerian Federation) was created. The circumstances for the movement arose when oil was found in commercial quantities in the Bomu oilfields (in the village of K-Dere) in 1958. This resulted in opening up Ogoni lands to further exploration and exploitation in the oil fields of Bomu, Bodo West, Tai, Korokoro, Yorla, Lubara Creek and Afam;[22] the concessions were owned by Shell (Saro-Wiwa, 1995: 67), the Petroleum Development Company. The intensive exploitation of oil in Ogoni territory further aggravated pressures on the land in one of the most densely populated parts of Nigeria. The small space of Ogoni land was thickly concentrated, with six oil fields, two oil refineries, a huge fertiliser plant, petrochemical plants and an ocean port,[23] leaving the people in poverty, unemployment, pollution and misery. According to estimates by the Movement for the Survival of the Ogoni People (MOSOP), about $30 billion worth of oil was extracted from Ogoni lands within 30 years, while the Ogoni contributed as much as 5% of Nigeria's total oil production in 1973. There were also strong feelings among members of MOSOP that because the Ogoni were ethnic minorities they were being denied their rights to oil by a federal government dominated by the big (three) ethnic groups in Nigeria. It was these feelings of alienation and anger, and the quest to give voice to Ogoni aspirations for self-determination and control of their environment, that gave birth to MOSOP in 1990. The expectations of the Ogoni people to realise their dream of self-realization, with the formation of a regional state of their own and direct access to oil within their territory, were destroyed when, during the war, the federal military government transferred the control of oil revenues to itself through legislation.[24]

The ecological damage of oil production had begun to manifest itself on Ogoni land following an oil blowout on 19 July 1970, which destroyed cassava farms, yams, palms, streams and animals for miles, through which oil flowed like a river, and polluted even rivers, the only source of drinking water. Though many letters were sent to Shell, British Petroleum (BP) and the State government by various groups about Ogoni land, little was done to ameliorate the impact of the ecological disaster that struck during the harvest period. Compensation for crops destroyed was not adequate and the clean-up of the spilled oil was not comprehensively addressed.[25] The Ogoni were thus further marginalised, both in relation to the highly centralised Nigerian federation after the war and with regard to the control of their land, which became exposed to oil exploitation, pollution and environmental degradation. Apart from losing out in terms of the allocation of oil revenues to the States of the federation, the Ogoni were adversely affected by the Land Use Decree of 1978. The Land Use Decree (later Act) vested all land in each State of the federation solely in the governor of the state (who, during military rule, was appointed by the federal government). According to the Constitutional Rights Project (CRP) report, the decree (section 28.2) provided that the right of occupancy could be revoked in the public interest, including 'the requirement of land for mining purposes or oil pipe lines or for any purpose connected therewith';[26] this brought to a head the alienation of the Ogoni people from their land. In an area of fragile ecosystems, mangrove swamps and relatively scarce land, the power to grant oil concessions rested with the federal government and officials far away in the federal capital. Concessions were given without consulting the local inhabitants whose lives were tied to the land. Thus, they were forced to give up their farmlands, fishing grounds and ancestral shrines to create a right of way for the pipelines of the oil industry, which offered no real employment to the locals, who had few or no skills to sell to the capital-intensive and powerful oil multinationals (Obi, 2005: 8).

The situation was further aggravated by the fact that those directly dispossessed ended up with little or no compensation. With Nigeria under military rule at the time of the Land Use Decree and the collapse of the democratic experiment of the Second Republic (1979–1983) after barely four years, the complaints of the Ogoni were never heard or addressed. Thus, they suffered the consequences of their political powerlessness and the domination of their lands by the partnership of the federal government and Shell, which excluded them from direct access to oil revenues, while bearing the full environmental impact of oil production. In this situation, with the purpose of renegotiating power relations in the oil-rich Niger Delta, the people of Ogoni formed MOSOP. It was an umbrella body of Ogoni affiliate organisations like the Federation of Women's Associations (FOWA), the National Youth Council of Ogoni People (NYCOP), the Council of Ogoni Churches (COC), the Council of Ogoni Professionals (COP), the Council of Ogoni Traditional Rulers Association (COTRA), the National Union of Ogoni Students (NUOS), the Ogoni Students' Union (OSU), the Ogoni Teachers Union (OTU) and the Ogoni Central Union (OCU).[27] It sought to contest and block further exploitation, pollution and marginalisation of oil-rich Ogoni lands and the Ogoni people by the State–oil business alliance and to assert Ogoni rights to claim and control their own resources. MOSOP adopted a high-risk confrontational strategy against Nigeria's military federal government and deliberately targeted Shell.[28] MOSOP also tapped into global discourse on the environment, indigenous peoples and human rights to empower its local claims and protests and put international pressure on Shell and the Nigerian State to respect the rights of the Ogoni to control their environmental space and land. MOSOP's 'high-risk' strategy was predicated upon the mobilisation of social power to block the extraction of oil from under its land until its complaints were addressed. This was because of the strategic importance of oil as the provider of over 80% of Nigeria's national revenue and over 90% of export earnings. By catching the attention of the government through their blocking power, MOSOP issued a list of demands through the Ogoni Bill of Rights (OBR) on 2 October 1990, which included among other things political autonomy, including political control of Ogoni affairs by the Ogoni people, the right to control Ogoni resources for Ogoni development and the right to protect the Ogoni environment and ecology from further degradation. The OBR was debated at all levels of Ogoni society in the local dialects and was adopted and signed after massive grass roots mobilisation by traditional Ogoni rulers and leaders. Since they did not get any reply to the OBR, an addendum to the OBR was sent by MOSOP to the federal government of Nigeria on 26 August 1991, after another round of broad social mobilisation, consultation and adoption (Obi, 2001: 124–5, 2005: 9). The addendum went beyond OBR to include criticism of the 1979 and 1989 Nigerian Constitutions for legitimising the expropriation of Ogoni rights and resources because they were a minority group. The addendum also sought restitution for the harm done to the health of the Ogoni people as a result of the flaring of gas, oil spillages, oil blowouts and related problems caused by Shell, Chevron and their Nigerian accomplices. Again, MOSOP received no real response from the Nigerian State or the oil companies, which continued with business as usual. It was at this point that MOSOP internationalised its local struggle.

In 1992, MOSOP contacted the Unrepresented Nations and Peoples Organization (UNPO), based in the Netherlands, and began networking with NGOs from other parts of the world. It presented the Ogoni case before a global assembly, the United Nations Working Group on Indigenous Populations, bringing forth a picture of the Ogoni as an indigenous people suffering discrimination, expropriation and imminent genocide as a result of the wanton destruction of the environmental basis of their existence by the oil industry and the repressive Nigerian military government (Obi, 2005: 8). It made use of news media, public lectures, publications, documentaries, the internet, personal contacts, letters and the lobbying of pressure groups, politicians, parliaments and foreign governments. On 4 January 1993, MOSOP successfully organised a peaceful rally against the State–oil alliance in which over 300,000 Ogoni people participated as part of the celebration of the UN's International Year of the World's Indigenous People. The success of the rally underscored the strength of MOSOP as an environmental movement contesting the power of the State–oil alliance over its oil-rich land. In the months that followed, conflict ensued between MOSOP as a local force of resistance and the State–oil alliance, which wanted to continue the process of oil-based capitalist accumulation. On 30 April 1993, Ogoni villagers, protesting damage done to their farms by an American oil service company working on behalf of Shell, were fired upon by soldiers. Many were wounded and one was killed. In June 1993, Saro-Wiwa, the spokesperson for MOSOP, was arrested and detained by security forces. At the same time, the leadership of MOSOP was immersed in a struggle between moderate and radical elements. Ogoni territory was militarised by the State, leading to repression, intimidation and a climate of fear. The tactics of the security forces included beating, detention of activists and MOSOP supporters, shootings, burning of houses, rape and even murder. Misunderstandings between the Ogoni and their neighbours were exploited and manipulated to punish the Ogoni. Similarly, cracks within the leadership of MOSOP were exploited by the State–oil alliance to divide and weaken the environmental movement of resistance. Saro-Wiwa and nine other MOSOP leaders were arrested and charged for a murder case and were later hanged. Following this, waves of repression were unleashed against the Ogoni, while numerous activists were detained, forced underground or escaped into exile. Ogoni refugees were found in neighbouring countries and dispersed across Europe and North America, thereby seriously weakening the environmental movement of the Ogoni, then into retreat. After the return of Nigeria to democratic rule in 1999, MOSOP has been trying to overcome divisions and rebuild itself. Shell withdrew from Ogoni land in 1993 as a result of popular pressure and there were signs of changes for Ogoni. A development Commission has been established for the Niger Delta, while federal revenue allocations to oil-producing States have been raised from 5% to 13% on the basis of the principle of derivation.[29] A Federal Ministry of Environment has been established, while the Department of Petroleum Resources, the monitoring arm of the Ministry of Petroleum Resources, has been granted autonomy. However, the power relations between the State–oil alliance and the Ogoni, which are skewed against the latter, remain unchanged.

The experiences of the Ogoni people reveal that the existence and even life of these people were problematic, and not just their political identity. Though their requirement for a regional state was fulfilled in 1967, they were not self-sufficient in other political needs like the control (power) over their environment (oil-rich), right for access to oil within their territory and a pollution-free environment. In addition to these needs, basic issues like the dispossession of the Ogoni people of their living lands, farmlands, fishing grounds and ancestral shrines, consequent to the large-scale oil extraction by the multinational company without any compensation, created the context for a mass political movement. The absence of a democratic political setup and the unjustifiable political tie between the military government and the oil company worsened the situation. The federal military government was not found to be responsible to the people of the State, as one would expect from a democratic government. The interim period of four years of democratic rule during 1979–1983 was so short a time period, within which the Ogoni hardly could move people to achieve any of their demands. The realisation that they were weak in terms of power and strength inspired them to unite and mobilise themselves to protest for their rights and, thus, to confront the military government with the joint effort of all other groups who face similar difficulties. The decision of the Ogoni people to contact other local and international organisations in other countries was the result of the awareness that similar political contexts exists all around the world. Thus, such a movement with strong support worldwide could only make the company withdraw from their land in 1993 and take steps to give consideration to the Ogoni people and their environment at the administrative level by 1999 and thereafter by bringing back democratic rule.

4.2.2 People versus State and industries

(i) Movements against wood-based industry

Forests were being depleted all over India even after independence, as trees were needed in large amounts to meet industrial demand (Guha and Martinez-Alier, 1997: 6–7). Generally, paper, rayon and plywood companies, apart from the subsidies they were granted from the government, tried to acquire firm control over the forests. Though Indian law prohibited large-scale ownership of land by private companies, the joint sector companies (units jointly owned by the State and private capital) provided the most feasible option. In the wake of the Chipko movement, there arose a wide-ranging debate on forest policy, with scholars and activists arguing that State forest policies had consistently discriminated against the rights of peasants, tribals and pastoralists, while unduly favouring the urban–industrial sector.[30] Another factor was the promotion of eucalyptus plantations in State-owned lands by the Forest Department from the early 1960s. As part of this, in many parts of India, rich, diverse natural forests were felled to make way for single-species plantations; the inspiration for this choice was clearly dictated by industry, for eucalyptus is a rapidly growing species sought after by both paper and rayon mills since regeneration is much easier to achieve and is not a grazing option for cattle and goats.

The establishment of Harihar Polyfibres, a rayon-producing unit located in the north of Karnataka by Birla and the happenings that occurred consequent to it are an example of how a political struggle emerged for a localised cause (for details see Guha and Martinez-Alier, 1997: 6–11; Sheth, 1997: 233–7). The company started its production unit in 1972 on the bank of the river Tungabhadra in Dharwad district, Karnataka. From its inception it polluted the river, the water of which was used by about one lakh people in that village, including fishermen, shepherds, farmers and labourers (Sheth, 1997: 233). Cases of disease were also reported due to the polluted water. On 14 November 1984, the Karnataka government entered into an agreement with Harihar Polyfibres to form a joint sector company called Karnataka Pulpwood Ltd. (KPL), in which the government had a holding of 51% and the latter had 49%. KPL was charged with growing eucalyptus and other fast-growing trees for use by Harihar Polyfibres. For this purpose, the State identified 30,000 hectares of common land spread over four districts in the northern part of Karnataka. This land was nominally owned by the State, but the grass, trees and shrubs standing on it were extensively used in surrounding villages for fuel, fodder and other materials. The land was granted by the State to KPL on a long lease of 40 years at Re.1 per acre per year. This consent was against the laws of the land, particularly the Forest Conservation Act. As much as 87.5% of the produce was to go directly to Harihar Polyfibres, and the private sector company also had the option of buying the remaining 12.5%. The government of Karnataka was even willing to stand guarantee for the loans that were to finance KPL's operations: loans to be obtained from several nationalised banks, one of which was the National Bank of Agriculture and Rural Development.

Within months of its establishment, the new company became the object of severe criticism, especially in the context of the wider, all-India debate. In December 1984, the State's pre-eminent writer Dr Shivram Karanth wrote an essay in the popular *Kannada Daily*, calling on the people of Karnataka to totally oppose the joint sector company KPL. The opposition grew after 15 July 1986, the date on which the State transferred the first instalment of land (3,950 hectares) to KPL. When the company was preparing the ground for planting eucalyptus, many petitions, representations and letters from individuals and organisations protesting the formation of KPL were sent to the Chief Minister. Meanwhile, protest meetings were organised at several villages in the region. The matter was also raised in the State legislature. At the forefront of the movement against KPL was the *Samaj Parivartan Samudaya* (SPS; Association for Social Change), a voluntary organisation working in the Dharwad district of Karnataka. On 2 October 1984, SPS held a large demonstration outside the production unit of Harihar Polyfibres. In December 1985, it filed public interest litigation in the High Court of Karnataka against the State Pollution Control Board for its failure to check the pollution of the Tungabhadra by the Birla factory. Before that petition could come up for hearing, SPS filed a public interest writ against KPL in the Supreme Court of India in New Delhi. SPS was motivated to do so by a similar writ in the state High Court, filed by a youth organisation working among the farmers in the Sagar taluk of the adjoining Shimoga district. In this petition, submitted in early 1987, the petitioners spoke on behalf of the 500,000 villagers living in the region of KPL's operations, the people most directly affected by the action of the State in handing over common land to one company. The petition described the difficulties of the villagers and exposed its violation of two provisions of the Indian Constitution, the right to fair procedure guaranteed by Article 14 and the right to life and liberty of the village community vested under Article 21 of the Constitution. Finally, the petitioners contended that the planting of monocultures of eucalyptus, as envisaged by KPL, would have a 'disastrous effect on the ecological balance of the region'. The petition argued that claims of time and tradition were counterposed to the legal status quo, through which the State both claimed and enforced rights of ownership. Thus, the petition was perfectly in line with popular protests in defence of forest rights. On 14 March 1987, the Supreme Court responded to the petition by issuing a stay order, thus preventing the government of Karnataka from transferring any more land to KPL. Encouraged by this preliminary victory, SPS turned to popular mobilisation in the villages. In May, it held a training camp in non-violence at Kusnur, a village in Dharwad district, where 400 hectares of land had already been transferred to KPL. A parallel organisation of villagers, the *Guddanadu Abhivruddi Samiti* (Hill Areas Development Committee), was created to work alongside SPS. The two groups held a series of preparatory meetings in Kusnur and other villages nearby for a protest scheduled for 14 November 1987, to coincide with the third anniversary of the formation of KPL. On 14 November, about 2,000 people converged at Kusnur, who resorted to a novel protest, termed the *Kithiko-Hachiko* (Pluck-and-Plant *satyagraha*). They moved to the disputed area and first uprooted 100 saplings of eucalyptus before planting in their place tree species useful locally for fruit and fodder.

The next major development in the KPL case was the partial vacation, on 26 April 1988, by the Supreme Court of the stay it had granted a year earlier, allowing the transfer of a further 3,000 hectares to KPL. Such interim and ad hoc grants of land were also allowed in 1989 and 1990. As a reaction to the court action, SPS prepared once more for direct action. They commenced training camps in the villages, planned to culminate in a fresh Pluck-and-Plant *satyagraha*. Meanwhile journalists sympathetic to their movement intensified the press campaign against KPL. In the context of mounting adverse publicity and the prospect of renewed popular protest, the government of Karnataka tried to set up a committee and commission to enquire into the issue and submit a report, until which time the KPL had to suspend its operations, a decision made in a meeting attended by representatives of SPS, KPL and the Forest Department. But this government action was seen as merely a tactic to defuse and contain popular protest. The commission was never set up and SPS started organising another Pluck-and-Plant *satyagraha* in August 1988. This time, the protesters were arrested and removed before they could reach KPL's eucalyptus plot. In later years, non-violent direct action continued to be a vital plank of SPS's strategy. In an attempt to link issues of industrial pollution and alienation of common land more closely, in August 1989 it organised in the towns of Hangal and Ranibennur public bonfires of rayon cloth made by Harihar Polyfibres. The following year, SPS reverted to the Pluck-and-Plant *satyagraha* again.

While these protests kept the issue alive at the grass roots level, SPS continued to make use of the wider political and legal system to its advantage. It obtained copies of four orders issued by the Chief Conservator of Forests, transferring a further 14,000 hectares of forest land to KPL, an area far in excess of what the Supreme Court had allowed. On the basis of these 'leaked' documents, SPS filed a further Contempt and Perjury petition in October 1988. Meanwhile, SPS persuaded public-sector banks to delay the release of funds to KPL pending the final hearing and settlement of the case in the Supreme Court. It also effectively lobbied the government of India in New Delhi to clarify its own position on KPL-style schemes. In February 1988, an official of the Union Ministry of Environment and Forests, making a deposition in the Supreme Court, stated that the raising of industrial plantations by joint sector companies required the prior permission of the government of India. The following year, a new National Forest Policy was announced that explicitly prohibited monoculture plantations on grounds of ecological stability. Within Karnataka, resolutions asking the government to cancel the KPL agreement were passed by local representative bodies, including several Mandal Panchayats, local councils and others of Dharwad. This was followed by a letter to the Chief Minister, signed by 54 members of the State legislature and sent on 11 July 1990, asking him to close down KPL so as to reserve village common land for the common use of villagers. With public opinion and the Central government arrayed against it, the government of Karnataka decided to wind up KPL. The final order of the Supreme Court in this case was issued on 26 March 1992, based on the government of Karnataka's order of 24 October 1991 confirming the winding up of KPL and a detailed affidavit of 12 March 1992 recognising the people's rights over the common lands.

This case is an example of the misappropriation of political power by a State government for exploiting natural resources with socio-political and environmental consequences. The controversy here is that the government, which is supposed to ensure the protection of the rights of the people in the State, itself created the circumstances that forced the common people to fight for their rights, both to live in a healthy environment and to use minor forest produce that forms their livelihood. It seems that the politically inactive position of the Karnataka government forced the people to protest in both contexts. In the first case, it allowed the company to continue functioning in the State, despite the pollution problems it created in its surroundings. The second situation of conflict is the result of the illegal plot made between the State and the company. The people in authority in the government misused their official power to satisfy their own private interests. The participation of the NGOs, especially SPS, was the main factor that led this struggle to success. Their continued protests in varied forms and use of different strategies actually helped the struggle to sustain its spirit throughout the years, highlighting its political significance. The intervention of the Supreme Court marked a turning point in this issue, which helped to disclose the conspiracy between the State government and the company and to resolve the issue, thereby ending the protest of the people for justice. The members of the Legislative Assembly also acted politically by raising questions regarding the issue and succeeded in making the concerned parties reveal their roles in this deceit. Media also played an important role by publicising the issue and thereby making people aware about it. Though this struggle is a localised one, examples of similar political contexts are common in many places in India, which required the people to come forward politically to fight for their rights.

(ii) Movement against Union Carbide Corporation

The Bhopal gas tragedy has become known the world over for the severe environmental disaster it caused and the role played by a multinational corporation in this case (for details see Sheth, 1997: 224–6; Raina et al., 1999: 140–7). The Union Carbide Corporation (UCC), a US-based multinational corporation, started working in Bhopal in 1969 with a small unit for pesticide formulations. Within a few years, it decided to expand and go in for the manufacture of a range of methyl isocyanate (MIC) based pesticides from a carbaryl base, under the trade-name Sevin; the new plant was set up in 1978. The company claimed that the new formulations would be safer, more effective and would handle a much larger spectrum of crops and pests. On 3 December 1984, an accident occurred, caused by the introduction of water into the toxic MIC storage tank. This resulted in a powerful and uncontrollable reaction generated by the liberation of heat, and as a result the deadly MIC escaped in the form of gas. The tank's vent gas scrubber and flame tower did not have the capacity to either neutralise or incinerate the immense volume of gases released. A large mass of poor people living around the Union Carbide plant were most affected by the accident. As the gas began to escape, about 3,000 people died on the spot within minutes, while another 50,000 sustained chronic lung damage, and many developed vision defects. Initial effects of gas exposure were inflammation of the lungs, acute dehydration coupled with oedema and severe corneal burns. However, the Union Carbide authorities only accepted at a later stage that the leak had occurred, and they also claimed that the leak had been plugged quickly when it really did not come into effect.

Union Carbide's MIC plant had a poor safety record from its inception. Six accidents had already been recorded, which the workers in the industry alleged was an under count (Ramaseshan, 1984: 2109–10). The first accident occurred, according to the government's records, on 24 November 1978, when naphtha stocks caught fire from sparks from a welding rod. The second occurred on 26 December 1981, resulting in the death of a maintenance department worker, who during his work inhaled phosgene. Another major accident was on 10 February 1982, when a mechanical seal on the phosgene pump failed, resulting in the leakage of phosgene. Twenty-five workers inhaled the chemical and all had to be hospitalised, though there were no deaths on this occasion. A fourth major accident occurred on 5 October 1982, when MIC was released and the workers ran for shelter. They complained of breathlessness and irritation in the eyes, the same symptoms as in the 1984 accident. On each occasion an inquiry was conducted by the government, which often ended up giving instructions to prevent such hazards. No evaluation was done about follow-up actions or whether any safety procedures had been adopted at all. In its efforts to increase productivity and profit, the authorities of the Bhopal plant avoided maintenance practices (Raina et al., 1999: 142–3). Norms were frequently violated, equipment rarely checked and raw materials not tested. The economising had been carried to such an extent that the plant's refrigeration unit was switched off during the overhaul. The government paid no heed to the warnings of the investigations regarding the possible danger that could occur. Union Carbide provided certain privileges to ministers and bureaucrats, and they never took the company to task for safety violations. When the issue of threat to Bhopal city was raised in the Legislative Assembly, the State's Labour Minister was dismissive. The government made no attempt to indict any UCC or Union Carbide India Limited (UCIL) official nor did it take any steps to investigate Union Carbide operations in India. The conspiracy to save the guilty was already visible when, a fortnight after the leak of 1984, the company reportedly funded a TB clinic in a gas-affected colony, which was inaugurated with much publicity by the then-chief minister, in order to dilute the case against Union Carbide for punitive damages. In addition, UCIL always received preferential treatment from government agencies. Financial institutions vied with each other to sanction loans to the company, which were often underwritten with extremely favourable terms. It also enjoyed several unlawful tax benefits and gained substantially from short-term withdrawal of industrial embargoes on licenses.

The issue was taken up by human right activists, environmentalists and humanitarian groups, who spontaneously rose against the callousness of the multinational companies (MNCs) that tried to play down the extent of the tragedy (Sheth, 1997: 224–5). The companies' negligence was exposed by the NGOs. Supported by national and international media, the NGOs expressed their anger against the administration and the medical authorities,[31] which were suspected to have underestimated the magnitude of the disaster. Regional, national and international NGOs, jurists and environmental/human right activists networked in a concerted way and brought pressure to bear upon the initially hesitant State and Union governments. Documents, videos and other evidence showed the blatant underplaying of the reality and the ghastly sufferings of mostly poor people and workers. As the news about the disaster spread all over the world, a lawsuit of $15 million was filed against the company by two Indian families in the United States on behalf of the victims; they retained a human rights champion as their lawyer (Raina et al., 1999: 144). This opened the gates for compensation claims; following this, lawsuits claiming damages worth $45 billion were filed in US courts, threatening to wipe out Union Carbide's entire global business. In March 1985, the Bhopal Gas Leak (Compensation Claim) Act was passed by Parliament, which made the government of India the sole representative of the victims seeking punitive damages from Carbide. The government took up some 6,000,000 claims in US federal courts. The judge ordered interim relief of $5–10 million to the victims at the first pre-trial hearing of the consolidated Bhopal litigation. Carbide only reluctantly agreed to pay the sum as it started playing tricks to delay the case. The case dragged on as the government of India and Union Carbide haggled over the compensation amount. Union Carbide lawyers shifted the case to the Indian courts, since they expected that they would have to pay far less compensation than if the case were fought in New York. The litigation went on until February 1989 when the Congress (I) government led by Rajeev Gandhi suddenly agreed to an out-of-court settlement of $470 million, a paltry sum that could not cover the long-term healthcare needs and restitution of the victims. The settlement was upheld by Supreme Court, which absolved UCC of all civil and criminal liability in the disaster.

The grossly unfair settlement raised a public outcry and the National Front government challenged the verdict in the Supreme Court in 1990 (Raina et al., 1999: 145). Anticipating a judicial review, the MP government had, just before the 1989 elections, conducted a fresh medical survey of gas survivors. The survey listed only 19 persons as permanently and totally disabled; 155,000 people, whose records were examined, were found to have suffered no injury at all. The medical fraternity and human rights groups were outraged, and their sustained opposition forced government to modify the survey's findings. But the apex court, in its final verdict on the Bhopal case passed in October 1991, cited these very findings in rejecting the appeal against the paltry settlement. However, it ordered reinstatement of criminal proceedings, first moved in 1985, against UCC and UCIL to sell its Bhopal plant lock, stock and barrel and move out of the city, as if it had never been. Carbide has since wound up all its operations in India. The case against the company was diluted even more when in September 1996 the Supreme Court, partially reversing its 1991 order, quashed charges of culpable homicide against UCIL officials and directed that fresh charges be framed for causing death due to negligence.

The Bhopal disaster is an incident that generated worldwide reactions against its human rights violations. This is a clear example that reveals the extent to which a government can be insensible to and negligent of its peoples' affairs through misuse of political power. In this case, many contexts exposed the conspiracy between the government and the company for personal benefit or 'to conserve foreign exchange' (Ramaseshan, 1984: 2109). It is evident from the study reports that the government has never tried to prevent the industry from getting established in a thickly populated area like 'slum' or to enforce it to function as per the norms or to adopt the protective measures properly, though it was functioning illegally challenging the norms. The industry had been using raw materials such as monomethylamine (m-MA) and phosgene and the ingredients in the various stages of production of MIC, such as carbon monoxide and chloroform,[32] which multiplied the severity of the issue. It is clear that the irresponsible attitude of government authorities resulted in the unlikely happenings in the capital of MP. The political insincerity of the government is also reflected in the ways they tackled the earlier accident cases. The government always seemed to protect the Union Carbide authorities, forgetting its duty towards the people. Though the workers in the industry could have knowledge about the risk involved in their job, the mass of people who were living outside were ignorant of it. Here both industry and government were politically flawed in ensuring protection of the people by refusing their right to know about the probable danger to their living place. The government also seemed insensitive to its duty towards the victims and remained passive even after the major accident. The act of obstructing the medical camp held jointly in Bhopal by three voluntary groups in order to provide medical relief to and detoxification measures for the gas victims[33] is an example of the government's political play. The ways in which the government handled the cases regarding compensation claims against UCIL also point towards its liability to the company rather than to its people. It is the complexity of this political context, where the people who are the victims remained helpless, either due to the company or the government, the real culprits, that pushed them to fight for their rights to live and to get medical help or other compensation. These circumstances led to worldwide protests against the human rights violations in this case. It was the intervention of human right activists, environmentalists, media and others that helped to expose the power play between government and industry. The intervention of the court also did not help in achieving satisfactory compensation due to the government's inaction. Hence, the fight for justice continues, since no justifiable solution to date has yet been made by the authorities.

4.2.3 People/State versus industry

(i) Anti-pollution movement in Gujarat

In 1991, the Maradia Industrial Complex started producing chemicals in Sayla taluk, in the Surendranagar district of Gujarat, which is spread over 1,300 acres of land (for details see Sheth, 1997: 238–44). It had not made arrangements for pollution control and as a result, nearby water sources like wells and reservoirs were coloured. Untreated liquid effluents flowed along with rainwater and polluted nearby ponds, causing the death of many cattle. In addition, from 12 am to 4 am the managers would dispose of the gas produced during the production process, the pungent smell of which caused people to suffocate and leaves to burn, even those of huge trees. In the beginning, the authorities ignored the complaints of the villagers. Though the Gujarat Pollution Control Board (GPCB) warned about establishing effluent treatment plants, the owners put forward claims that were wrong. Things took a turn when on 18 June 1996, torrential rain caused the waters of the polluted pond to overflow and reached the Saburi dam, about 6 km away, changing the colour to red and making it undrinkable. The danger of this lay in the fact that if the rain had continued, the water would have flowed to the nearby Nayika and Dholidhaja dams, the water of which was used by about 4 lakh people of both towns and about 35 villages in the vicinity. About 40% of the district's population depends on these two dams for their drinking water. The people gathered and protested, which prompted the District Collector to provisionally order 17 plants of the complex to be closed down, under Article 143 of the Indian Penal Code. Water samples from the Saburi dam and the surrounding wells and dunkies (hand pumps from borewell) were tested in laboratory. Five out of six samples of water were found to be completely undrinkable; even the waters of the dunkies were found to be red, meaning that waters deep underground were also polluted. The water was found to have very high levels of Chemical Oxygen Demand (COD). A case was filed against the Maradia Complex as public interest litigation because the vital interest of many people was involved. In 1995, the Gujarat Ecology Commission (GEC) appointed a committee of two experts to study the problem in the context of the people's growing complaints. Its report clearly brought out that in spite of the GPCB, this industry had flouted environmental laws on a large scale from the first day.

The Central Pollution Control Board found that the Maradia Complex had started production without receiving permission from GPCB; the company only obtained it in 1995. Even then, it cheated the authorities and people by manufacturing naphthalene-based chemicals without permission, which were hazardous to the environment. In 1995, the committee recommended that the industry consider the adoption of modern technology to treat the polluted water, cautioning about possible dangers to the dams; it blamed the GPCB for approving the location for the chemical complex without prior investigation of the environmental impact. The Chairman of the Maradia Group tried to defend his industry by arguing on behalf of the workers and pointing out the loss per day in case of closure. Many political parties demanded action against the industry. However, despite the GPCB's orders to close down four plants manufacturing environmentally hazardous chemicals like H-acid and J-acid and to stop the process of treating some chemicals collectively, the industry continued its production processes. The political hold of the industry chairman was such that he could manipulate the regulatory power structures of the state, like the GPCB, and he even challenged CBI inquiry. At this stage, only the uprising of the people during June–July could make a breakthrough. At this time, leaders of the main political parties and people of all the strata joined together to constitute *Maradia Hatao Ladat Samiti* (the Committee to Fight for Removal of Maradia), with which many leaders of other villages also united. The industry filed an application in the High Court requesting that it be permitted to run its closed units as it had invested crores of rupees and the closure would affect the company's financial condition. It brought workers to pressure the court despite having been directed not to adopt such tactics. Another petition was filed by the farmers of the areas adjoining the chemical units pleading for continuance of the closure orders. The counsel for GPCB brought to the notice of the court that the industry was highly polluting and thus it had recommended the closure of its units to the government under Section 5 of the Environment Protection Act. The government ultimately started taking back the land from Maradia, signalling the end of this anti-people enterprise.

This anti-pollution movement is an example of the victory of the people's protest against a strong chemical industry, this time with the help of the government. It also points out the part played by a government, which is bound to protect the people's rights and nature. This case reveals that the industry was initially able to establish itself for two reasons. Firstly, its unholy nexus with the top political leaders gave it the opportunity to ignore laws related to the working of an industry. Secondly, the politically irresponsible approach of the GPCB cleared the way for the establishment of the industry. The initiation of a movement made by the people for the protection of their right to an unpolluted environment and drinking water created the context for challenging the working of the industry in such a location. Even when people started protests against the firm, the department of pollution control remained inactive and did not take any action against it. However, some officers like the District Collector who were 'politically' motivated intervened and acted responsibly by taking people's complaints seriously, finally ordering the industry to close some of its plants. The utilisation of political power by political parties to demand the closure of the industry provided support for the people's protest. At a later stage, the intervention of the court, the favourable stand taken by the GPCB and the enquiry reports of the committee opened the way for the victory of the people by permanently closing the chemical units down and having the government take the land back.

4.3 'Political' in political process

This section deals with the formation of Green parties and their entry into the political process in response to the experience of new social movement politics. The participation of Green parties in the mainstream political arena in many countries reveals the necessity of getting into power or forming part of the political structure or government in order to address issues of environmental concerns. This kind of situation seems to arise from the traditional (that is, partisan party politics) political system's inability to resolve environmental problems. Party politicians are often perceived as having little interest in solving difficult environmental issues or pursuing principled activities (Doyle and McEachern, 1998: 107).

Green party

Green political parties were formed in many countries in Western Europe, the United States and Australia in the early 1980s in response to the experience of new social movement politics (related to anti-nuclear and feminist mobilisation, concern with the environment, the student revolt and so on) or the lobbying practices of environmental NGOs. Between 1980 and 1984, new Green parties were founded in 12 Western European countries (Muller-Rommel, 2002: 1). By the late 1980s, these parties had gained significant electoral and parliamentary success. Since 2009, Green parties in most of these countries, except the UK (only 2.77%), have succeeded in the European Parliament with a double digits percentage that shows their ratio in total number of seats reserved for the respective country (Horvat and Tomašević, 2011: 19). The representation of Green parties for these countries in the period 2009–2011 is as follows: France (18.05%), Luxembourg (16.66%), the Netherlands (12%), Denmark (15.38%), Finland (15.38%), Germany (14.40%), Belgium (13.63%), Austria (11.76%) and Sweden (11.11%) (18–19).

Sweden's *Miljöpartiet de gröna*, founded in 1981, was among the first Green parties to secure national electoral success in Europe (Haq and Paul, 2012: 9). In the

1988 national elections they won 5.5% of the vote and took 20 seats in parliament, though they were unable to succeed in the 1991 elections (Muller-Rommel, 1994). The *Finnish Green League* that emerged in Finland secured parliamentary recognition in 1991 and in 1995 became the first Green party in Western Europe to enter a national government (Haq and Paul, 2012: 9); the Greens in Finland are still in the government.

The German Green party is Europe's most successful ecology party. In West Germany, a history of radical protest in the midst of obvious environmental problems and the nuclear threat of an active phase in the Cold War caused the formation of a Green party[34] in 1980; from 1980 to 1982 it had enough electoral support to be represented in various State parliaments and in 1983 it entered the Federal Parliament in Bonn (Doyle and McEachern, 1998: 1). The radical style of the West German Greens, with their commitment to participatory democracy, leadership rotation and gender equality, contrasted sharply with the normal politics of the rest of West Germany's conventional parties (O'Neill, 2000: 166). In 1980, a diverse alliance of activists launched the national West German Party but polled only 1.5% in their first national contest. A national programme based on 'four pillars' (ecologism, grass roots democracy, social responsibility and non-violence) was adopted for the 1983 national elections, securing 5.6% of the national vote and 27 seats. In 1987, this representation grew to 44 seats (Doyle and McEachern, 1998: 117). Though the German Greens held on to their grass root aspirations, only a fraction of the party (Fundis) supported more radical declarations to change the consciousness of society. The other group, the Realos, emphasised reform and, upon entering party politics, experimented with alliances with the Social Democrats (SPD) (Lippelt, 1991: 5; see also Sarkar, 1986). Thus, the German Green party turned out to be very pragmatic by the 1990s, causing the Fundis to quit the party (Lippelt, 1991: 5). From the late 1990s to 2005, the German Greens have been part of the ruling government (Horvat and Tomašević, 2011: 19). However, the coalition of the Greens and Social Democrats was defeated in the 2005 parliamentary elections; in 2009, however, the Greens improved. Though Greens remained part of coalition governments for the next few years, by 2017 they had kept their place in the opposition.

In Britain, the ecology party formed in 1973 by a group of small activists from Coventry was renamed the Green party in 1985. It has numerous branches in both local and national electorates. The late 1980s to the mid-1990s were characterised by mixed results and internal politics.[35] Though at the national level, the Greens polled 14.9% of the vote in the 1989 European Union Election, they could not enter the parliament (Doyle and McEachern, 1998: 116).

The French Green Movement had achieved remarkable electoral results as early as 1978, even before they united into a stable structure. The French Green party (Les Verts) was officially founded in 1984. The French Greens scored their first significant electoral victory during the 1989 European election in which they gained some 11%. In the 1997 national elections, the Greens gained 5.1% of the total vote and for the first time were asked to participate in the formation of a new French National Government (Boy, 2002: 64–5). In France, the Greens have operated successfully with their strategic behaviour in government, along with the Socialist party, abandoning or banning some projects that could have significant adverse impact on the environment. For example, abandonment of the high capacity Rhine–Rhone canal project, closing of the fast breeder Super-Phoenix, implementation of a moratorium on genetically modified cultivation (Boy, 2002: 68) and so on.

Green parties have existed in Australia since the formation of the United Tasmania Group in the late 1970s. They existed at the local, state and national levels. The national Australian Green party was formed in 1992 (Doyle and McEachern, 1998: 115). Green electoral politics in the United States is relatively poor. Several Green parties have been formed at the local and state level. At the national level, the 'Green Politics Network' was formed in June 1995 (115–16). In both Britain and United States, there is little prospect of Greens gaining representation at the national level. Here, Green parties use elections to attract media attention to their cause. There are also financial gains in playing party politics (122).

In Western Europe, as various data reveal, the electoral as well as the parliamentary performance of Green parties has proved that the Greens have developed into a stable element in most European party systems. The principles that the Greens hold as a movement and the objectives they aim to achieve distinguish them from conventional political parties. Yet in order to execute political programmes in favour of society and environment, the Greens resort to the usual political procedures to gain entrance into the parliament and thus become part of a 'national' government. The Green parties introduced this kind of a socio-political approach, referred to as the 'new politics dimension', to European party systems, and it has consolidated itself over the past 20 years.[36] However, there is an evident discrepancy between the well-established Green parties and their quite effective performances in the 'West' on one side and their unstable performance in East or Mediterranean countries (Greece and Spain are exceptions) on the other, where they face severe difficulties in finding their way to national parliamentary representation (Horvat and Tomašević, 2011: 16).

4.4 Analysis

From the case studies discussed in the earlier section, it follows that environmental problems generally arose as an outcome of government policies or decisions that victimised a group of people, usually poor and backward classes. In cases where the government acted politically, that is, responsibly and equitably towards its people, it helped to resolve the issues immediately. The anti-pollution movement against the Maradia industry is a good example of the victory of the people with the support of the government. In other cases, it seemed the government remained either insensitive or inactive, moved to action only when pressured by the people's protests. The duration of each struggle was determined by the time before the authorities took action to resolve the issues, especially in favour of the people's movements. The fishermen movement in Orissa was one of short duration due to meaningful and timely intervention and decision taken on the issue by the government. But the Narmada issue, by contrast, seems to be the longest due to the power politics played by different governments. The case studies considered here point towards the fact that the viewpoints and interests of those in power are a crucial factor in decision-making processes. That is, the approach of the government towards its people, natural resources and environment and the attitude to the idea of 'development', foreign aid and so on function as determining factors in the emergence of a political struggle. The political complexity of each case depended on the power relations established between the agents involved in any issue. In cases of intervention by powerful agents such as industries, multinational companies, political parties, media and others, these all influenced the government, thereby causing delays in resolving the issue. Hence, the political positions taken by the government are most important when dealing with people's problems. As a democratic institutional set up, the approach of the government should represent the stakes of all of the groups of people who are the real beneficiaries. The government should identify and understand the problems in-depth by collecting relevant data, and steps should be taken to determine solutions in accordance with the collected information. Thus, the government is expected to protect the interests of the real sufferers in each issue by ensuring they receive justice. But as is evident in the above examples, other networks make the functioning of the government very complex.

The natural or urban settings in which people have long been settled is their lived space; they depend on this in various ways, but not in a linear manner. It is their habitat; though not necessarily natural, it becomes one by regular interaction. In addition, there is the aspect of being part of a system of relations in which living beings interact with the environment and among themselves in a particular setting. Therefore, this habitat can rightly be called an 'eco-habitat', in the sense of people both intervening in and depending on it. The lived space, that is, the eco-habitat, is also a space with which the people form an emotional bond. Their identity is something they come to attain in this process and is affirmed, from time to time, by their lived experience in their eco-habitat. This adds value to eco-habitats as culturally significant systems. Now the eco-habitat of people can be defined as a system (1) in which people find themselves in a relation of co-existence with the rest of the environment, (2) on which they are physically dependent for their livelihood and (3) that provides an enduring setting for their cultural identity. Therefore, when there is external interference or a disturbance in the eco-habitat, it will have an impact on the life of the people. It is against this backdrop that the significance of the 'political' dimension of the domain of human agency–environment must be seen. To describe the changes in the environment as partly or largely due to human activities only partially represents what actually happens. Most often, the 'human' is not the people in their eco-habitat. Interference detrimental to the eco-habitat of a group of people mostly comes from 'human' agency authorised by the State or those who obtain legal sanctions from the State. It is the authority to intervene in an environmental setting that renders human agency with its political significance.

When the impact of such activities negatively affects the eco-habitat of a local people, and they recognise this and decide to resist the move to intervene in their eco-habitat, then their reaction also assumes 'political' significance. In other words, intervention from external agencies and resistance to it on the part of the people when their eco-habitat is affected reveal that the 'political' dimension is internal to the eco-habitat. It points to people's tacit recognition of the arrangement of a given eco-social life and an understanding that the power to continue or change it lies solely with the people. Human beings peopling an eco-habitat are perceived to have an inalienable right to preserve, continue or change the eco-social life that it gives rise to in the course of life. This is the 'political' in the eco-habitat, and it is reflected in many environmental movements around the globe. Eco-habitat can be defined not only locally but also globally, as is applicable in the case of the sustenance of the eco-social life of human beings threatened by the consequences of global warming and others. For example, the impact may be local in cases where deforestation affects livelihood or development leads to the displacement of people in an eco-habitat. But the lives of all living beings on earth may be affected in the case of ozone layer depletion. The details of the various environmental movements given in the earlier section serve the function of capturing graphically the 'political' dimension of the domain of human ecology.

Notes

1 Sections of this chapter are based on Devi, T. V. Geetha. 2012. 'The 'Political' Dimension in the Protest Movements of the Indigenous Groups', in Vineetha Menon (ed.), *Environment and Tribes in India: Resource Conflict and Adaptation*, New Delhi: IGRMS, Bhopal/Concept Publishing Company, 180–7. Used with permission.
2 North American environmentalism is considered 'apolitical' due to the following reasons: (1) it lacks a human political dimension, (2) there is little criticism of existing political systems, (3) the pluralist system is so dominant that people do not perceive it as a political model. See Doyle, T. and McEachern, D. 1998, *Environment and Politics*, New York: Routledge, 69.
3 Kendlebacher, 'A New World Order: Deep Ecology and Mental Environment', See www2.uah.es/iuen/friends_of_thoreau/documents_pdf/Julia%20Kendlebacher/Chapter%203_2.pdf.
4 Earth first! does not rule out militant actions (most specifically property damage) in its efforts to 'protect Mother Earth'. This method is known as 'eco-sabotage'. See Doyle and McEachern, 1998: 91.
5 The apocalyptics did not expect the continuation of the existence of the human race after the apocalypse. They worried that the world would be overtaken by famine, genocide, war, totalitarianism, plagues and economic collapse. This group considered overpopulation to be one of the key factors that threatens ecological balance.
6 Mass mobilisation strategies are aimed at widespread change, including alterations in mass consciousness and individual value systems. Doyle and McEachern, 1998: 91.
7 Some scholars remark that Silent Valley can be considered as a shola forest rather than a tropical rain forest, since it does not have year-round rainfall, and there is no rain for at least a couple of months every year. Sholas are the thick vegetation found only at the base of valleys in the western hill of south India, and Silent Valley is a good example of this. See D'monte, D. 1991, *Storm over Silent Valley*, Ahmedabad: Center for Environment Education, 15.

8 See Prasad, M. K. et al., 1979, *Silent Valley Hydro-Electric Project: A Techno-Economic and Socio-Political Assessment*, Thiruvananthapuram: Kerala Sastra Sahitya Parishad, 9–24.
9 Report of the Joint Committee set up by the Government of India and Government of Kerala. 1997 (1982). *The Silent Valley Hydro-electric Project: A Techno-Economic and Socio-political Assessment and Ecological Aspects of the Silent Valley*. Kochi: Kerala Sastra Sahitya Parishad (KSSP), 53–83.
10 Collins, G. F. S. 1921, 'Modifications in the Forest Settlements: Kanara Coastal Tract', Part I, Karwar: Mahomedan Press, cited in Gadgil, M. and Guha, R. 1995, *Ecology and Equity: The Use and Abuse of Nature in Contemporary India*, New Delhi: Penguin Books, 40.
11 The Chipko movement is said to have originated in an incident that occurred three hundred years ago (in 1763), in Rajasthan, when the members of the Bishnoi community sacrificed their lives to save their sacred Khejri trees being felled under orders from the Maharaja of Jodhpur. Guha is of the opinion that this analogy obscures Chipko's origins, which are specific to the conditions of Uttarakhand. Guha, R. 1989, *The Unquiet Woods: Ecological Change and Peasant Resistance in the Himalaya*, New Delhi: Oxford University Press, 173–4; Shiva, V. 1988, *Staying Alive: Women, Ecology and Survival in India*, New Delhi, Kali for Women, 67.
12 Yugvani, 24 June 1973, cited in Guha, 1989: 156.
13 Some authors describe the Chipko movement as 'women movement'. See Shiva, 1988: 67. Guha argues that it is simplistic to characterise Chipko as a feminist movement. In many cases of protest in UP it is only in Dungri-Paintoli that women took the responsibility of fighting against the State due to the conflict with the men of that region. Even the protest in Reni cannot be taken as an example of women's major participation, since the situation necessitated their involvement in this case. He points out that the hill women have traditionally borne an extraordinarily high share of family labour and their participation in Chipko may be read as an outcome of the increasing difficulty with which these tasks have been accomplished in the deteriorating environment. See Guha, 1989: 175.
14 According to Shiva, in the early stages of the Chipko movement, when the exploitation of forest resources was carried out by non-local forest contractors, the women's concern with forestry for survival was temporarily merged with a largely male concern for commercial interests, as they collected raw materials like resin and timber for factory purposes. However, a separation took place between local men's interests and local women's interests with the intervention of social activist Bahuguna, who turned the women's concern to the conservation of natural forests, since they are life-supporting systems and to the Chipko struggle as a struggle to conserve them. See Shiva, 1988: 70–1.
15 Gadgil and Guha point out that in the aftermath of Chipko there were efforts to modify the forest policy, and as part of it, the National Forest Policy of 1988 included an official acknowledgement that the biomass needs of the village people must have primacy over the commercial demands of others. Some attempts have also been initiated to set up management systems involving local communities, but these policy initiatives had not been put into practice. Throughout these periods the traditional selection felling methods of timber harvesting and the subsidised supply of forest raw material to industries continued, while large masses of village people still depended on open access lands for their biomass needs. Gadgil and Guha, 1995: 23–4.
16 About 90 companies were said to be active in importing logs from Southeast Asia, of which the top five giants were Mitsui, Marubeni, Itochu, Mitsubishi and Sumitomo. Wong, A. 1998, 'The Anti-Tropical Timber Campaign in Japan', in Kalland, A. and Persoon, G. (eds.), *Environmental Movements in Asia*, Surrey: Curzon Press, 138.
17 It was stipulated that the NSP would be built mainly for the regulated releases of about 4MAF water for the SSP and that the benefits of the SSP were dependent on the proper completion of the NSP. See Sangvi, S. 2002, *The River and Life: People's Struggle in the Narmada Valley*, Mumbai: Earth Care Books, 16–17.

The question of 'political' 149

18 Up-to-date information (post-2002) regarding the Narmada issue has been provided by Philip Mathew, an activist in the Narmada Movement.
19 Nyoman Nuarta Studio 1993, 1. Bali Post, 17/7/93, cited in Warren, C. 1998, 'Symbols and Displacement: The Emergence of Environmental Activism on Bali', in Kalland, A. and Persoon, G. (eds.), *Environmental Movements in Asia*. Surrey: Curzon Press, 190.
20 Beinart, W. 1999, 'African History, Environmental History and Race Relations', Inaugural lecture delivered at the University of Oxford, 6 May, 9, cited in Obi, 2005, 'Environmental Movements in Sub-Saharan Africa: A Political Ecology of Power and Conflict', *Programme Paper No. 15 on Civil Society and Social Movements*, United Nations Research Institute for Social Development, January, 3.
21 Mamdani, M. 2000, 'Democratic Theory and Democratic Struggles (in Africa)', in Nnoli, O. (ed.), *Government and Politics in Africa – A Reader*, Harare: African Association of Political Science (AAPS) Books, 229, cited in Obi, 2005: 3.
22 Saro-Wiwa, K. 1995, *A Month and a Day: A Detention Diary*, Lagos: Penguin Books, cited in Obi, 2005: 7.
23 Obi, C. 2000, 'Globalization and Local Resistance: The Case of Shell versus the Ogoni', in Gills, B. (ed.), *Globalization and the Politics of Resistance*, New York: Palgrave Macmillan, 287–8, cited in Obi, 2005: 7.
24 Decree No. 15 of 1967; Offshore Oil Revenue Decree No. 9 of 1971; and Decree No. 6 of 1975. See Obi, C. 2001, *The Changing Forms of Identity Politics in Nigeria Under Economic Adjustment: The Case of Oil Minorities Movement of the Niger Delta*, Research Report No. 119, Nordiska Afrika institutet, Uppsala, cited in Obi, 2005: 7.
25 Robinson, D. 1996, *Ogoni: The Struggle Continues*, World Council of Churches, Nairobi, Geneva and All Africa Conference of Churches, 32–46, cited in Obi, 2005: 8.
26 Constitutional Rights Project (CRP), 1999, *Land, Oil and Human Rights in Nigeria's Delta Region*, CRP, Lagos, 3, cited in Obi, 2005: 8.
27 Barikor-Wiwa, D. 1997, 'The Role of Women in the Struggle for Environmental Justice in Ogoni', *Cultural Survival Quarterly*, 21(3), Fall, 46–9, cited in Obi, 2005: 9.
28 Carr, S., Douglas, O. and Onyeagucha, U. 2001, 'The Ogoni People's Campaign over Oil Exploitation in the Niger Delta', in Thomas, A. et al. (eds.), *Environmental Policies and NGO Influence*, London: Routledge, cited in Obi, 2005: 8.
29 Obi, C. 2002, 'The politics of the Nigerian Industry: Implications for Environmental Governance', in Osuntokun, A. (ed.), *Democracy and Sustainable Development in Nigeria*, Frankad Publishers for Friedrich Ebert Foundation, cited in Obi, 2005: 10.
30 Anon, 1982, *Undeclared Civil War: A Critique of the Forest Policy*, New Delhi: Peoples Union for Democratic Rights; Guha, R. 1983, 'Forestry in British and Post-British India: A Historical Analysis', *Economic and Politic Weekly*, 29 October and 5–12 November. For these citations refer Guha and Martinez-Alier, 1997: 7.
31 Though the forensic team was almost certain that the killer poison was cyanide, a fact confirmed by traces found in some cells, and the administration was advised to use sodium thiosulphate as an antidote, the doctors did not heed it because of Union Carbide's strong influence. If the easily available antidote had been used, perhaps hundreds of lives could have been saved. See Raina, V. et al. (eds.), 1999, *The Dispossessed: Victims of Development in Asia*, Hongkong: Arena Press, 142.
32 It is argued that the government cannot claim that it did not have the sort of data that would have required it to enforce stringent checks on the plant. The State electricity board was in possession of all the requisite documents, which were handed over to it perfunctorily the first time and every time subsequently when Union Carbide applied for an enhancement of the power supply. Also, at every stage since the inception of the plant, the government has been fully aware of the noxious character of the materials the plant was using for the manufacture of pesticides. What it lacked was the will and the intent to come down strongly on Union Carbide. See Ramaseshan, R. 1984, Government Responsibility for Bhopal Gas Tragedy, *Economic and Political Weekly*, 19(50), 15 December, 2019.

33 *Economic and Political Weekly* (editorial), 1985, XX (27), July 6.
34 The Green Party in Germany was called 'Die Gruenen'/ Die Grünen, which denotes 'The Greens'.
35 Hutchings, V. 1994. 'Support Your Local Village Green', *New Statesman and Society*, March 11, 7, 293: 20–1, cited in Doyle and McEachern, 1998: 116.
36 Muller-Rommel, F. and Poguntke, T. (eds.), 1995, *New Politics*, London: Dartmouth, cited in Muller-Rommel, 2002: 6.

PART IV
Knowledge

The broad aim of Part IV is a characterisation of the domain of human-environment interaction, following that of second and third parts, though in a considerably different way from both. Alternatively, it addresses the question of explaining the events or phenomena that occur at the intersection of humans and the environment. This part tries to characterise the domain not through a formal definition but by highlighting as well as juxtaposing the salient features of the theoretical efforts (of interdisciplinary character) made by several scholars (including ecologists and social scientists) to explain the happenings in the domain. Since in this part the emphasis is on 'explanation', this characterisation will have its focus on the scientific status of the studies. The strategy followed in this part is to group together a number of varied and multidisciplinary efforts to explain phenomena that fall under a broad domain, in which human and environmental factors enter into a causal relation. These efforts can be treated as exemplary for, and the methodologies adopted as appropriate to, a distinct discipline even when they differ from each other in their presuppositions or methods employed. 'Human ecology' is an appropriate term to name such a discipline for the single reason that it mainly concerns the difference humans make to the domain of ecology. However, the term has been in circulation since the 1920s in Europe, and many studies, theoretical as well as empirical, have claimed the title of 'human ecology'. However, these ideas will not hinder an attempt here to redefine or refashion human ecology with new significance. In this venture, our approach is more inclusive than exclusive, and earlier efforts made by scholars and theoreticians are gathered together at the conceptual level to make sense of an emerging discipline. Differences among scholars are treated as constructively informing the idea of the discipline rather than destructively disintegrating the idea.

In 'human ecology', the weight seems to fall on 'ecology', thus appearing to subsume the discipline under ecology. However, the conceptual history of the discipline does not bear out this evidence. In fact, the first two decades in the history of the idea of human ecology were characterised by a flood of sociological imagination, which seemed to represent human ecology as primarily a branch of social science. Hence, 'ecology' did not figure in such representations in a thorough sense. Yet by way of analogy, and factual reference, ecology played a decisive role in shaping the concept of human ecology. The science of ecology covers the impact of human agencies to the extent that it helps us to account for the changes human beings bring about in the ecosystem. In other words, ecology as a science informs us about the area of human–environment intersection, with explanations for the consequences of human actions resulting in climate change, pollution, desertification, global warming and so on. Ecological science provides us with the conceptual tools and methods to explain the diversity and intensity of these 'ecological' problems. Yet such explanations alone prove inadequate for providing a satisfactory account of the ways in which human beings interact with and influence their surroundings as human (social) agents, with their socially mediated actions. Often through such series of human interventions, 'ecological' problems get converted into a complex set of environmental issues. Therefore, it is reasonable to imagine a discipline called human ecology to fill the vacuum, or it can be said that the rationale for such a discipline is already present in the above circumstances.

An important challenge at this juncture is to conceive of human ecology as an independent discipline. One question that could be reasonably asked is whether it forms an independent discipline beyond constituting an area of (interdisciplinary) research. By considering it as a discipline, this does not mean simply addressing questions that can be answered independently by either one or other social sciences or ecology. Rather, the kind of questions human ecology is expected to address should be unique to itself. Therefore, it is relevant to presume human ecology is a discipline with certain defining features distinct from ecology or sociology. Another possibility that may question its disciplinary status is treating it as a sub-discipline of the science of ecology, extended to include human factors, or taking it as part of the sociological endeavour. These questions can be answered only after examining the methodology of ecology and various proposed definitions of human ecology that are historically given, on the one hand, and, on the other, actual research works conducted under its label. In this effort, we also consider studies that fall more or less in the same domain as that proposed for human ecology. This last point implies that researchers from varied disciplines have already been conducting their research with a human ecological orientation. The task in this part of the book is to delineate features of such studies that may characteristically enter into the definition of human ecology.

This part comprises two chapters. Chapter 5 includes analysis of various ideas of human ecology as discussed in the historical literature. This is followed by an inquiry into the ecological components of human ecology, including methodological and conceptual issues, the methodological shift and theory building in ecology as well as references to its developmental history. Chapter 6 examines the actual research works in both natural history and human ecology with the purpose of delineating the characteristics of such studies for the construction of the methodology of human ecology.

5

THE MAKING OF HUMAN ECOLOGY

A historical perspective

5.1 The human ecological imagination in the historical literature

The earliest efforts to understand the discipline of human ecology started from the last decades of nineteenth century itself. Pioneering attempts by early sociologists and geographers and later anthropologists, psychologists, political ecologists and economists ended up including an ecological perspective in their studies from the point of view of their own disciplines; what follows is an account of these ideas that emerged in this period. Human ecology has been depicted as a field, invented by a group of sociologists in the Department of Sociology at the University of Chicago in the early 1920s (Gross, 2004: 575). Even in the 1890s, there were efforts on the part of sociologists and geographers to develop an idea of human ecology.[1] Yet it was the idea of a unique discipline of ecology that led to a hybrid catchment area claimed by both disciplines (577). The historical literature has generally portrayed human ecology as an extension of plant and animal ecology to the human realm, as it is conceived in sociology and urban studies of the 1920s (575).

Small and Vincent,[2] pioneers in sociology, placed emphasis on the centrality of geography, maps and depictions of people in their natural environment in *An Introduction to the Study of Society*. They also examined the relation of society to the material environment. They did not consider the complexities of this relation, but regarded society as having a two-fold relation to nature, since nature leaves an impression on society and the latter subjects nature to an endless series of modifications. Small later subsumed the material environment with an influence on human society as part of 'social forces' and thus defined material environment as part of the process of human association. In Goode's opinion, human ecology is the interface between geography and sociology,[3] that is, human ecology as the new hybrid field, where geography builds the factual foundation and sociology the abstractions from geographical facts. Earlier, he considered human ecology to be a part of ontography, along with plant and animal ecology; he described the latter as the geographical science of the relations between living beings in general. Hayes[4] pointed out that explaining the distribution of social phenomena by reference solely to conditions supplied by peculiarities of the earth's crust is insufficient; he stressed the need for a sociological explanation that would correlate the four factors of physiologic, technic, geographic and psychic into one description (Gross, 2004: 588). Hayes's suggestion was to study social activities in a two-step approach, that is, sociological phenomena should be analysed in a descriptive way as regards the processes of human association, and sociologists should subsequently explain these phenomena 'in the light of all that affects them'.[5] Hayes viewed human society as active and as acting not only upon its social and natural environment but also on and with technology (Gross, 2004: 588). Hayes reiterated in 1914 that

> prevalent social activities are moulded by conditions of four kinds (1) geographic or the natural physical environment, (2) technic or the artificial environment, (3) psychophysical or the hereditary and acquired traits of population and (4) social conditions or the causal relations between the activities of associates [... and that ...] geographic conditions or the natural physical environment inhabited, must be recognized as including aspects, soil, water supply, other mineral sources, flora, fauna and topography.[6]

It was Eugenius Warming who promoted the term ecology and made it known in the wider circles of academia through his pioneering work (*Oecology of Plants: Introduction to the Study of Plant Communities*) (Gross, 2004: 577, 599) in the field of plant ecology in 1896, though the term 'ecology' was first coined by German biologist Ernst Haeckel in his *Generelle Morphologie*, as early as 1866 (Odum, 1971: 3). Though Warming conceived of his book as an introduction to ecological plant geography, he also discussed human influence on the environment and the importance of the human species in ecological studies (Gross, 2004: 577). Warming used the term 'social adaptation' to describe the communal life of plants, and he emphasised the pivotal role played by human societies in influencing 'the struggles between plant associations' and their influence on human societies in return (577). This is probably the first instance in which the human species is treated as analogous to plant species, though the similarities drawn are merely functional. In another move of comparable significance, L. F. Wards,[7] one of the forerunners of human ecology, expanded the biological idea of symbiosis into a larger principle of synergy.

Park and Burgess,[8] who co-authored *Introduction to the Science of Sociology*, have excerpted a number of basic bio-ecological works[9] and made an effort to apply the concepts of plant and animal ecology, so isolated, to human collective life. Park developed the idea of human society later in much more detail. He views human society as distinct from plant and animal society and organised on two levels, the biotic and the cultural: symbiotic society based on competition and a cultural society based on communication and consensus (Park, 1961: 28). The function of the cultural society is to suppress competition through co-operation and consensus. He examines in a human context such basic biological ecology concepts such as web of life, food chains, mutual interdependence, community symbiosis, balance of nature, succession, dominance and competition, with strong emphasis on the last two (28). Park notes that human ecology differs in several important aspects from plant and animal ecology, though he applied a series of principles from biological ecology to human populations and communities (Hannigan, 2014: 31):

> Firstly, humans are not so immediately dependent upon the physical environment, having been emancipated by the division of labour. Secondly, technology has allowed humans to remake their habitat and their world rather than to be constrained by it. Thirdly, the structure of human communities is more than just the product of biologically determined factors; it is governed by cultural factors, notably an institutional structure rooted in custom and tradition.

Park defines human ecology fundamentally as an attempt to investigate

> (i) the process by which the biotic balance and the social equilibrium are maintained once they are achieved and (ii) the processes by which, when the biotic balance and the social equilibrium are disturbed, the transition is made from one relatively stable order to another.[10]

The influence of biological ecology is seen later in the works of biologically oriented authors like Adams,[11] who considered human ecology as part of animal ecology. That is, human communities are one more animal community in the natural environment, which can be characterised by the features of general ecology. Adams suggested that the study of the human community and social relations could be made possible from the study of the ecological community. Thus, in his view, sociology was also to be seen as part of general ecology. Therefore, Gross's remark that biological ecologists were solely interested in ethology, instincts and physiology and not in culture, perceptions and consciousness (2004: 589) seems to be relevant. Darling earlier takes an ambivalent position since he believes that there is only ecology and not a human ecology, but at the same time he recognises certain unique properties of human communities that resist traditional ecological analysis, such as human political organisation and their subjective values.[12] At this stage, the focus of concern seems to have shifted to the human from the plant and animal world, which is the dominant factor. Thus, Darling defines human ecology principally as the study of man's impact on the rest of the life world. Young summarises the observations of the bio-ecologists and offers a definition of human ecology from a bio-ecological standpoint (Young, 1974: 8). It is the study of man as (1) the ecological dominant in plant and animal communities and systems, (2) simply another animal affecting, and being affected by, his physical environment and

(3) a human being, different from the rest of the animal world in general and interacting with physical and modified environments in a distinctive and creative way. Gibbs and Martin (1959: 34) observe that in a certain sense human ecology is an application of biological principles in a specified context. 'Biological variables are the key to one of the mechanisms that underlies ecological relations. If populations are to survive, their mode of sustenance organization must meet certain indispensable biological needs' (34). Gibbs and Martin emphasise here the property of collective organisation by man, since man survives through collective organisation (1959: 30). They find a wide variety of organisational forms, and it is in the variability in the characteristics of sustenance organisation among populations that human ecology finds its fundamental problem, which contemporary ecology largely ignores. Population as an aggregate of individuals is taken as the primary conception of sustenance organisation that is engaged in activities that provide them with a livelihood. Thus, the sustenance activities of individuals form the primary data of human ecology, the ultimate goal of which is to describe the characteristics of sustenance organisation for the population as a whole. That means the patterning of social relationships within the population are manifested in sustenance activities (Gibbs and Martin, 1959: 30).

Hawley argues for the necessity of a close working relationship between human ecology and general or bioecology (1944: 400). However, he opposes the approach of human ecologists to take competition as the theoretical element in human ecology, which he alleges results from the desire of the former to achieve a thoroughgoing natural science treatment of human behaviour. Moreover, 'competition, because of its essentially unconscious or asocial character, is assumed to provide a definitely natural science, that is, objective and impersonal, avenue of approach' (400). Hawley takes community as the subject of ecological inquiry, the form and development of which are studied with particular reference to the limiting and supporting factors of the environment (1944: 404). Thus, human ecology may be defined as the study of the 'development and form of communal structure' as it occurs in varying environmental contexts and 'the distinctive feature of the study lies in the conception of the adjustment of man to habitat as a process of community development' (404). However, some researchers observe that the form and development of the community is both too broad and too narrow to be considered as the proper subject matter of the field (Gibbs and Martin, 1959: 29). In addition, a community represents a configuration of widely diverse activities, phenomena that are far too heterogeneous to be treated in terms of one general theory. Furthermore, when community is considered as one unit of observation in defining human ecology, more microscopic units such as regions and nations would be excluded. Hence, the suggestion put forward by Gibbs and Martin is to place its emphasis on 'societal organization' since it is difficult to ignore societal factors in seeking to explain events in a community (29).

According to Hawley, human ecology has the distinctive features[13] of (1) emphasising population as a point of reference with the view of organisation as a property of a population, (2) treating organisation as a more or less complete and self-sustaining whole and (3) working with the hypothesis that organisation arises from the interaction of population and environment. He deduces the following principles of ecological organisation from the above: (1) interdependence, (2) the key function, (3) differentiation and (4) isomorphism (Hawley, 1968). Another tendency of sociological human ecologists who have organisational concern is to look in to how aggregates of people have organised themselves in space; thus, spatial analysis has played a prominent part in the development of human ecology (Young, 1974: 16).

Concepts which dominated the theories of human ecology from Park to Hawley, like competition, have never had their empirical referents clearly established in the human sphere and consequently have produced only purely verbal explanations. Other concepts such as invasion and succession, far from providing adequate explanations, have only served to further the almost exclusive concern with spatial distribution. In either case, plant and animal concepts, taken as a whole, have almost questionable relevance for human ecology, since they do not get at the fundamental attributes of sustenance organisation in human populations.

Robson[14] attempted a sociological approach to urban ecology and utilised geography and human ecology to provide a framework where nature of the relations between space and urban social structure can be empirically examined. Young places this work within the established sociological approach to urban ecology (1974: 36). The Chicago school of sociological human ecologists considered 'city' as a subject for ecological analysis in their early works. In those studies, city is declared an 'ecological fact', explainable in terms of the tendency of all life to 'live in communities', to form 'associations, groups, communities, societies', that is, in the case of man, a tendency to live in urban aggregates (Young, 1974: 14). For example, Robert Park and his colleagues first pioneered urban ecology; they applied their principles of human ecology to the processes that create and reinforce urban spatial arrangements (Hannigan, 2014: 31). They visualised city as the product of three such processes: concentration and deconcentration, ecological specialisation and invasion and succession. 'The building blocks of the city were said to be "natural areas" (slums, ghettoes, bohemias), the habitats of natural groups, which were in accordance with these ecological processes' (31). Schmid developed human ecology as a sociological research technique with a spatial emphasis (Schmid, 1988: 432) as part of the ecological approach to study human society. The most distinctive characteristic of this approach is its emphasis on the spatial or distributive relationships of human beings and social forms and the principles and factors that determine these relationships. The fundamental methodological procedures and techniques used in ecological research are concepts of natural area, concentric zones, concept of gradient, census tracts, census county divisions, mathematical techniques for the analysis of spatial and areal problems (like centrographical and related techniques), indexes and other statistical techniques, correlations and related techniques, isoline maps, gravity potential and related concepts and techniques (1988: 432–47). Nevertheless, Quinn (1939: 164) questions the idea that human ecology is synonymous with studies of spatial distribution. He objected to this idea due to the following two reasons: (1) certain spatial studies are not ecological and (2) ecology includes aspects, which are not spatial.

Hawley opines that the research that is focused on community life and plotting their distributions on maps should come under the discipline of geography but not under ecology (1944: 402). In addition, in mapping when the aim of the study is the determination of the degree of correlation, it is not ecological; rather, it is more in the nature of a statistical study in psychological behaviourism. He points out that in such cases, ecology has sometimes been treated as 'method', to be compared and contrasted with so-called statistical, case study and historical methods,[15] which leads to the mistake that one of the techniques of ecological research-mapping has been taken for the discipline itself. Hawley attributed the origin of this peculiarity (that is, the emphasis put upon spatial relations or spatial aspects of human interdependencies) to the early definition of human ecology (1944: 402), suggested by McKenzie as 'a study of the spatial and temporal relations of human beings as affected by the selective, distributive and accommodative forces of the environment'.[16] Hawley finds here a subordination of interest in symbiotic relations to a concern for the spatial pattern in which such relations are expressed (1944: 402).

The attempt to apply the ideas of ecology in geography is generally considered to have begun with Barrows (Young, 1974: 33). He tried to broaden the catchment area of geography and human ecology by 1922 by declaring human ecology as the unique field of geography, since the latter deals with plants and animals as elements of the natural environment affecting man, rather than with the relations of plants and animals to their natural environment.[17] The main objection to Barrow's ideas is that this approach is deterministic, though Young observes that he took equal effort to also avoid the taint of determinism (1974: 33). However, for a period, a fear of environmental determinism kept geographers away from applying ecological concepts in geographical methodology, and mostly those who turned their attention to the human side of geography were confronted with this dilemma. While on the one hand they focused on geology, meteorology or geophysics, on the other they tried to overcome the accusation of one-way environmental determinism acting upon human societies (Gross, 2004: 591). Goode pointed out the hybrid character of geography, that is, studying both the physical and the social environment. For him, 'progress in social evolution is a record of a changing ratio between the influence of the physical environment and this growing social environment'.[18] For Hayes it was something more than environmental determinism; hence, he viewed society as active and as acting upon its social and natural environment with technology (Gross, 2004: 588). The idea of climatic determinism was put forward by Huntington by linking the effects of different climatic regions to the progress of civilisation,[19] and by Eyre in relation to the causes of certain vegetation and soil types.[20]

White and Renner[21] viewed human ecology as synonymous with geography. They limited their field to a study of the direct relations between men or groups and their environments. They investigated problems such as (1) the effects of climate upon human health and energy, (2) the influences of resources and topography upon human occupations, homes, institutions and inventions, (3) influences of natural routes and barriers upon social isolation and contact and (4) possible effects of natural surroundings upon customs, attitudes and beliefs. Gibbs and Martin (1959: 34) are of the opinion that human ecology is not identical with human geography, though the subject matter of the latter is of relevance to the former. The difference between both lies in the fact that human ecology incorporates more variables within its universe of inquiry and strives for the status of a generalising science. Moreover, the organisational characteristics of human populations are of primary rather than secondary concern for human ecology. Quinn also opposed the conception that human ecology is synonymous with human geography, which proves inadequate for sociology (1939: 163), because human geographers traditionally study many problems that sociologists would regard as outside their own field of interest and vice versa. Sociologists approach human ecology

> as a valuable means of studying certain aspects of human interrelations per se; they study the relations of man to man as influenced by limited supplies of environmental resources rather than the direct relations of men or groups to environment.
>
> *(1939: 163)*

All these viewpoints are limited to the idea of how natural forces affect man, which traditional geography studied.

Thornthwaite[22] tried to present a view involving co-operation of geography, sociology, demography, anthropology, social psychology, economics and many of the natural sciences as well. In his opinion, geography involves a higher order of integration; human ecology also involves integration but on a still higher plane. For him, the concern of human ecology is based on the notion of community, that is, 'the development of human communities and the interrelations of these communities with the totality of the environment' (Young, 1974: 34). Morgan and Moss[23] also emphasised the application of ecological concepts, particularly the community, in the study of physical or biological geography. Young proposes an idea of the possibility of incorporating ecological concepts (with pronounced spatial attributes) with geography's idea of spatial analysis concepts such as interaction, environmental perception, community and ecosystem (Young, 1974: 37).

Gettys points to the problem of biological/geographical determinism that human ecology holds in human affairs (1940: 470). Firstly, the hypothesis of human ecology usually emanates from the natural sciences, and these are set up as postulates from which we are asked to construct a science or sciences of human actions and relationships (473). Secondly, the factual studies conducted for testing hypotheses are shown to be too narrow, confined to a single and somewhat unique area, for example, the large American city. Thirdly, the development of a conceptual and theoretical framework in human ecology is not according to the law that conceptual and theoretical generalisations should be derived inductively and should grow naturally and logically from factual studies. This failure is a result of inconsistent and biased theoretical assumptions, too many a priori conclusions and discrepancies between the theoretical formulations and the factual observations (473). Gettys's suggestion is that human ecology must be free from its primary dependence upon organic ecology and has to 'concentrate on the study of the distributive aspects of human beings and their institutions by methods suited to such material and then analyse and interpret its data in terms of its ecological conceptual scheme' (474). Moreover, if human ecology is to be a significant social science discipline, it has to focus on the description, measurement, analysis and explanation of the spatial and temporal distribution of social and cultural data (475).

Before 1970, though sociological human ecology was largely derived from the work of Hawley, the field was also enriched by the strand of thought developed by Duncan and Schnore. As part of his effort to apply insights from general ecology to sociological human ecology, Duncan developed a concept called 'ecological complex', from the biologists' concept of 'ecosystem' (Dunlap and Catton, 1979: 251). Duncan's 'ecological complex' focuses on the web-like interdependence among Population, Organisation, Environment and Technology (P, O, E, T); it stresses that each element is reciprocally related to every other element (Duncan, 1959: 684).[24] Dunlap and Catton opine that it offers a useful conceptual device for viewing the interactions of human societies with their environments (1979: 251). Schnore (1961) challenged the prevailing myth of human ecology, that ecology is somehow marginal to sociology; instead, human ecology represents one effort to deal with the central problem of sociological analysis and that its real potential lies in its contributions to a macro-sociology (Young, 1974: 17). According to Young, however, sociological human ecology could not be developed into usable theory since an adequate theoretical structure was not developed (17).

In the 1970s, sociology's own response to the emergence of environmental problems led to the development of the field of environmental sociology (Catton and Dunlap, 1978; Dunlap and Catton, 1979).[25] This view emerged by questioning the existing assumptions of the domain of sociology, such as the supposed irrelevance of the physical environment for understanding social behaviour (Dunlap and Catton, 1979: 250). The obsolete assumptions of traditional sociological worldviews are called the Human Exceptionalism Paradigm (HEP) by those who stressed the ecosystem-dependence of human species, the latter being referred to as 'New Environmental Paradigm' (NEP) (250). Those sociologists who support HEP overemphasise humans as a species in the sense that they are taken to be unaffected by ecological principles and by environmental influences and constraints due to their exceptional characteristics, including culture, technology, language and elaborate social organisation; environmental sociologists deny this position (250).

Environmental sociologists take the following assumptions as the basis of NEP:

(1) Human beings are but one species among the many that are interdependently involved in the biotic communities that shape our social life.
(2) Intricate linkage of cause and effect and feedback in the web of nature produce many unintended consequences from purposive human action.

(3) The world is finite, so there are potent physical and biological limits constraining economic growth, social progress and other societal phenomena (Catton and Dunlap, 1978: 45).

Hannigan remarks that Catton and Dunlap's HEP–NEP distinction, the most influential theoretical insight within the area of environmental sociology, has failed to generate much excitement outside of this specialty area, in disciplines like psychology, political science and environmental education (2000: 12).

5.1.1 Critical summary

Small and Vincent in their work recognise a relation of what may be called reciprocity between society and material environment. However, since their aim was to outline the study of society, they subsumed material environment under social forces, that is, part of the human association. Goode recognises the hybrid nature of the study of human ecology in which geography provides the factual foundation and sociology abstracts from geographical facts. But as Hayes noticed in his criticism of this view, it failed to recognise the need for a sociological explanation. The recommendation instead is to explain the processes of human association in light of all that affect them. The conditions that mould social activities are (1) geographic, (2) technic, (3) psychophysical and (4) social. Sociologists like Hawley emphasised the organisation of people into groups, in certain environmental settings, in Young's words, in space. In all these recommendations, the uppermost concern is to arrive at a model of explaining the social world; the domain is social organisation of a community. Human ecology in this sense is a focus on the organisational properties of a social group such as having been in one way or another determined by environmental factors.

In the works of Park and Burgess, we come across the earliest attempt to apply certain biological ecology concepts – such as web of life, food chain, mutual interdependence – to the understanding of social processes. What makes human ecology different from plant ecology must be the characteristic ways in which human beings come into contact with, or depend on, the physical environment. This seems to be a right move in conceiving of a new type of inquiry called human ecology. From the above discussion, we can construe three ways by which humans differ from most other members of the animal kingdom: (1) dependence on the environment is mediated through division of labour, (2) evolving technology reshapes the habitat and (3) human communities are largely governed by cultural factors. Park's explanatory model centres on the notion of biotic balance and social equilibrium and suggests that a subject of human ecology should study the processes involving biotic balance and equilibrium. Apart from the theoretical problems this approach may incur, that is, the presupposition of social equilibrium, it may also unnecessarily narrow down the range of questions that can be raised in human ecological research. In another biologically oriented definition of human ecology, Adams tended to subsume the latter under animal ecology. One can use the model of general ecology to characterise human community. Thus, as a branch of knowledge that claims to study human community, sociology is a part of general ecology. This can lead to ecological determinism. With regard to the notion of community, though it may be illuminating to view human community as characterised by the place it occupies in the ecosystem, explaining social relations in terms of ecological factors will be oversimplifying. But, more importantly in using ecological concepts in the explanation of sociological phenomena, it only ends up in sociology, not human ecology. Darling is more concerned about the impact human actions have upon the rest of the life world. Therefore, the domain of human ecology can be conceptualised as distinct from that of sociology. This is a methodological advance.

A further development can be viewed in Hawley's remark about taking competition as the theoretical element in human ecology, i.e., as a natural science treatment of human behaviour. This was a sign of the fact that conceiving the status of the discipline has moved away from biological determination. In his approach, the emphasis is now placed on the 'community' in environmental context, in the sense that the study focuses on human beings' adjustment to their habitat as a process of community development. However, community development is an idea that has only a very narrow scope if it is taken as the key notion in defining the domain of human ecology, although it may define an area of sociological interest. As Gibbs and Martin observed, it can form only 'one unit of observation', but not in the sense in which 'regions' and 'nations' make other units. More specifically, it may not simply be what happens 'in' or 'to' the community that matters in human ecology. Though Martin and Gibbs rightly pointed out that 'biotic community' has no real equivalent in a complex society, 'sustenance organization', the idea proposed by the authors, is an equally inadequate notion to be used in the domain of human ecology.

In Robert Park's conception of urban ecology, 'ecological' meant more or less the processes by which natural groups tend to live in communities in 'natural areas'; slums and ghettoes of the city are examples. This could be seen either as an extension of the use of the term 'ecology' or as capturing a real aspect of the domain of human ecology. In the latter sense, urban ecology is not just an instance of ecological approach to the study of human society. However, if we treat urban habitats as continuous with natural ones, that is, capable of giving rise to environmental issues as a consequence of the interaction between human agency and environment, it would be a study of urban ecology that belongs to the domain of human ecology. Nonetheless, for Schmid, human ecology is again a tool in sociological research. As we noted earlier, as a tool it is specifically applied to the study of spatial or distributive relationships of human beings and social forms and to the principles and factors that determine these relationships. But as Quinn has rightly pointed out, equating human ecology with the study of spatial distribution will be inadequate because there are spatial studies that are not ecological and ecology includes aspects that are not spatial.

Similarly, Hawley's criticism of treating studies that are characteristically geographical as human ecological is also worth noting. Mapping is a method used in ecological/human ecological research, though such methods should not be mistaken for the discipline itself. The geographical conception of human ecology is comparable to the sociologically informed one. From a geographical point of view, human ecology may be seen as resulting from applying ecological concepts in geographical methodology. It is the human response to the physical environment, which came under focus in the early ruminations of geographically oriented human ecological thinking. But this rather led to a one-way deterministic view (Barrow, Huntington, Eyre and others). The focus on the human component in geographical studies using ecological concepts at the most yields a 'human' geography, which White and Renner wrongly claim as human ecology. Human ecology from this point of view will study the direct relations between human groups and their environment (White and Renner), but here the influences flow from environmental factors to the social world. While Gibbs and Martin question the identification of human ecology with human geography, they still think of the organisational characteristics of human populations as the central concern of human ecology, which is no improvement on the sociologically oriented conception of human ecology. This attitude is clearly manifested in Quinn's rejection of the claim that human ecology is synonymous with human geography. For Quinn, it is not the direct relation of human groups to environment but relations among humans as influenced by the limited supplies of environmental resources that concern human ecology. This, however, is a characteristically sociological concern. Thornthwaite, however, recognises human ecology as involving a higher order of integration, that is, involving co-operation of geography, sociology, demography, anthropology, economics and so on. Duncan's idea of 'ecological complex' rightly integrates the notion of interdependence (among population and environment) implied in 'ecosystem', which is an important step in a human ecological study. The NEP is well founded by defining the place of humans in the ecosystem and the reciprocal relations between humans and environment, which can be considered as the basic premise on which an idea of human ecology can be built up.

5.2 Status of ecology as science

5.2.1 Methodological issues

The critical issue that persists within the field of ecology is with regard to its status as science (causal–explanatory),[26] like other natural sciences, and the way scientific research is done in this field of study. The latter focuses on whether the current methods followed in ecological research would help explain and predict natural phenomena, especially in the context of the recent idea that communities may not be near equilibrium and the recent re-emphasis on the necessary role of historical explanations (Weiner, 1995: 153).[27] The most serious criticism against ecological theories was that they are not theories at all, but rather deductive games that provide untestable 'insight'.[28] In those cases where theoretical models have made predictions, they have been rejected.[29] These failures in ecological experiments are shown to have resulted from the difficulty in applying the Popperian model of deductive logic and testability in both theoretical and empirical works in ecological studies.

In formalism, suggested by Popper,[30] correct explanations cannot be proven deductively except by eliminating all possible alternatives, but incorrect explanations may be disproved by contradictory experiments or observations. Popper argued explicitly that estimates of probability are unfalsifiable and thus not subject to scientific testing under criteria of disproof. In general, propositions not subject to rejection by contrary observations are denied status as scientific theories in the Popperian model. In this sense, most biological laws fall in this category. Three major classes of problems are identified in studying highly overlapping mechanisms of ecological (and evolutionary) change into a rigid hypothetico-deductive mould:

(1) 'Formal hypotheses generally cannot usefully be posed in a way that allows meaningful disproof of a finite number of discrete possibilities. Possible contributing causes are not "hypotheses" of hypothetico-deductive reasoning, because in patterns with multiple causes, it is not possible in principle to perform "critical tests" to distinguish between the "truth" of processes occurring simultaneously.
(2) Treating possible contributing causes as distinguishable hypotheses leads to univariate critical tests. However, the behaviour of a multivariate process may not be safely inferred from any combination of univariate tests if there are strong interactions among contributing causes'.
(3) It is related to the use of 'null hypotheses' in the study of natural communities. It is shown that in practice, reliable null hypotheses may often be impossible to construct, and even if a 'null hypothesis' can be posed, it has no probability of being strictly correct, and a sufficiently sensitive critical test will necessarily lead to rejection. Thus, testing a null hypothesis would appear to have no value in formal deductive logic (Quinn and Dunham, 1983: 604).

Some conceptual, logistic and ethical problems are also identified during the application of the hypothetico-deductive scheme, and they are discussed below (Mentis, 1988: 6–9). The conceptual problems concern formulating appropriate falsifiable hypotheses and establishing the grounds on which a given hypothesis is to be considered refuted. Different forms of hypothesis testing and the grounds for their refutation are as follows (7).

(1) One type of problem arises in relation to hypotheses or models used explicitly for prediction. The conceptual problems here include how to define the level of accuracy and how to remedy it in the case of failure.
(2) A second type involves assessing explanatory power. For evaluating any single explanatory hypothesis, competitive theories are needed. Hence, the generation of viable competitors, the relative weighting of the various criteria for

refutation and determination of what constitutes a satisfactory explanation are raised as conceptual problems here.
(3) A third type concerns the classical statistical concept of a null hypothesis. Problems are shown to arise with incommensurable variables.

The logistic problems are with respect to replication and temporal and spatial scales (8–9).

(1) The problem of pseudo replication (that is, non-independence of samples or replicates) as seen in studies of large-scale systems (lakes, catchments, drifting continents and others). It is observed that numerous situations arise in ecology where there is a bundle of inseparable correlates and the attempt to unravel cause and effect is hindered by inherently poor falsifiability.
(2) Long-term studies have many obstacles compared to short-term studies, which are also more practicable. In the case of the former, the future is uncertain and even scientific paradigms may change over decades to render obsolete some research questions and the data collected in relation to them. Short-term approaches include retrospective studies, the substitution of space for time, extrapolating from systems with fast to those with slow dynamics and modelling.
(3) Regarding problems with spatial scale, while microcosmic studies are possible, effects at a biospheric scale of such phenomena as acid rain, increased atmospheric carbon dioxide content and nuclear winter are not amenable to direct manipulative experimentation.

An ethical problem arises when a thorough testing of ecological hypotheses implies the application of experimental treatments which are of a type or scale that is socially unacceptable, for example, an experimental nuclear winter is not a feasible way of testing various predictions (9).

Inductive approach – For the above-mentioned reasons, ecological research largely follows inductive method as different from the Popperian deductive model (Quinn and Dunham, 1983: 603). It relies on the statistical hypothesis testing method, in which potential causal processes are identified and their probable contributions evaluated, weighted and tentatively generalised to other situations (603). However, hypothesis testing adopted in an inductive method is rarely appreciated. The object of investigation is the proportion of observed variation that may be explained using one or more predictors (like food limitation, predators, soil nitrogen and so on) and the proportion to be ascribed to 'chance'. Since the predictors of 'statistical hypotheses' are chosen based on qualities such as simplicity, measurability and tractability, it would represent deliberately oversimplified caricatures of the assumed underlying processes, with 'chance' referring less to true physical phenomena. Hence, this kind of hypothesis testing is incomparable to the deductive logic of 'strong inference' (603).

The practice of generalising from empirical data through various kinds of correlation analysis and curve fitting operations are also criticised (Macfadyen, 1975: 385). It is pointed out that as a test of fit to theoretical ideas, this practice is irrelevant because (1) the judgement of the 'fit' is usually subjective, (2) the practice does not lead to hypothesis testing because it is too easy to get a fit; it is insufficient in the sense of Medawar and Popper and (3) a set of relationships which are all operating together is confounded and made to appear simple. This practice, when applied to field populations of insects, is criticised, since the production of a formula on this basis is no indication of causal relationships but rather purely descriptive.[31]

Weiner (1995: 154), criticising Peters' position,[32] points out that although the phenomenological (for example, curve-fitting) and statistical models – called calculation tools (by Loehle)[33] – seemed to be helpful in generating testable predictions, they are atheoretical and inadequate as a functional (mechanistic) model[34] or as explanatory theory. Mechanistic explanation is not only consistent with the goal of producing testable predictions, but these theories give rise to much broader and therefore stronger predictions. However, calculation tools are helpful in making more accurate predictions in narrower domains in many instances.

Other problems

The routine application of the scientific method to ecology raises two types of criticisms.

(1) The application of analytical techniques, which is appropriate to physical sciences, for example, cases where the factor-by-factor approach is followed to determine the effect of physical quantities on distribution, growth or physiological performance; the problem involved in it is that it ignores the non-linear effects on ecological parameters of factors acting both simply and in combination, the important characteristics of threshold levels and of synergism.
(2) The failure to reflect in an experimental situation all the relevant parameters required by the theory (Macfadyen, 1975: 384–5).

Some argue that laboratory experiments have a minimal part to play in the study of ecology if it is to be relevant to field conditions, since all the behavioural and other influences cannot be known fully.

5.2.2 Models in ecology

It is suggested by ecologists that deductive mathematical models can make major contributions to explanatory theories in ecology. The following uses of models are recognised in ecological studies: (1) to explain population and community dynamics, (2) to forecast future population and community change, (3) to generate interesting, testable hypotheses as topics for investigation and (4) to serve as idealised standards against which real-life ecological processes can be measured (Pielou, 1981: 18).

However, many theories have failed to make testable predictions, including Lotka–Volterra population models[35] and models such as niche theory, non-linear dynamics, lottery models, non-equilibrium thermodynamics, fractals, energy and others (Weiner, 1995: 155). Some attribute this failure to the effect of highly random inputs present in the ecosystems, such as weather (Odum, 1971: 278). When basic inputs frequently cannot be measured or predicted, it is unreasonable to construct models of high predictive power. As a result, ecological models are often judged in terms of generality and ability to guide research efforts rather than on numerical predictive power (precision). Conversely, it is also shown that in applied ecological problems in which prediction is the goal, realism and generality are often sacrificed for precision. 'Considering the immense complexity of interactions between plants and animals and the difficulty of identifying and measuring these interactions, some mathematical ecologists have concluded that models cannot be both realistic and general'.[36]

Pielou (1981: 17) observes that though the original task of models is to explain nature, this is the task they perform least well; he recommends 'investigating' as a better method to yield advances in knowledge. Investigating is the method of gathering and interpreting appropriate field data (21) and for providing answers to single 'unit' questions, whereas a model is expected to answer such questions simultaneously. According to Pielou, it is not informative to postulate answers, to construct a model from the postulates and then to try and judge whether the real-life system under study is a realisation of this particular model and none other (21). Two specified methods of investigating (as opposed to modelling) are standard multivariate data analyses and spectral analyses (25).

Another problem is with regard to the usefulness of mathematics in theory construction. When a field of research is so technically i.e., mathematically, advanced, there is a risk of losing sight of the purpose of the phenomenon under study (Fagerström, 1987: 261). Fagerström points out that in such a situation, the theory itself is considered the object to be analysed rather than the ecological system that the theory is supposed to represent; Lotka–Volterra equations for competition represent such a case. He mentions certain cases where the authors appear to consider the equations themselves worthy of elaboration and analysis without consideration of the ecological phenomenon of competition. Hence, Fagerström suggests that mathematics should be used as an aid in theory construction, not as a substitute for it (1987: 261).

Weiner (1995: 154) points towards the lack of agreement between data and theory as the cause of failure in the production of successful theories. The usual criticism (Popperian) is that though the role of data is to test hypotheses, ecological data are often collected without any clear theoretical questions in mind. In his opinion, they often seem to be collected and treated like case studies, which are then put into apparently causal narratives that give us the feeling of understanding processes and phenomena (154). Fagerström (1987: 261) notices that ecological theories are not primarily judged due to their agreement with data and that the truth of a theory does not matter to ecologists; rather, consistency, productivity, simplicity and beauty are the criteria primarily used for evaluating a theory.

In order to solve the issue of incompatibility between data and theory, Weiner puts forward certain suggestions. According to him, the aim of data collection should be to search for patterns in nature like patterns in community structure and food webs; correlations among traits in different species and environments; and allometric trends (Weiner, 1995: 155). The subject of ecological study is to be shifted to natural patterns, and not to individual facts or models. Patterns can be used to generate calculation tools and may provide clues about underlying processes. The existence of many patterns makes ecology a predictive as well as a descriptive science (155). He also emphasises the need to fuse the efforts of theoreticians and empiricists (Weiner, 1995: 157), that is, modellers should learn about the natural history of the systems they are trying to model and empiricists about any models that may be relevant to their research. Moreover, he warns against the tendency among researchers in ecology to get distracted by other fields of study like mathematics, statistics, physiology and so on. In order to bridge the gap between theory and experiment (data), many ecologists recommended pluralistic approaches in ecological research (Caswell, 1988: 43; Aarssen, 1997: 178). But this attempt to solve the issue of incompatibility between theoretical and empirical approaches was alleged to arise from the wish of some ecologists to retain 'ecology' as a 'pure science', and this position was attacked by ecologists themselves (Aarssen, 1997: 178; Weber, 1999: 526).

All these point towards the crisis that persists in ecological studies and the confusion among ecologists themselves, who 'appear to be endlessly uncertain and critical of the scope and methodology of their discipline' (Aarssen, 1997: 177). Now, it seems that the discipline 'ecology' has no standing on its own and that there is a necessity for inquiring what constitutes it as a discipline. In these circumstances, some ecologists have expressed the opinion that hypothetico-deduction is just one approach to ecological endeavour and alternative approaches are to be adopted in ecological research to get meaningful and reliable results.

Weber argues for a different view of science, which emphasises disunity, methodological diversity and a complex relationship between theory and experimentation against the narrow view of physical science (1999: 526). Macfadyen puts forward a modified definition of the scientific method, as is suitable to ecological studies (1975: 382–3). He argues that the scientific method is not confined to the study of so-called causal relations. According to him, science is concerned with a description of consistent patterns of behaviour of the material world. Therefore, a reasonable perception of patterns is important, and this forms the key to understanding hypothesis formation. A pattern that is not suited to the conditions would imply that, of the possible outcomes of a particular experiment, some were excluded or that the system is subject to constraints. By mapping the boundary conditions of a system, whether deterministic or stochastic, one can evaluate if all possible states of the system are equally probable or not. Macfadyen suggests this as an alternative definition of 'scientific method', where there is no mention of causality, no need for the repeatability of particular phenomena and no precise specification of the nature of a satisfactory explanation. This science includes the analysis of historical phenomena as well, such as those that are encountered in ecosystem studies, in areas of human ecology and also studies of human history itself. There are ample references to the methods of field observation and natural history works as alternative approaches in ecology (Noss, 1996; Applegate, 1999: 587; Weber, 1999, 526). According to Weiner (1995: 156), the relationship between ecology and natural history is central to one's conception of ecology as science and therefore to its practice. Graham and Dayton evaluate the erasure of the history of ecology as having caused the present crisis in the discipline of ecology (Graham and Dayton, 2002: 1486).

5.2.3 Making of ecology – an historical perspective

Ecology is said to have originated, during the nineteenth century, from the old tradition of natural history, on the one hand, and from the then new 'scientific', that is, physiological biology, on the other (Jax, 2001: 2). The influences of natural history can be traced back to early plant geography in the tradition of Alexander Von Humboldt and his successors in the first decades of the nineteenth century; the influence of science is visible in the definition of ecology provided by Haeckel and later in the branch of study called autecology (physiological ecology) (2). Both approaches together gave form to the hybrid character of ecology.

Natural history

Natural history in its earlier form was primarily concerned with description and classification, especially during the eighteenth century. 'Natural historians sought to uncover the large-scale patterns of living nature, through collecting in the field and classifying in the museum' (Nihart, 2000: 426). In the early modern period, and before that, classification of the objects of nature was made based on their relationship to man. Thus, animals were often considered as symbols or mirror images of human relationships.[37] Even in the eighteenth century, the French naturalist Buffon tried to create a natural order for arranging animals according to their degree of relationship to man (Thomas, 1983: 53). Gradually this tendency gave way to new and more objective principles of classification. Thus, European botanists tried to group plants based on their intrinsic structural characteristics rather than their human uses. John Ray, the English botanist, made a natural system of classification in the late seventeenth century, which, though it started with the seed, attempted to take into account the plant's whole structure (65). By the mid-eighteenth century, Linnaeus had developed an artificial system of plant classification – the *Systema Naturae* – based on the number, situation and proportion of the parts of fructification (65). While collecting and cataloguing exotic species from the farthest corners of the world formed the natural history study, especially of British scientists, others focused more on the microcosmic study of nature, which later contributed to studies in field ecology.

The *Natural History of Selborne*, written by Gilbert White, was published in 1789 and describes the wildlife, seasonal changes and antiquities of his parish in Selborne, which laid the foundations for the natural history essay in England and America (Worster, 1995: 5). While focusing on the microcosm, the natural order of his parish, he also tried to grasp the complex unity in diversity that made Selborne environs an ecological whole, that is, to see how many creatures the Selborne parish contained and to understand how they were all united in an interrelated system (7). Another element White found out through his study was arcadian harmony with nature (9). The famous figure Linnaeus presented a static portrait of the geo-biological interactions in nature in his essay 'The Oeconomy of Nature' (34). He presupposed a cyclical pattern in nature that keeps returning to its point of departure. At the very foundation of this natural order, he conceived the hydrological cycle, the perpetual circulation of water from the 'exhalations' of seas and rivers into the form of rainfall and snow and thence to the sea once more. For Linnaeus,

> this model is repeated throughout nature, it is the template or paradigm from which all environmental phenomena take their form: the round of the seasons, the birth and aging of a man, the course of a day, the formation and weaving away of the very rocks.
>
> *(34)*

Instead of a static view, Thoreau's age emphasised ecological change and turbulence (Worster, 1995: 66). This idea was reinforced by the historical study of the ecological changes in regions (for example, New England), where civilised man has radically altered the ecological system. As a naturalist, he also tried to bring together all the natural phenomena of his home environs into a single interrelated whole, arranged by nature in perpetual balance (66), but which is not self-perpetuating and consists of a fragile 'system of relations' (75–76). Darwin's studies on Argentine Pampas are potent evidence of how human settlers can disrupt the vital interdependencies of a local natural order, for example by displacing vegetation, local animals and so on by introducing alien species. While on his journey to the Galapagos Island in 1835, he had unravelled before him the dark side of nature such as conflict, depravity, terror and extinction, he continued to maintain a certain degree of faith in natural processes (Worster, 1995: 122–8).

Role of biogeography

Study of biogeography, that is, large-scale patterns of floras and faunas across the globe, formed an important part of natural history during the eighteenth century. Early biogeographical thought was intimately tied up with travel and access to exotic specimens (Browne, 2001: 1). The explorers of the eighteenth and nineteenth centuries collected much data, which provided information on various animal and plant species. Linnaeus was one of the first to give it a scientific status by cataloguing many thousands of foreign organisms received from Uppsala, Sweden (1). Buffon proposed a scheme which explained that animals originated very early in the arctic circle when the earth was warm and later dispersed southwards according to the environment (1–2).

In the early nineteenth century, Humboldt, during his exploration of River Orinoco, tried to focus on vegetation at different places in relation to environmental conditions like degree and angle of insulation, latitude, rainfall, temperature range, barometric pressures and so on (Browne, 2001: 2). He identified characteristic bands of plant life that exist at successive heights on a mountain in Central America, which he called 'physionomie' of vegetation. Based on these studies, botanists like Augustine De Candolle and Alphonse De Candolle arrived at the idea that distinct communities of plants, such as coniferous forest, deciduous woodland, heath or moorland, were associated with particular environmental conditions (2). Darwin and Wallace[38] also contributed to biogeographical studies, which emerged from their expeditions. Thus, Darwin found the animal inhabitants of South America (both westward and southward) and of Galapagos islands to be similar but not identical. Wallace[39] pondered geographical variants of birds and butterflies during his exploration in 1848–1852 to study the natural history of the Amazonian basin, noting how each distinct race lived in its own territory, separated from others by the tributaries of the River Amazon (2).

In the nineteenth century, a demographic understanding of animal and plant distribution became very common. This was a matter of compiling statistical data on the distribution of species around the world and then deriving from such data a system for classifying geographic regions (Worster, 1995: 194). A technique called 'botanical arithmetic' i.e., the numerical proportion of species to genera and other quantitative relationships, was made by Humboldt, Robert Brown and Augustine De Candolle and later formed an essential part of the cataloguing enterprises (Browne, 2001: 4). In addition, numerical demographic techniques were used for describing foreign insect and bird distributions wherever possible. Gradually, the focus shifted to the adaptations of organisms to their environments; the school studying this aspect came to be known as 'physiognomic', then physiological and finally 'ecological' geography (Worster, 1995: 194).

Origin of plant ecology

Plant ecology came into prominence as a discipline in the early twentieth century, primarily as a result of the efforts of botanists and plant geographers. Humboldt, the German plant geographer, who has the legacy of naturalist tradition, though emphasised on the interdependence in nature, tried to give the integrative vision of ecology, a more precise, manageable form, in his 'Essay on the Geography of Plants' (1807) (Worster, 1995: 134). The central concept of this essay was that along with the taxonomic relations of the plants it is also important to see how they are grouped in relation to the geographic conditions in which they live. Humboldt called these groups 'divisions physiognomiques'. By this, he emphasised the visual patterns in vegetation, and thus each region as a unique ecological assemblage dependent on local or regional conditions; as a result, there are ecologies of deserts, of steppes, of tropical jungles and of arctic wastes (Worster, 1995: 135). August Grisebach transformed Humboldt's physiognomical system of plant forms into the first truly ecologically oriented system of vegetation units, which he called 'formations', in the mid-nineteenth century (195). However, it is Eugenius Warming's *Oecology of Plants: An Introduction to the Study of Plant Communities* (1909) that is considered as the starting point of self-conscious ecology (Cittadino, 1990: 3–4).[40] In this book, he centred his ecological studies on the present set of relationships between the assemblages of plants and their physical environments (Cittadino, 1990: 148).[41] This complex network of interactions between plant communities and environments is called synecology (147–48). His work, together with Schimper's – *Plant Geography upon a Physiological Basis* (1903) – fused plant geography with plant physiology and marked the beginnings of modern studies in ecology (Browne, 2001: 5).

Methodological shift

As the above account shows, towards the end of the nineteenth century, natural history lost its original character as many aspects of it became incorporated within the framework of existing sciences and thus fragmented into a set of separate branches and separate disciplines (Farber, 1982: 148).[42] That is, there was a gradual expansion and diversification of the biological sciences which made natural history just one of several orientations that a biologist could pursue (Nihart, 2000: 439). For example, the German 'scientific' zoologists of the 1850s successfully lifted life history studies out of natural history and recast them in a closer relationship to morphology, which in 1870s and 1880s re-emerged as a distinct biological problem area (441).

However, the division of natural history into many new fields was accompanied by a change in the methods of inquiry. For example, a naturalist, besides identifying a bird or animal being observed, would also note what it was doing and eating and try to discern some order in its habits and behaviour (Lewis, 2003: 41). These observational practices of the naturalists and their focus upon the interactions between plants, animals and their environments were followed by the scientists in Germany, Britain and the United States,[43] even after natural historical study in its early form went out of fashion. This shift in the method of study is visible in the case of botanists and zoologists after the 1890s, who rather than studying dead specimens or collecting individual plants began to look at communities of organisms naturally occurring in the field or interactions between members of a population of animals (Lewis, 2003: 41). Thus, the traditional zoologist/botanist used to understand the form and functions of animals/plants and, based on these characteristics, placed them into taxonomic categories within a larger (Linnaean) framework (Lewis, 2003: 38). Thus, ecologists in the late nineteenth and early twentieth centuries are different from taxonomists and more traditional naturalist–zoologists,[44] with the former's emphasis on the interaction aspect among different species in the natural environment.

Thus, the two trends in nature study – that is, natural historical and physiological biology – have widely differed in their methods of research. While the distinctive feature of physiology was that of an 'exact' science, searching for general laws and drawing heavily on experiments and the identification of mechanisms, the natural history approach focuses on the particular and uses both actualistic explanations of phenomena – referring to currently active causes – and also historical ones (Jax, 2001: 2). The latter follows the method of description, comparison and classification. Universal laws are taken for granted and used to explain particular patterns and events instead of themselves forming the focus of research. It was the merging of the two traditions by the end of the nineteenth century that allowed the creation of ecology as a distinct discipline (2).

New ecology

Plant ecology was the first of the various branches of ecological science to be developed as a discipline in its own right. Animal ecology, limnology, marine ecology, population biology, community ecology and other ecological fields developed more or less independently or somewhat later than plant ecology (Cittadino, 1990: 3). A general science of ecology[45] only started to appear in the 1930s, and a unified ecological science emerged only after 1960. Clements investigated the composition of plant communities in the first decades of the twentieth century. Two interrelated themes dominated his writing: the dynamics of ecological succession in the plant community and the organismic character of plant formation (Worster, 1995: 209). He pointed out the importance for an ecologist to be a natural historian in order to understand the change in nature's communities, chronicling the succession of plant societies that appear for a while and then disappear (209). The works on nature between 1920 and 1945 brought a model of the environment that depended on both modern economics and thermodynamics, which came to be known as 'New Ecology' (256–7). Charles Elton is said to have laid the foundation of the new ecology (294).[46] In his work, *Animal Ecology*, he highlights the notion of the interactive (animal) community (Jax, 2001: 3), the form or organisation of the community forming the central problem (Worster, 1995: 295). In addition, he describes the subject of his study as 'the sociology and economics of animals' (295). He distinguished a set of 'organising principles' to describe and explain the pattern and dynamics of communities; important among these are the concepts of food chain, food web and the ecological niche (Jax, 2001: 3). Elton was still relying on old-fashioned, descriptive habits of the field for his study, in addition to the experimental laboratory data and mathematical precision. He even referred to this kind of study as 'scientific natural history' (Worster, 1995: 299).[47]

The idea of 'ecosystem' was proposed by Arthur Transley in 1935 (Jax, 2001: 5). He tried to study organisms living in integrated units as physical systems instead of organic wholes. By shifting the method of studying nature using the laws of physico-chemical activity, Transley tried to view ecology as an adjunct of physical science (Worster, 1995: 302). Hence, the emphasis was on energy flow in his new approach to ecology. Research based on 'modern' ecosystems was begun with the application of the ecosystem concept to the study of a senescent lake in Minnesota by Raymon L. Lindeman in 1942 (Jax, 2001: 5). In this work, he emphasised the flux of matter and energy in ecological systems as a central topic for ecology.

Theoretical ecology

Mathematics was adopted in ecology, and mathematical (theoretical) ecology was established in the 1920s and 1930s, with the arrival of many physicists to the field of ecology (Lundberg, 2004: 1). Until 1960, theoretical and mathematical development in ecology was paralleled by a similarly strong build-up of mathematical theory in evolutionary biology,[48] especially population and quantitative genetics. It is only after the 1960s that the two fields began to merge to become the strong field of theoretical evolutionary biology, as it is known today (Lundberg, 2004: 1). The application of system analysis[49] procedures to ecology came into practice as part of this in the 1960s, and systems ecology became a major science in its own right for two reasons: (1) it comprised extremely powerful formal tools in terms of mathematical theory, cybernetics, electronic data processing and so forth and (2) formal simplification of complex ecosystems provided the best hope for solutions to man's environmental problems that could no longer be trusted to earlier methods, for example, trial and error (Odum, 1971: 276).

Ecologists made use of this by designing mathematical models of ecological systems to predict patterns of change or stability. Using modelling, scientists could predict what would happen if very small behavioural changes occurred over the course of thousands of generations, and ecologists conducted computerised experiments that simulated evolutionary (geological) time (Lewis, 2003: 159–60). Models for life-history strategies (for example, where an organism devotes its energy to growth, reproduction and so on) were also developed based upon trade-offs and the optimisation of resources, using mathematical modelling (160). Theoretical work in ecology[50] has so advanced that it went far beyond empirical work such as observational or experimental work in the field or the laboratory, whereas in others theory development and data analyses have been more parallel (Lundberg, 2004: 1–2). The study of spatially complex systems with many species is cited as an example for the former and the study of single-population fluctuations in time, for the latter (2). The last development in ecology can be probably said to be the revival of the natural history approach for studying nature; two factors reinforce this approach: (1) the temporal and spatial scale of ecological phenomena is often so large and many phenomena are apparently so unique that experimentation is impossible and (2) ecological processes also have had a strong historical contingency through the course of evolution since the origin of life (Lundberg, 2004: 5).

Revival of natural patterns

In the context of the growing criticisms within ecology, non-experimental methods (that is, observational, comparative and quasi-experimental) are suggested for gaining knowledge in natural history, especially when addressing large-scale phenomena (Graham et al., 1999: 1004). By these methods, pattern finding in nature can be done as part of field ecology; wildlife ecology is the process of looking for patterns in nature. Patterns in nature are often said to be correlative, not causative (1004). Non-experimental designs describe correlation. Therefore, accurate natural histories of organisms provide the conditions for finding new patterns and developing theories from these patterns. It is also argued that natural historians make more testable predictions than do theoreticians; that is, field ecologists can make strong claims about the management history and testable predictions of the future course of succession or the effects of specific grazing regimes, fertiliser applications and so on, in a field which they never visited before (Weiner, 1995: 156). For Weiner, one of the goals of ecological science is to transform such intuitive knowledge into scientific one and to extend this knowledge (1995: 156). Weiner also stresses the importance of searching for patterns and theories in narrower domains, pointing out that testable theories in ecology (concerning plant defences, causes of succession in particular classes of habitats and food webs) seem to address somewhat narrower questions than the general abstract models of the 1960s and 1970s (1995: 157). According to Aarssen, the subject of ecology is concerned with patterns and effective processes in the abundance, distribution and diversity of organisms, taxa, biomass and productivity in nature and the practice of ecology is the interpretation of these patterns and processes by practitioners followed by further interpretation (1997: 178).

5.2.4 Critical summary

The above discussion on methodological and conceptual issues, the methodological shift and theory building in ecology, and references to its developmental history, help us realise the nature of the component of ecology in human ecology. It reveals the lack of consensus among ecologists over methodological orientation and exposes the uncertainties that prevailed among them regarding what should form the subject matter of ecological study. Here it would be relevant to recall Weiner's recommendation that the subject of ecological study is to be shifted to natural patterns. This has the consequence, as Weiner has remarked, that data collection should be a search for patterns in nature. But the attributive space remains the same: one still looks for information about community structure, food webs, food chain, correlation among traits in different species and environments and allometric trends, each of which is a conceptual apparatus of ecology. That is, while methodology shifts and the purpose for which one looks for data changes, the concern of ecology remains the same. Similarly, when Pielou preferred standard multivariate data analysis and spectral analysis to model testing as a method of investigation, it was the content of knowledge in ecology that was in question.

Description of patterns does not necessarily involve establishing causal relations. Methods closer to such a venture are historical. As Weiner said, the relationship between ecology and natural history is central to one's conception of ecology as science and therefore its practices. Graham and Dayton even attribute the cause of the present crisis in the discipline of ecology to the erasure of the history of ecology. The point is that ecology in its early stages is largely built on natural history findings. A theme that is found to recur in natural history works was the relation between the properties of geographical or environmental regions and certain characteristics of the biological phenomena in that region. This was evident in Humboldt's physiognomic concerns, that is, treating each region as a unique ecological assemblage dependent on local or regional conditions. In Grisebach, this concern was transformed into ecologically oriented systems of vegetation units. Warming's synecology was also an example of recognising the complex network of interaction between plant communities and environment. Such concerns and pattern finding paved the way to modern ecology. Natural history is both the method and the subject of such concern. Studies focusing on the shifts in plant communities, as some ecologists pointed out, for example, imply giving an account of changes in the succession of such communities, which is a historical venture; here the subject is the patterns identified in nature. In Clements's writings, thus, two interrelated themes dominated: (1) the dynamics of ecological succession in plant community and (2) the organic character of plant formation. In Charles Elton, the form or organisation of the community came under focus. He developed a set of 'organising principles' to describe and explain the pattern and dynamics of communities, concepts such as 'food chain', food webs and ecological niche. Though Elton may be rightly called the founder of new ecology, he referred to the kind of study he engaged in as scientific natural history.

When Arthur Transley proposed in 1935 the idea of ecosystem and emphasised the need for studying the physical systems into which the living of organisms is integrated, more theoretical works followed in this direction, with mathematical modelling dominating the scene. However, it became clear that theoretical works tend to exceed the observational work in the field. Moreover, observation or comparative methods seem to be more suitable to studying ecological phenomena if we consider their temporal scale and spatial scale. As has been observed in defence of the natural history approach in ecology, ecological processes have a strong historical contingency through the course of evolution. In field ecology, a major concern is pattern-finding. Such patterns are correlative rather than causative. Therefore, non-experimental methods such as observation and comparison are to be resorted to for identifying patterns. This is the basis on which ecological theorising can be built in the future. One could see that this line of thinking historically proceeded from an internal criticism within the discipline of ecology. Thus, Weiner stresses the importance of the search for patterns and theories in narrower domains such as plant defences and so on, which contrasts with the general abstract models of the 1960s and 1970s. One can also recall the suggestion made by Aarssen that the practice of ecology must be defined as the interpretation of the patterns and processes using any approach of human endeavour that generates inspiration among practitioners for further interpretation of pattern and process in nature.

Notes

1 J. P. Goode, E. C. Hayes, A. W. Small and G. E. Vincent are important among them.
2 Small, A. W. and Vincent, G. E. 1894, *An Introduction to the Study of Society*, New York: American Book Co., cited in Gross, M. 2004, 'Human Geography and Ecological Sociology: The Unfolding of Human Ecology, 1890 to 1930 – and Beyond', *Social Science History*, 28(4), 578.
3 Goode, J. P. 1911, 'A College Course in Ontography', *Annals of the Association of American Geographers*, 1, 111, cited in Gross, 2004: 582–4.
4 Hayes, E. C. 1908, 'Sociology and Psychology, Sociology and Geography', *American Journal of Sociology*, 14, 371–407, cited in Gross, 2004: 584.
5 Hayes, E. C. 1906, 'Sociological Construction Lines: V', *American Journal of Sociology*, 12, 65, cited in Gross, 2004: 587.
6 See Hayes, E. C. 1914, 'Effects of Geographic Conditions upon Social Realities', *American Journal of Sociology*, 19, 813, cited in Gross, 2004: 587–8.
7 Ward, L. F. 1903, *Pure Sociology*, New York: Palgrave Macmillan, 607, cited in Young, G. L. 1974, 'Human Ecology as an Interdisciplinary Concept: A Critical Inquiry', in Macfadyen, A. (ed.), *Advances in Ecological Research*, Vol. 8, London: Academic Press, 11.
8 Park, Burgess and McKenzie are widely recognised as the 'founders' of human ecology within Sociology. Park, R. E. and Burgess, E. W. 1921, *Introduction to the Science of Sociology*, Chicago, IL: University of Chicago Press, 1040, cited in Young, 1974: 5.
9 Clements, F. E. 1916, *Plant Succession*, Washington, DC: Carnegie Institution. Referring to Clements, Park explained the potential of plant ecology for constructing a sociological perspective and as a point of view for understanding social processes. See Park, R. E. 1918, 'Education in its Relation to the Conflict and Fusion of Cultures: With Special Reference to the Problems of the Immigrant, the Negro and Missions', *Publications of the American Sociological Society*, 13, 38–63, cited in Gross, 2004: 591. McKenzie also drew heavily on Clements in his work, 1924, 'The Ecological Approach to the Study of the Human Community', *American Journal of Sociology*, 30, 287–301, in Young, 1974: 5.
   1 Warming, E. 1909, *Oecology of Plants*, Oxford: Oxford University Press.
   2 Wheeler, W. M. 1910, *Ants: Their Structure, Development and Behavior*, New York: Columbia University Press.
   3 Darwin, C. 1859, *The Origin of Species*, New York: Appleton, 552.
   For all these citations see Young, 1974: 5.
10 Park, R. E. 1936, 'Succession: An Ecological Concept', in *American Sociological Review*, 1(2), 171–9, cited in Young, 1974: 12.
11 Adams, C. C. 1935, 'The Relation of General Ecology to Human Ecology', *Ecology*, 16, 316–35, cited in Young, 1974: 6–7. Also, see Gross, 2004: 589.
12 Darling, F. F. 1967, 'A Wider Environment of Ecology and Conservation', *Daedalus*, 96, 1003–19, cited in Young, 1974: 8.
13 Hawley, A. H. 1968, 'Human Ecology', in *International Encyclopedia of the Social Sciences* (David L. Sills ed.), vol. 4, New York: Palgrave Macmillan and Free Press, 328–37, cited in Young, 1974: 16.
14 Robson, B. T. 1969, *Urban Analysis*, New York: Cambridge University Press, 304, cited in Young, 1974: 36.
15 Schmid, C. F. 1939, 'The Ecological Method in Social Research', in Young, P. V. (ed.), *Scientific Social Surveys and Research*, New York: Prentice-Hall, Cha. XII, cited in Hawley, A. H. 1944, 'Ecology and Human Ecology', *Social Forces*, XXII, 402.

16 McKenzie, R. D. 1925, 'The Ecological Approach to the Study of the Human Community', in Park R. E., Burgess, E. W. and McKenzie, R. D. (eds.), *The City*, Chicago, IL: University of Chicago Press, 63–4, cited in Hawley, 1944: 402.
17 Barrows, H. H. 1923, 'Geography as Human Ecology', *Annals of the Association of American Geographers*, 13, 114, cited in Gross, 2004: 592.
18 Goode, J. P. 1904, 'The Human Response to the Physical Environment', *Journal of Geography*, 3, 343, cited in Gross, 2004, 582.
19 Huntington, E. 1919, *World-Power and Evolution*, New Haven, CT: Yale University Press, cited in Gross, 2004: 589.
20 Eyre, S. R. 1964, 'Determinism and the Ecological Approach to Geography', *Geography*, 49, part 4 (225), 369–76, cited in Young, 1974: 35.
21 White, C. L. and Renner, G. T. 1935, *Geography: An Introduction to Human Ecology*, New York: Appleton, cited in Quinn, J. A. 1939, 'The Nature of Human Ecology – Reexamination and Redefinition', *Social Forces*, 18, 163.
22 Thornthwaite, C. W. 1940, 'The Relation of Geography to Human Ecology', *Ecological Monograph*, 10(3), 343–8, cited in Young, 1974: 34.
23 Morgan, W. B. and Moss, R. P. 1965, 'Geography and Ecology: The Concept of the Community and Its Relationship to Environment', *Annals of Association of American Geographers*, 55, 339–50; Morgan, W. B. and Moss, R. P. 1967, 'The Concept of the Community: Some Applications in Geographical Research', *Transactions of Institution of British Geographers*, 41, 21–32. Both are cited in Young, 1974: 35.
24 Duncan, O. D. 1959. 'Human Ecology and Population Studies', in Hauser, P. M. and Duncan, O. D. (eds.), *The Study of Population*, Chicago, IL: University of Chicago Press, 678–716, cited in Dunlap, R. E. and Catton, W. R. Jr. 1979, 'Environmental Sociology', *Annual Review of Sociology*, 5, 251.
25 Schnaiberg advocated several years ago that the study of interaction between environment and society is the core of environmental sociology. Dunlap and Catton explain that this involves studying the effects of the environment on society (for example, resource abundance or scarcity on stratification) and the effects of society on the environment (for example, the contributions of differing economic systems to environmental degradation). See Schnaiberg, A. 1972, 'Environmental Sociology and the Division of Labor', Department of Sociology, Northwestern University, mimeograph, cited in Catton, W. R. Jr. and Dunlap, R. E. 1978, 'Environmental Sociology: A New Paradigm', *The American Sociologist*, 13, 44.
26 The dominant view of scientific explanation was the hypothetico-deductive model, mainly advocated by Popper, which offers deductive causal explanations and tests them by way of predictions. This is more often called the method of hypothesis, for it does not achieve absolute certainty for any of the scientific statements which it tests; rather, these statements always retain the character of tentative hypotheses, even though this character of tentativeness may cease to be obvious after they have passed a great number of severe tests. See Popper, K. R. 1961, *The Poverty of Historicism*, New York: Harper & Row. Platt characterised explicit formal hypothesis testing in science as 'Strong Inference'. See Platt, J. R. 1964, 'Strong Inference', *Science*, 146, 347.
27 Many ecologists have pointed towards this problem as requiring serious consideration. See Macfadyen, A. 1975, 'Some Thoughts on the Behaviour of Ecologists', *The Journal of Ecology*, 63(2), 379.
28 Peters, R. H. 1991, *A Critique for Ecology*, Cambridge: Cambridge University Press, cited in Weiner, J. 1995, 'On the Practice of Ecology', *Journal of Ecology*, 83, 153.
29 Hall, C. A. S. 1988, 'An Assessment of the Historically Most Influential Theoretical Models Used in Ecology and the Data Provided in their Support', *Ecological Modelling*, 43, cited in Weiner, 1995: 153–4.
30 Popper, K. R. 1959, *The Logic of Scientific Discovery*, New York: Basic Books. Popper, K. R. 1983, 'A Proof of the Impossibility of Inductive Probability', *Nature*, 302, 687–8. For these citations refer Quinn, J. F. and Dunham, A. E. 1983, 'On Hypothesis Testing in Ecology and Evolution', *The American Naturalist*, 122(5), 602–3.

31 Varley, G. C. and Gradwell, G. R. 1970, 'Recent Advances in Insect Population Dynamics', *Review of Entomology*, 15, 1–24, cited in Mentis, M. T. 1988, 'Hypothetico-Deductive and Inductive Approaches in Ecology', *Functional Ecology*, 2, 385.
32 Peters recommends statistical fitting and extrapolation of empirical relationships as the best ways for generating testable predictions. As an alternative to mechanistic model, Peters advances a sort of positivist 'behaviorism', in which there are no explanatory theories, only black box predictions: inputs and outputs fitted by regression. See Peters, 1991: 154.
33 Loehle, C. 1983, 'Evaluation of Theories and Calculation Tools in Ecology', *Ecological Modelling*, 19, 230–47, cited in Weiner, 1995: 154.
34 The original aim of ecological modelling is to explain, for example, why fluctuating populations behave the way they do. The salient property of a dynamic fluctuating system is the change it undergoes, at varying rates; therefore, an explanatory model must account for these changes and their rates. See Pielou, E. C. 1981, 'The Usefulness of Ecological Models: A Stock-Taking', *The Quarterly Review of Biology*, 56, 18.
35 These models were originally devised to describe and explain the behaviour of simple laboratory microcosms, which have been an outstanding success. However, the basic assumptions or preconceptions underlying the models are shown to be unnatural, and to what extent such models can reasonably be applied to large systems are highly debatable. The three most conspicuous defects pointed out in this model are the following, which assume that (1) environmental conditions do not change with time, (2) population growth rates respond instantly, with no time lag, to the changing densities of the interacting populations being modelled and (3) the space occupied by the interacting populations is homogenous and sufficiently small for all the contained individuals to interact with one another in the same manner. See Pielou, 1981: 18. In Smith's opinion, in the field of population dynamics, though there is a useful and valuable stockpile of concepts, little of the experimental work is at all conclusive. Most of the ideas should be regarded as hypotheses, not theories. See Smith, F. M. 1952, 'Experimental Methods in Population Dynamics: A Critique', *Ecology*, 33(4), 442.
36 Levins, R. 1966, 'The Strategy of Model Building in Population Biology', *American Scientist*, 54, 421–31, cited in Odum, E. P. 1971, *Fundamentals of Ecology*, Philadelphia: Saunders College Publishing, 278.
37 For example, the natural historians of the Renaissance periods like Conrad Gesner, Camerarius and Aldrovandi took an emblematic view of nature. Their works emphasised the intricate web of relationships that interconnect humans and animals. See Ashworth, W. B. Jr. 2000, 'Emblematic Natural History of the Renaissance', in Jardine, N. et al. (ed.), 2000, *Cultures of Natural History*, Cambridge University Press, 17–37.
38 Darwin's and Wallace's theory of evolution by natural selection provided a strong theoretical base for the nascent subjects of biogeography and ecology. See Browne, J. 2001, 'History of Biogeography', in *Encyclopedia of Life Sciences*, John Wiley & Sons, 4. www.els.net.
39 Wallace is considered the father of evolutionary biogeography, to which his most famous contribution was the identification of 'Wallace's Line', the boundary between the faunas of the Australasian and Oriental biogeographic regions. See Berry, A. (ed.), 2003, *Infinite Tropics: An Alfred Russell Wallace Anthology*, New York: Verso, 1. His 'Geographical Distribution of Animals' (1876) provided a model for evolutionary naturalists studying biogeography. See Browne, 2001: 5.
40 This treatise commenced with a thorough review of the impact of habitat factors like light and heat on the growth patterns of plants, focusing especially on the nutritive organs. Warming named the process of structural and physiological adjustment to habitat 'epharmosis'. See Worster, D. 1995, *Nature's Economy: A History of Ecological Ideas*, New York: Cambridge University Press, 198.
41 While American, British and continental European botanists followed this tradition, during the 1880s and 1890s the Germans dealt with the relationship between the minutiae of internal structures and factors in the external environment of the plant, such as

moisture, temperature and light, and rapidly came to include studies of vegetation found in exotic regions. The Germans called this line of research 'plant biology', which now falls within the province of plant ecology, specifically autecology or physiological plant ecology. Refer Cittadino, E. 1990, *Nature as the Laboratory, Darwinian Plant Ecology in the German Empire, 1880–1900*, New York: Cambridge University Press, 2.
42 For more details, see Graham, M. H. and Dayton, P. K. 2002, 'On the Evolution of Ecological Ideas: Paradigms and Scientific Progress', *Ecology*, 83(6), 1486–7.
43 German botanist Ernst Haeckel named this type of study 'oecology' in 1866. American scientists transformed it to 'ecology' in 1890s. See Kingsland, 1995, *Modelling Nature: Episodes in the History of Population Biology*, 2nd edn., Chicago, IL: University of Chicago Press, 11, cited in Lewis, M. 2003, *Inventing Global Ecology: Tracking the Biodiversity Ideal in India, 1945–1997*, New Delhi: Orient Longman, 41.
44 Salim Ali can be considered as the first 'ecologist' in India, in this sense. He acknowledged the importance of taxonomy as the precondition for all other work, but also pointed out the importance of careful and rational fieldwork (in living birds) in their natural environment, known as bird ecology. See Ali, 1997, *The Book of Indian Birds*, New Delhi: Oxford University Press, xxiii, cited in Lewis, 2003: 45.
45 The science of ecology dealt with the principles and concepts pertaining to the ecosystem, energy in ecological systems, biogeochemical cycles, limiting factors and the structure and function of different levels of biological organisation like food chains, food web, trophic levels, community, population, species and the individual. See Cittadino, 1990: 3.
46 Some point out that Darwin's and Wallace's influence can be seen in the way zoological attention turned to the biotic and abiotic features of the natural environment, to food chains and ecological balance. Refer Browne, 2001: 6.
47 It is pointed out that much of the ecological literature of the first half of the twentieth century had the character of natural history. See Cittadino, 1990: 152.
48 Evolutionary biology was naturally introduced into ecology through the subfield of population biology. Along with the evolutionary biology approach, a lot of theories in community ecology, for example, island biogeography, population dynamics, theories of life-history strategies, R and K selection and others formed part of 'modern ecology'. See Lewis, 2003: 168.
49 The process of translating physical or biological concepts about any system into a set of mathematical relationships and the manipulation of the mathematical system thus derived is called system analysis. See Odum, 1971: 277.
50 Since the 1950s and 1960s, after theoretical ecology had become an established subdiscipline of ecology, it has revolved around the following general problems:

Single-species population dynamics; multispecies interactions and their influence on the persistence and stability of communities and ecosystems; the number of species and their relative abundance in a community; the ecological niche and the mechanisms of species co-existence; the implications of individual behaviours for population and community dynamics and spatial structure and scale. See Lundberg, P. 2004, 'Theoretical Ecology', in *Nature Encyclopedia of Life Sciences*, Nature Publishing Group, 1.

6
'HUMAN ECOLOGY' AS A DISCIPLINE

Methodological reflections

The foregoing account reveals that from the eighteenth century on, ecologists often drew up their elaborate schemes of classification without considering the presence or influence of humans (Worster, 1995: 217). That is, their inquiries were solely confined to plants and animals and never dealt with an additional 'human factor'. As a result, the models and methodology required to study human ecology are distinct from those of ecology and hence inadequate. However, human ecological studies adopt the method of pattern-finding in nature from natural history studies.

Natural history studies are conceived here as those based on the key idea of 'ecosystem',[1] interconnecting flora, fauna, geographical and other physical features. By tracing these entire factors, one can presuppose the historical connections that resulted in the (natural) changes that occurred in relation to any specific natural happenings: for example, any catastrophe, extinction of species, desiccation of any river and so on. Natural history provides us with a historical sketch of what has happened in these cases; in other words, it tries to find out a pattern. It may be the case that similar patterns can be traced in other places as well, where similar conditions persist. Not only the natural history of organisms but also the natural histories of rivers, landscapes, whole geographical areas with their human settlements and the histories of productive activities in a geographical area can be studied by using natural history methods. Such studies might suggest patterns which will later help us to explain changes in the environment or explain differences or contrasts or account for disasters that occur in a particular ecosystem in which human actions play a determining role.

6.1 Studies in natural history: some representative case studies

In this section, three instances of natural history research are chosen as case studies for highlighting methodological features. All of these cases, of either general or particular nature, pertain to a natural phenomenon, and each takes 'pattern-finding' as the dominant method directing the study. Additional methods are also used in these studies, which are specific to the theme of inquiry, to help them arrive at a conclusion. These case studies put forward different treatments of 'pattern-finding' technique as exemplified here, which has a bearing on human ecological studies.

6.1.1 Case study I

A study on the biodiversity patterns in Amazonia was conducted based on information from multiple disciplines (Rossetti and De Toledo, 2006: 215–3). The researchers claim that the integration of biodiversity patterns with both geological and fossil data provide the necessary background for understanding current biological interactions.

Marajo island separated from the mainland (Central and Southern Brazil) as a consequence of geological processes (that is, subsidence, possibly combined with relative sea level rise, followed by renewed sediment deposition) during the Plio-Pleistocene and Holocene. The island has been shown to have a bipartite vegetation pattern (that is, open vegetation dominates in areas with Holocene sedimentation, while closed forests prevail in older Quaternary and Pliocene terrain). In order to analyse the reason for this phenomenon, depending on geological and geomorphologic data, the researchers reconstructed the processes that detached the Marajo island from the mainland and made the vegetational differences. They arrived at the conclusion that there are differences in the type of sediments (deposits) formed within different geological contexts of the Plio/ Pleistocene/Holocene palaeovalley, which resulted in different vegetational patterns. Again, based on the following palaeo-ecological information, they established the existence of a former connection between this island and the mainland areas, with an open vegetation structure. They are (1) the presence of Mastodont species remains on Marajo island and (2) the presence of the cervid species (i.e., pampas deer) living in natural populations in areas with open vegetation located in the southeastern side of Marajo island, the occurrence of which is recorded in historical times in most of the natural grass lands below the equator. Thus, in this study, the explanation for the bipartite vegetation is provided with the help of assumptions made from geological and palaeo-ecological data and by comparing this with fresh data from the current biodiversity patterns.

This case of natural history studies aims to discover order in a natural phenomenon by connecting different processes constructed from geological, paleontological and geographical data, in a chain-like manner. This kind of study does not aim to discover any general laws or to deduce other laws from it. Rather, it is comparable to the method followed in the discipline of history, that is, arranging concrete events in an order, which may sometimes take the form of causal explanation. In other words, the inference may be deduced from the conditions (situations) stated previously. As a result, we may be able to evaluate a similar event, occurring at a different time, in the light of this analysis. However, they do not claim any predictive power, and hence these studies are not classically scientific. In addition, when there are chance occurrences, explanations and predictions are impossible, since contingent factors can influence natural processes and impede the natural order.

6.1.2 Case study II

Goudge puts forward a model of causal explanation in natural history (1958: 194–202) with the purpose of justifying the relevance of this method for that of the scientific method (that is, of physics). In this model, he uses a piece of reasoning related to the individual phenomenon of developing limbs in the case of amphibians. The reasoning he applies proposes a theoretical pattern composed of (1) accepted statements of facts (for example, the Devonian, the period in which the amphibians originated, was a time of seasonal droughts), (2) statements inferred from these statements of facts (at times the streams would cease to flow ... If the water dried up altogether and did not soon return ...) and (3) statements, which are plausible conjectures about various occurrences (the amphibians ... could crawl out of the shrunken pool, walk up or down the stream bed ... learn to linger about the drying pools ... etc.).

The author claims that the phenomenon in this pattern is connected in an orderly way to the states of affairs that led up to it. This model (theoretical pattern) necessitates a possible sufficient condition of the phenomenon to be explained; the plausibility of other events introduced into the pattern depends on the relevance they have to the overall sufficient condition as well as their compatibility with the general body of scientific knowledge and the internal coherence imposed by the sequential character of the total narrative. Goudge's example is a case in which the explanatory model does not claim to be deductive. The sequence of events is such that one cannot be deductively inferred from the other when we know it. Events specified do not constitute just the necessary condition. Logical relations among many of the component statements are merely conjunctive, not implicated. Hence, the author considers this explanatory pattern as more of a portion of a complex historical network with an enormous number of cross connections rather than as a causal chain of events. Therefore, he specifies the kind of study as narrative.

6.1.3 Case study III

There are cases of studying natural patterns that follow a rigorous scientific model, for example, a study conducted by Chettri et al. (2005: 235–43) on the relationship between bird communities and habitat in the Sikkim Himalayas. This study was conducted with the major purpose of identifying areas of significant conservation interest, and hence birds were selected as one of the taxa, which are efficient indicators for measuring and monitoring biological diversity. Thus, to understand bird community structures and their relationships with variations in vegetation types, this study importantly relates the bird community to changed habitats. As the first step, different vegetation types (different species types present in the closed and open forest canopy) and bird species diversity (that is, of various kinds) and richness (numbers) were taken as variables, and the relationship among these variables and between these variables were analysed. Finally, by making deductions from the relations between bird species and their habitat (in terms of plant species diversity), the relations between bird species and vegetation types were inferred.

In this case, instead of understanding a pattern through an exhaustive description, a process is studied by finding out the co-relation between certain factors (characteristics) that determine this pattern. These different factors are taken as the variables, the relationship among which is to be found out through the study. The samples of these variables will form the data to be analysed. The particular relations between these variables are then generalised by analysing the data and inferences are drawn from the results of these relations. Thus, this model seems to follow the scientific method, that is, deduction of laws from a general law, and hence is determinate in nature.

In the case studies just described, the first is a study of the biodiversity patterns in Amazonia that specifically explains the bipartite vegetation pattern on Marajo island. Data deduced from geological, geomorphological and paleo-ecological methods are examined to construct natural history. In the second study, Goudge's model of causal explanation in natural history is discussed. In the last example, the study conducted by Nakul Chettri et al., the correlation between different factors determining the observed patterns is established using deductive theorising. These studies exemplify how 'natural patterns' are analysed in varied ways.

6.2 Studies in human ecology: some representative examples

In this section, a new set of case studies is considered for the exemplification of human ecological inquiries. All of these studies are drawn from different disciplines or are interdisciplinary in the sense of using different methods that sometimes define a specific discipline (such as archaeology, geology, geography and so on). However, they all focus on the area that intersects human actions and their relation to environment in some determinate sense. Thus, these studies all have some relevance for delineating the methodology of human ecological discipline.

6.2.1 Case study I

The study of Amazonian environmental history made by Raffles and WinklerPrins (2003: 165–87) highlights the role of human beings in manipulating the Amazon basin, in spite of the prevailing conception that the local native Amazonians are part of nature and the physical environment of the region is largely unmodified by human intervention. In this study, the researchers present both new and previously published material on the manipulation of Amazonian landscapes by local populations. Here they try to substantiate the fact that Amazonians routinely intervene in fluvial systems and that these changes modify landscapes on a wide variety of scales. In addition, they argue that these practices have contributed to dramatic changes to regional landscapes, ecologies and social organisation in a manner consistent with that of terrestrial interventions. They made use of the descriptive study of Raffles as an evidence of how the residents of one community of the Amazon estuary have substantially changed the course, dynamics, volume and significance of local rivers and streams. They also describe new data collected by WinklerPrins near Santarem in the Lower Amazon, a site where local people take advantage of natural sedimentation processes to create land in the difficult conditions of the flood plain.

The researchers' main intention in this work is to provide a systematic account of fluvial manipulation in the Amazon region. With this purpose, they draw on bibliographic research, rely on personal communication with their colleagues and conduct fieldwork to present a range of examples that indicate the scope and variety of these interventions. The fluvial manipulations include the cutting of *furo* (stream) by fishermen, digging of drainage trenches and canals by cattle and buffalo ranchers, cutting of a series of passages called *valas* by *caboclos* (local term for Amazonians of rural origin) and so on. Hydrographic and biogeographical mappings form another source, providing information on regions in which fluvial manipulation occurs. In addition, they rely on the works of archaeologist Clark Erickson,[2] who brings evidence of large-scale, pre-Columbian water management, specifically raised fields and fish weirs; William Denevan's[3] geographical account, which draws on both archaeological and ethnohistorical sources to document fluvial interventions in this area; and also work by Erland Nordenskiold,[4] a Swedish anthropologist, who argues that the practice of canal-making was passed from indigenous Amazonians to their Jesuit administrators. It is also noted that in the lower reaches of the Amazon, it is extractive logging rather than agriculture that has driven large-scale fluvial management, as by the Dutch company BRUMASA during the 1970s and 1980s. Another human intervention documented by Denevan is the digging of 'river-connecting canals' that 'facilitate water travel by joining different river systems or lakes or by connecting areas of settlement with navigable streams' (1966: 74). Research reports and other evidence reveal the presence of government support in digging canals and streams during the second half of the nineteenth century.

The researchers point towards the vast differences between the ways in which the indigenous people manipulate the river, like the *valas* of Acre, and the later grand schemes (both government-supported and transnational) to create a transregional internal water way. This difference of scale, according to their analysis, is linked to structural changes like institutional context and social relations of the social life of the people. The most serious issue regarding the contemporary Amazonian landscape is shown to arise from the shift in the political interest of a section of the society, of both indigenous groups and outside people, to imagine the region as wilderness – a culturally empty natural space.

6.2.2 Case study II

Gadgil and Thapar (1990: 209–23) trace the history of the various stages in human life in the Indian Subcontinent, from the period of hunter–gatherers and shifting cultivators to the post-independence period. They critically look at the ecological changes that occurred in accordance with each successive stage. The information regarding the early history of the Indian subcontinent, before the arrival of the genus *homo*, is provided with the support of geological data. The earliest evidence of human occupation during the Pleistocene (middle) period appears in the form of artefacts such as hand axes. The life of hunter–gatherers and agricultural–pastoral people, and their ecological niche and social relationships, are all described based on speculation, which at times is supplemented by evidence from various places provided by other studies.

The assumed history of hunter–gatherer life shows that in this society, the material cycles are largely closed, and stable productive environments with relatively fixed territories would therefore be expected to develop cultural traditions of sustainable utilisation of their resource base. The social relationships of such a tribe would be governed by kinship and mutual help, and social and religious practices were developed to safeguard the health of their resource base. However, environmental changes might have occurred due to both over-utilisation of resources and climatic changes. The food crisis resulted due to climatic change, and the creeping back of the forest cover associated with it is assumed to have prompted hunting–gathering societies to domesticate animals and cultivate plants, which gathered momentum some 10,000 years ago.[5] The husbanding of plants and animals radically transformed the life of agricultural–pastoral people in terms of stored surplus harvests, which encouraged material flow over spatially much larger scales. Thus, this group would tend to be stronger than the hunter–gatherer, eventually eliminating them from regions suitable for agricultural–pastoral people. The agricultural settlements developed over the period 6000 to 1000 BC along the watercourse in the drier tracts of northwestern India, the Indus Plains and the Deccan Peninsula.[6] The first urban civilisation of the Indian subcontinent embraced a very wide region of the northwest. Archaeological evidence suggests that this culture was familiar with the use of the plough. The agricultural surpluses produced by cultivation permitted the establishment of many towns, where the surplus served to promote further processing and exchange of materials, as well as artisanal and trade activities. It is found that iron, along with fire, made it possible to bring the middle Gangetic plains under intensive agricultural–pastoral colonisation, with wet-paddy cultivation as a key element.[7] Indeed, fire-based sacrificial ritual and extensive agricultural settlements might have catalysed the destruction of forests and wildlife and the suppression of tribal peoples during the agricultural colonisation of the Gangetic plains. Buddhism, Jainism and later the Hindu sects may have been responses to the need for a reassertion of ecological prudence once the more fertile lands were brought under cultivation. British rule radically changed the focus of the country's resource use pattern from production of a variety of biological resources for local consumption to the production of a few commodities largely for export. The resulting ecological squeeze was accompanied by disastrous famines and epidemics between the 1860s and the 1920s. The counter-flows to tracts of intensive agriculture have reduced such disasters since independence. However, these are quite inadequate to balance state-subsidised outflows of resources from the hinterlands. These imbalances have triggered serious environmental degradation and tremendous overcrowding of the niche of agricultural labour and marginal cultivators all over the country.

Information on the urban civilisation (Indus valley) – for example, use of the plough – is derived from archaeological evidence, geological changes and palaeobotany etc. Archaeological evidence of important discoveries like iron, fire etc. helped researchers to assume the kind of society that succeeded thereafter. From these details, they construct the ways in which people interacted with nature and how the resources were utilised. History of the later periods is written with support of the data available from various writings and documents. This study, while it describes how the human beings in the hunting–gathering stage led towards a settled and organised life, also presupposes their needs at each stage and the ways they might have been satisfied. Based on this, the authors evaluate the technologies they used and their relations with nature, i.e., whether it is co-operative or exploitative. Though mainly historical, the study concerns ecological aspects of human actions and may be termed human ecological in a broad sense.

6.2.3 Case study III

A study was conducted to understand landscape changes (that is, significant decrease in herbaceous cover and an increase in forests) that occurred in the Madres and Mont Coronat in the Eastern Pyrenees, France, between 1953 and 2000 (Roura-Pascual, 2005: 252–61). The researchers' intention was to probe into underlying interaction processes between environment and society that would contribute to understanding these dynamics.

The landscape history of the Madres has shown that during the period between 1861 and 1914, the population decreased considerably, leading to abandonment of the furthest cultivated lands and a decrease in livestock. Consequently, shrubs and trees started to encroach upon open areas. From 1945 to 1965, croplands were transformed into rangelands and herds became the only managers of the territory. At the end of the 1960s, population decline was at its greatest and land abandonment became more pronounced.[8] At the end of the 1980s, some new breeders established themselves in the study area, favoured by mountain policy, which in 1995 applied the European Commission's Agri-environment measures. Against this background, this study aimed to quantify vegetation changes in the study areas between 1953 and 2000 and to understand the influences of socio-ecological constraints (environmental factors, pastoral structures and public policy in mountain areas) on these changes.

The main source of the study was photographs taken more or less every 15 years, since 1953, the manual interpretation of which is done for the evaluation of landscape changes.[9] The photographs were used to produce vegetation maps to monitor landscape dynamics. Years were chosen according to the availability and quality of the images, in order to reconstruct the history of the area. To correct the errors in mapping, other cartography of the region was used and field surveys were made to correct the photo interpretation. Landscape data were analysed using Map Info and Excel Software. Variables like total area, total number of patches and mean patch size were taken into consideration. They also took into account the aspect of fire frequency and pastoral and administrative units to understand landscape changes in the study area. Finally, to estimate the relationships between socio-ecological conditions and landscape dynamics, the vegetation maps were overlapped with the cartography of different socio-ecological factors.

The following relations between the variables were analysed:

(1) The relationship between landscape dynamics and environmental variables (including north-facing zones, north-facing slopes, south-facing zones and seasons like winter, summer and others); for this purpose, they examined aspect and pastoral units.
(2) Because of the relationship between the disturbance regime and landscape patterns,[10] the zones suffering regression in the lignification process were compared with data on the fires that occurred in these areas (prescribed burnings and wildfires), and from the results, the researchers found spatial similarities between them.

The general trends inferred from the study are:

(1) The grass lands decreased (by 73% across 47 years) whereas forests (dense forests increased by 50% and open forests by 13%, although there was a slight decrease for the period 1953–1969), woodland and shrub land increased during the study period.
(2) The high loss of grass lands until 1988, which resulted due to changes in exploitation systems and rural emigration. The latter helped to transform the traditional agro-pastoral system into a pastoral one.
(3) Forested areas, particularly dense forest, increased throughout the period because of land abandonment and reduction in forestry activities. The greatest increase of dense forest was between 1953 and 1969 due to lignification of open forests. These open forests were the result of extensive woodcutting practices carried out until the 1950s for charcoal production and mine exploitation. Since then the introduction of new combustibles, especially gas for cooking and heating, and a more competitive economy have induced the decline and transformation of forest activities.

The study revealed that there are also local landscape particularities explained by their own socio-environmental constraints. In other words, the capacity of traditional activities to adapt to new socio-economic transformations and land ownership is shown as the most relevant factor in determining local landscape dynamics. For example, in the southeastern part of the study area, the cattle dealers kept herds of ovines and owned the most productive lands, which made it possible to maintain pastoral activity and therefore an open landscape. In the northern area, traditional activities underwent profound changes, for instance transition from ovine to bovines or caprines, underutilisation of the productive fields and economically non-viable forest activity. This favoured a more pronounced lignification in the northern areas and reduced the erosion process. In the southwestern part (Olette), farming activity was residual at the beginning of the 1950s and the most important activity was the cutting of forests, which has continued to be practised until now. It is concluded that as a result of these interactions between environment and society, the landscape of the Madres presents a mosaic composed of natural, semi-natural and cultural environments that change in space and time, while a high level of natural and cultural diversity is maintained.[11]

Though this study relies on methods like cartography for understanding the landscape patterns, in large part it followed the model of a scientific study, that is, the relationship between various factors is determined by generalising from the samples. In addition to this landscape study, there are indications of society's transformation from an earlier agro-pastoral society into pastoral one. There are also intimations of adapting society to the new socio-economic changes, which is reflected in their further engagement with forests.

6.2.4 Case study IV

In his work on 'Progressive Contextualization' (1983: 265–81), Vayda criticises the methods used in human ecology research such as commitment to long-term, expensive projects; rigid frameworks; traditional disciplinary goals; and unwarranted assumptions about the stability and purposiveness of units or systems. In this article, he presents an alternative method of explaining human activities in nature or people–environment interactions by placing them within progressively wider or denser contexts; this includes a rationality principle, comparative knowledge of context and the principle of pursuing the surprising. According to the rationality principle, those who engage in the activities or interactions of concern to the researcher are rationally using their knowledge and available resources to achieve whatever their aims are in the situations in which they find themselves.

These ideas are discussed regarding a study conducted to understand the forces contributing to deforestation in the Indonesian province of East Kalimantan on the island of Borneo. To achieve this goal, the investigators started by focusing on specific activities, such as timber cutting performed by specific people in specific places at specific times. They then traced the causes and effects of these activities outwards. The authors observed that in doing so, they remained committed to the holistic premise that adequate understanding of problems can be gained only if they are seen as part of a complex of interacting causes and effects. The advantages of this kind of approach are shown as following:

(1) It does not see as important a unit of research, that is, the researchers do not assume that people–environment interactions are necessarily components or expressions of some previously defined system. It allows the researchers the

freedom to gain understanding by proceeding empirically to put the interactions in question into context – for example, sometimes by going far beyond the boundaries of a nation–state or island.

(2) It avoids unwarranted assumptions about the stability of units or systems. The study under consideration does not take any social unit, such as ethnic groups, communities or tribes, as research units in advance on the assumption that they necessarily have key roles in managing resources or effecting people–environment interactions, since there is the possibility of shifting the units from one to the other during the period of study. For example, in East Kalimantan, along with Bugis migrants who cleared logged-over forests, they found ad hoc coalitions of urbanites and rural people from various ethnic groups making quick profit from cutting and selling timber. Researchers claim that progressive contextualisation, starting with specific activities such as timber cutting performed by specific people in specific places at specific times, enabled them to see and understand the activities and impacts of such coalitions and did not require them to make any assumptions about their performance or stability.

(3) They do not rely on strict quantitative methods; rather, they opted for ad hoc combinations of qualitative and quantitative methods for discovering variable complexes of interacting causes and effects within which people–environment interactions occur. The former includes informal interviewing and participant observation and the latter surveys of household composition, time allocation and land use. They point out that having the freedom to rely on their experiential judgement without the constraint of following routines of rigorous methods meant the investigators in the project could, for example, start by noting such activities as tree cutting or forest clearing by migrant farmers and Dayak tribesmen in East Kalimantan; they could then, in contextualising the activities, proceed to relate them to various factors.

Another point they highlight, as the second guiding principle, is the comparative knowledge of contexts, that is, the knowledge of another context in which apparently similar interactions take place. Thus, for example, their attempt to put forest clearing by Bugis migrants in East Kalimantan into context was guided by their knowledge of the historical contexts in which Bugis migrants in other provinces of Indonesia have cleared forests in order to grow perennial commercial crops.[12] A related point mentioned is that though comparative knowledge of contexts is an infallible guide, the knowledge may be misdirected, which may create a surprise; this very fact of surprise could form an important impetus for pushing inquiries in the direction of the new knowledge. For example, their research on forest conversion by shifting cultivators in the vicinity of Samarinda was guided at the outset by the knowledge that such conversion was proceeding in other parts of the world at the hands of rootless, landless people. However, they found instead that much of the timber cutting attributed to shifting cultivators in the Samarinda vicinity was being done by better-off, enterprising rural and urban residents interested more in making profits from land speculation and from cutting and selling timber than from farming. This approach also does not insist on disciplinary boundaries; rather, they argue that viewing from different disciplines will allow for a better understanding of the problem.

(4) In using progressive contextualisation, the researchers hope that they can directly communicate to the policy makers with questions of concern. Broad issues, such as how to reduce deforestation and how to make forest management in East Kalimantan more effective as well as environmentally and socio-economically sounder, can be readily broken down into more specific ones about timber cutting and other activities or interactions. The researchers point out that it is these activities or interactions that become the objects of progressive contextualisation, in the sense that the approach leads to concrete findings about who is doing what, why they are doing it and with what effects, and the very concreteness of the findings means that the policy implications are quite concrete, too, and readily communicable to the policy makers.

(5) Possible theoretical significance of the results is shown to have derived from the fact that it is suited to studying unstable and transitory phenomena as well as stable and persistent ones. By contributing to giving flux and process more of their due, its use can lead to a better-balanced view of life and the world.

The researchers do not claim any rigid frameworks, either spatial or temporal, with which the contextualisation can proceed. However, they argue that to insist on the rigorous methods of the experimental sciences will be counter-heuristic, taking into consideration the kaleidoscopic nature of the contexts, especially where people–environment interactions would occur. But in cases where other things being equal, they find it better to use the rigorous methods of the experimental sciences than not to use them.[13]

6.2.5 Case study V

This study by Muldavin examines how the economic policies of privatisation and deregulation in China were followed by exploitation of labour and resources (2003: 227–59). It provides a political ecological analysis in a socialist context: changes in political economy and patterns of resource use explain increases in environmental degradation. Political ecology emphasises the importance of political economy in understanding environmental degradation – a historically informed attempt to understand the role of the State, the social relations within which land users are entwined and resulting environmental changes. This study exposes the role of transnational agencies like the World Bank, which played a major part in destroying self-reliance in agriculture in China[14] and putting this country onto a production treadmill by introducing agricultural reforms between 1978 and 1995. The author challenges the claim of the World Bank that China is its number one success story for post-socialist transition by focusing on its environmental costs and, more generally, on the whole question of sustainability, which the World Bank defines strictly using short-term economic indicators of growth.

The agrarian reforms in China are the product of a new system, which is said to have emerged from a synthesis of command socialism and advanced capitalism – which seems to combine the worst of both systems, particularly in terms of environmental impacts and long-term sustainability. The nature of this system is described as simultaneously a cross between NIC, a Soviet-style industrialisation model, an export-led growth model, an import-substitution model and a sweat shop/subcontractor to the world's corporations. The reform period has brought a shift from collective to decollectivisation i.e., the dismantling of the commune system in rural areas and a move towards a market-oriented economy. The effects rural reforms have on long-term sustainability of production can be understood from the three arenas of change: (1) in the predominant mode of economic coordination (2) in the base unit of production and (3) in accompanying decision-making strategies and goals.

The most significant shift was from a predominantly planned economy to the decisiveness of market forces. Simultaneously, there is the introduction of the Household Responsibility System.[15] There has been a shift from collective production to the household and individual, an immense and historically important transfer of control over resources and means of production. The transfer corresponds to a shift in control at the highest level of government. Finally, a shift in decision-making strategies and goals supplants long-term egalitarian collective gains with short-term decision-making, combined with increased social inequalities: a shift from long- to short-term outlooks results from the transfer of risk in production from collectives to households and individuals. The result of this complex of changes was increased insecurity and instability throughout the economy, with immediate and ongoing material returns necessary for political legitimation for the State and a strategic reform for further reforms. Another important change was the restructuring of collective industries by transferring the collective assets to the elite or transforming political power into material inheritable wealth,[16] which resulted in the rapid social stratification in many rural areas. Thus, the control has been taken up by a few peasant households who were transformed into a new class of small industrial and commercial entrepreneurs. Communes gave up much of their regulatory power while distancing themselves from the risks associated with production. Privatisation undermines important revenue sources for the state, while leaving high expectations for delivery of social welfare services and infrastructure maintenance. The resulting gap between expectations and service provision undermines state authority and legitimacy.

China has developed a system of agriculture with sustainable organisational forms in farming and with proper maintenance and improvement of cultivated land across thousands of years. After liberation in 1949, there were efforts to turn back the desert, converting wastelands into productive croplands, reforesting denuded hillsides, controlling rivers and bringing water to arid lands. The large-scale organisation of labour by collectives, focused on building necessary bio-physical infrastructure, was very much responsible for the long-term gains in production that were achieved. During the reform period (1978–1995), grain production was at

'Human ecology' as a discipline **193**

its peak in 1984, but it fluctuated between 1984 and 1989.[17] Stagnation in grain production resulted from decreasing profitability, a subsequent shift to cash crops and unsustainable production practices. Much of the gain during the boom period (1978–1984) is attributed to technical factors of production, such as fertiliser application, rather than social reorganisation of production. Thus, problems associated with these technical factors loom large in subsequent periods of stagnation. When the state monopoly on agricultural inputs was lifted in the mid-1980s, the potential for huge profit in the black market undermined (many) of the expected benefits of freer input flows. In part, due to the long chain of middlemen, prices were so high that the already minimal profitability of grain production simply vanished. The trend during the reform period is to move away from historically more sustainable methods, compounded by economic changes favouring short-term decision-making and rapid utilisation of existing resources. The introduction of modern inputs to agriculture and the shift to cash crops such as oil seeds and tobacco, followed by an increased need for chemical fertilisers and pesticides, was characteristic of the reform period.

As a result, environmental problems like soil degradation, organic matter decline and water pollution occurred at a rapid rate, with overuse of fertilisers and chemical pesticides. Resource degradation took many forms, such as increased use of marginal lands, more intensive cropping patterns, increased and uncontrolled use of destructive chemical inputs, a decline in agricultural infrastructure investments, rapid exploitation of existing assets through industrialisation and accompanying pollution, land conversion and the rampant destruction of ecosystems through industrial mining and the search for construction materials. Muldavin finds that the possibility of a political ecological analysis in the Chinese context, focusing on long-term environmental effects, forces a re-evaluation of the impacts of short-term coping strategies under shifting regimes of accumulation – from plan to market, collective to individual, long-term to short-term. It also provides a framework for analysing indirect forms of resistance, such as claims by peasants on the state via 'natural' disasters.[18] The author recommends a hybrid framework combining aspects of political ecology and the new industrial geography, which allows a comprehensive multi-level analysis of environmental degradation.

As human ecological inquiries are of an interdisciplinary nature, the methods employed in research need not be specific to that discipline. In the many examples cited above, a wide range of methods was used. Case study one traces the Amazonian environmental history, which describes the role of human beings in fluvial manipulation in the Amazon region. In this study, different methods such as carbon dating and ethnography mappings of different kinds are implied where data has already been derived by using such methods. There, we find data from bibliographical research, fieldwork, hydrographic and biogeographical mappings, archaeology, geographical accounts drawing on archaeological and ethnohistorical sources, anthropology, economic history, political economy and so on. In case study two, Gadgil and Thapar examine the ecological changes that occurred at different stages in human life in the Indian Subcontinent; periods include that of shifting cultivators to post-independence. In this study, geological and archaeological data are mainly used. In the third study, landscape changes were linked to the interaction process between environment and social existence of humans for more or less 50 years. This study uses photo interpretation for quantifying vegetation mapping. Mapping errors were corrected by using other cartography of the region and field survey was used to correct photo interpretation. Vegetation maps were overlapped with cartography of different socio-ecological factors. The fourth study traces the forces that contributed to deforestation in the Indonesian province of East Kalimantan, the island of Borneo. In this study, an ad hoc combination of qualitative and quantitative methods was used for discovering variable complexes of interacting causes and effects within which the people–environment interactions occur. Qualitative methods here included informal interviewing and participant observation, and quantitative methods used were surveys of household composition, time location and land use. The fifth example is drawn from political ecology, which has already become an alternative approach to studying problems arising from human–environment interaction. It relates the increase in environmental degradation to changes in political economy and patterns of resource use in the context of agrarian reforms in China. Human ecology as a discipline can make a legitimate claim to this work. In this study, the human factors are the focus for its political–economic dimensions that have environmental implications.

6.3 Human ecology: methodological reflections

A consideration of the general methodological orientation of, and the specific discipline-based methods employed in, the works cited above would help us to imagine the discipline of human ecology on a broad base and recognise the inherently interdisciplinary character of human ecological endeavours. General methodological orientation concerns, as mentioned elsewhere in this part, the nature of the domain that is formed by the intersection of human activities and environment. Theorising the events that occur in this domain needs to consider the nature of human agency involved and the characteristic features of the environment that influence human actions and which in turn are susceptible to change due to human intervention. Obviously, a key notion that defines theorising on this domain is that of 'ecosystem', as suggested in the beginning of this chapter, derived from the study of ecology. In other words, the decisive step in theorising is taken by treating the area of human activities in an environment as forming one single interconnected whole. In making sense of the events occurring in this domain, the notion of ecosystem or rather interconnectedness can be used as a methodological tool, as a part of a frame of reference, which helps us to order the data about the field when we ask significant research questions about it. This approach will guide us to search for those features or aspects in the environment and human actions that are strongly correlated with or determine the events in question. However, it is a matter of methodological decision whether the principles and concepts used as a rule in connection with the ecosystem are to be used as rigidly as they were often employed in ecological studies. Yet it will be instructive to think of the equivalent of such principles in human ecological studies. Some of the ecological concepts are constitutive of the theory of ecosystem and therefore are directly relevant to studying the interconnectedness of problems arising in the domain of human ecology, such as the levels of biological organisation like food chains, food webs, trophic levels of community, populations, species and so on. Methodological use of such principles and concepts characteristically defines the inquiries in human ecology by limiting the cases the latter takes up for study. To ensure that this will not prevent inquiries from covering areas in which ecosystemic interconnectedness cannot be legitimately attributed, we should be wary of applying these notions rigidly in human ecological contexts. However, the notion of interconnectedness as such cannot be jettisoned. To clarify this point, one may refer to Vayda's innovative programme of progressive contextualisation in human ecology.

Although human ecology considers human agency and environmental factors in its explanatory work, it is about neither events in the social world nor environmental changes in the physical world. That is, the explanations do not properly belong to either social sciences or ecological or environmental sciences, as it was the case in the early history of human ecology. However, social theorising necessarily involves all those instances where explanation touches on causes and effects, in relation to human agency per se or connected to human agency in a causal chain. Innumerable factors that are conventionally considered in isolation in inquiries of independent social science disciplines enter into the account of human actions. Such factors are identified in theorising on social phenomena when they fall within the conventional boundaries of sociology, economics, political sciences and so on. However, the methodological orientation of the explanations thus obtained will not only differ along disciplinary lines but also vary according to the different frameworks used within the same discipline. This is not to claim that studies conducted on the same problem will yield always incompatible results if such studies use different frameworks. These studies may highlight different aspects of the phenomena and may look different in their conclusion, but may all illuminate the problem without contradicting each other. Our submission is that such differences in disciplinary terms as well as the theoretical framework are smoothly carried over to human ecological studies, when theorising on human ecological domain involves social theorising. That is, social theorising will not be characteristically different when it forms part of theorising in human ecology. Whatever theoretical debates about the nature of human agency exist in the social sciences, they will have similar repercussions in human ecological explanations. Therefore, the problem of theorising over domains that take human agency as a causal factor need not require separate treatment.

Political ecology, which arose partly as a critique of 'ecological anthropology' and 'cultural ecology', is a good example of how difference in a social theoretical framework is carried over to difference in 'human ecological studies'. Political ecology is a response to the theoretical need to integrate land use practice with local/global economy and is a reaction to the growing politicisation of the environment. The theoretical difference here is the awareness that the societies cultural ecologists studied were actually part of large, complex, open political economies like market and State involvement of various sorts, which in many cases undermined the ideas of equilibrium and homeostasis on which geographers and anthropologists had drawn. Although political ecology is broadly characterised by a political economical approach to ecological phenomena and thereby gives a different social theoretical thrust to explanation in the human ecological domain, the theoretical differences that exist in political ecology itself will lead to differences in explanation. The political ecology approach has been criticised for lacking historical depth (Peet and Watts, 2003: 12). If one accommodates an environmental history approach to political ecology it will yield different results. Political ecology is harnessed to a rather outdated view of ecology rooted in notions of stability, resilience and systems theory.[19] Botkin[20] and Worster[21] describe relatively new ecological concepts, which pose problems for the theory and practice of ecology. The shift from 1960s system models to the ecology of chaos, that is, chaotic fluctuations, disequilibria and instability, suggests that many previous studies of range management or soil degradation resting on simple notions of stability, harmony and resilience may have to be rethought (Zimmerer, 1994). On top of these, we also notice Escobar's version of post-structural political ecology, which acknowledges equally the cultural and the biological aspects. Now, if we treat political ecology as a specific social theoretical input to human ecology, the differences within political ecology itself will not make any differences to this claim. All these differences will reflect in human ecology. Political ecology is a consequence of the interpretation of 'human' in human ecology. It is a consequence of theorising on human agency. This is also the case with other frameworks such as structuralism, post-structuralism, reflexivism (constructive structuralism) and others.

The two foregoing observations concern the two components of human ecology: ecological and social scientific; the third major component is historical. In our discussion on the importance of the natural history approach to ecological studies, the historical component in ecology (and by definition, in human ecology also) is already acknowledged. Historical studies are primarily characterised by the application of historical methods to obtain data about the past events and to connect those data. Since any relevant data in human ecology is spread along a very long timescale, the historical method will be an essential part of its methodology, and at the level of theorising, the historical component has an important definitive role. In seeking interconnections between geographical features, other physical features of environment, flora, fauna and human organisations, policy decisions and actions along a specific timescale, it is a historical interconnection that is presupposed. What specific connections lead to changes in question is a matter of historical theorising, because the concrete events that come in succession, in linear or non-linear fashion, may be contingently connected. In such cases, explanation is description, and thus if an event is accounted for, it is historically done. When theory building is based on patterns discovered across different space and time, it may indicate ahistorical or synchronic explanations.

Human ecological explanation can be done on a higher order level, when its theorising is based on results of theorising in other disciplines, such as archaeology, geography, geology, anthropology, political economy or sociology. Such interlacing of explanations renders the human ecological study both theoretically exciting and technically intriguing. This also makes the methodology of human ecology more complex. When explanations from different disciplines touch upon a particular problem, one could use these explanations as raw material for further theory building with due care, supplementing them with new and necessary data.

Notes

1. The ecosystem is conceived here as interconnecting all the biotic and abiotic factors in the environment; any fluctuation at one level will result in both intended and unintended consequences at another level. But this conception does not presuppose an equilibrium on which ecological theories rested before the 1970s; rather, it presupposes that the different factors are interrelated in certain specific ways.
2. Erickson, C. 1980. 'Sistemas agrícolas prehispánicos en los Llanos de Mojos', *América Indígena*, 40, 731–55; 2000, 'An Artificial Landscape-Scale Fishery in the Bolivian Amazon', *Nature*, 408, 190–3, cited in Raffles, H. and WinklerPrins, Antoinette M. G. A. 2003, 'Further Reflections on Amazonian Environmental History: Transformations of Rivers and Streams', *Latin American Research Review*, 38(3), 176.
3. Denevan, W. 1966, 'The Aboriginal Cultural Geography of the Llanos de Mojos of Bolivia', in *Ibero-Americana*, 48, Berkeley, CA: University of California Press, 74–6, cited in Raffles and WinklerPrins, 2003: 176.
4. Nordenskiold, 1916, (Original in other language), 144–7, cited in Raffles and WinklerPrins, 2003: 176.
5. Hutchinson, J. et al. 1977, *Early History of Agriculture*, Oxford: Oxford University Press, 1977, cited in Gadgil, M. and Thapar, R. 1990, 'Human Ecology in India: Some Historical Perspectives', *Interdisciplinary Science Reviews*, 15(3), 212.
6. Possehl, G. L. (ed.), 1982, *Harappan Civilization*, New Delhi: Oxford and IBH; Dhavalikar, M. K. 1988, *The First Farmers of the Deccan*, Pune: Deccan College; Allchin, B. and Allchin, F. R. 1968, *The Birth of Indian Civilization*, Penguin Books. For these citations, see Gadgil and Thapar, 1990: 214.
7. Kosambi, D. D. 1970, *The Culture and Civilization of Ancient India in its Historical Outline*, New Delhi: Vikas, cited in Gadgil and Thapar, 1990: 214.
8. Becat, J. 1974, 67, (Original in other language), 1–59, cited in Roura-Pascual, N. 2005, 'Transformation of a Rural Landscape in the Eastern Pyrenees Between 1953 and 2000', *Mountain Research and Development*, 25(3), 254.
9. Dunn, C. P., et al., 1991, 'Methods for Analyzing Temporal Changes in Landscape Pattern', in Turner, M. G. and Gardner, R. (eds.), *Quantitative Methods in Landscape Ecology*, New York: Springer-Verlag, 173–98, cited in Roura-Pascual, 2005: 254.
10. Lloret, F., Calvo, E., Pons, X. and Diaz-Delgado, R. 2002, 'Wildfires and Landscape Pattern in the Eastern Iberian Peninsula', *Landscape Ecology*, 17, 745–59, cited in Roura-Pascual, 2005: 256.
11. Pino, J. and Roda, F. 1999, (Original in other language), 5–20, cited in Roura-Pascual, 2005: 259.
12. Lineton, J. 1975, 'Pasompe' Ugi': Bugis Migrants and Wanderers', *Archipel*, 10, 173–201, cited in Vayda, A. P. 1983, 'Progressive Contextualization: Methods for Research in Human Ecology', *Human Ecology*, 11(3), 273.
13. A study on 'Shifting Cultivation and Patch Dynamics' in an upland forest in East Kalimantan is cited, where they used rigorous quantitative methods. See Vayda, 1983: 273.

14 The Maoist development model of China included joint development of agriculture and rural industry supplemented by improved infrastructure, which would help to bring long-term productivity gains benefiting the entire community. The agricultural system was composed of a spectrum of organisational forms, from state farms to communes, and ranged from large-scale mechanised capital-intensive production on flat open plains, to small-scale non-mechanised labour-intensive production on narrow terraces. Communes and state farms were part of a national system planning; co-ordination was via top-down and bottom-up, communication and negotiation. See Gurley, J. G. 1976, *China's Economy and the Maoist Strategy*, New York: Monthly Review Press, cited in Muldavin, J. 2003 (1996), 'The Political Ecology of Agrarian Reform in China: The Case of Heilongjiang Province', in Peet, R. and Watts, M. (eds.), *Liberation Ecologies: Environment, Development, Social Movements*, London: Routledge, 230.
15 In this system, dismantling of the collective control of land is done through the introduction of subcontracting and land division, which parcelled out per capita shares of equivalent pieces of land to every family.
16 Cooper, M., 2003. 'Transformation in Contemporary Russia', lecture given at UCLA, 28 March, cited in Muldavin, 2003: 233.
17 Stone, B. 1988, 'Development in Agricultural Technology', *China Quarterly*, 116, 767–822, cited in Muldavin, 2003: 236.
18 Blaikie, P. et al., 1994, *At Risk: Natural Hazards, People's Vulnerability and Disasters*, London: Routledge, cited in Muldavin, 2003: 239.
19 Zimmerer, K. 1994, 'Human Geography and the New Ecology', *Annals of the Association of American Geographers*, 84(1), 108–25, cited in Peet and Watts, 2003: 12.
20 Botkin, D. 1990, *Discordant Harmonies*, New York: Oxford University Press, cited in Peet and Watts, 2003: 12.
21 Worster, D. 1977, *Nature's Economy*, Cambridge: Cambridge University Press, cited in Peet and Watts, 2003: 12.

PART V
Ethics, politics, knowledge
A multidimensional approach

CONCLUSION

This concluding part recommends a multidimensional approach to studying events in the domain of human ecology as well as solving problems arising thereof. This necessitates recollecting the aims and the main arguments of Parts II, III and IV to examine how they would contribute to the effort in this part to arrive at a multidimensional approach. In Part IV, we argued that human ecology has a unique domain to address. Moreover, we tried to show there that human ecology represents not just an interdisciplinary area of research but an independent discipline with the emphasis that it is inherently interdisciplinary in its methodology. The topic in Part IV forms an independent idea because the arguments in it can be established independently of and without reference to those in Part II and III. Similarly, Part II argues for the recognition of the irreducibility of the 'value' aspect of the domain constituted by human–environment interaction. Perspectives of different schools of ecological philosophies discussed there help us to problematise the events in the ecosphere in ways other than that of the scientific. The validity of the claims of such philosophies largely depend on the principles they recommend for making value judgements of the consequences or motives of human actions in the domain. Instead of concluding which claims are really valid, we confer on it a different significance: they all tell us about the question of value the domain throws up, which will not disappear or be answered once we explain the events in the domain. Part III is not a textual study; it is an arrangement of information contained in the reports on environmental struggles, on the basis of the antagonisms that characterise such struggles. What was internal to the relation between human agency and environment is now externalised in the form of environmental movements, that is, the political dimension of the domain. The arguments in this part also stand independently of other parts of the book from the point of view of the question it tries to raise.

This fifth part attempts to offer a different proposal, which could be established on the basis of the conclusions of the three previous parts alone. These arguments are now put together under one single topic to construct the core argument that the book intends to bring forth. The topic is the characterisation of the domain where human agency and environment interact. This domain, obviously, is the domain that human ecology, as a science, addresses or tries to explain. The explanation of this domain forms the topic of the fourth part. For a characterisation of the domain, however, a frame of reference or a theoretical framework, equipped to provide explanations of the events in the domain, may not be adequate. By the characterisation of the domain we mean drawing comprehensively the features of the domain with a view to capturing its significance to human actors, which is more than giving an objective account of it or merely addressing the epistemic dimension of the events that occur in nature, as done in Chapter 6. The question, how events occur in the domain, is of course a fundamental one to be asked to acquire an understanding of that domain. However, if human agency is involved in the occurrence of the events, then to understand those events as distinct from merely explaining them, we should know in what relation the human actions, events and the consequences of events stand to human (social) agents. This knowledge is not just an objective account of how events occur, but, in addition, what the events mean to the people involved. This knowledge, that is, understanding, informs part of the characterisation of the domain.

The task in this part is not to establish a theory with the above-mentioned particulars but rather to draw the outlines of such a theory, that is, a theory of understanding of the 'domain of human ecology'. The following points are to be noted as functioning as guidelines in this regard: (1) it is important, for a characterisation of the domain of human ecology, to know what it is, or the events in it are (referring to explanation), for humans, because the domain is constituted partly by human actions, 2) characterisation of the domain, understood in this sense, is of equal importance to humans as being able to account for the events taking place in the domain (as the causative agents), (3) scientific knowledge of the domain just mentioned does not cover the significance of the events happening in the domain, for humans, and (4) human beings have a pre-scientific (knowledge outside science) or post-scientific sense of the significance of their living and non-living environment and their own place in it (subjective) which is not dispelled when they can account for the events happening there (objective), including their own motives of actions. In other words, even when humans are aware of their role in causing some events to happen, they can study the events objectively by focusing on the explanatory part of the event, and this does not affect or reduce the significance of humans as affected agents.

Characterisation, then, can be an account of the domain in which significance and science (in the above sense) are properly synthesised to gain an understanding of the domain. *Understanding* applies to, and is relevant in, intersubjective contexts. To understand an action or a situation or an utterance or an event, one should know what it means and to whom. Eco-habitat *means* something to the people who live in it; actions, events and changes in it are of 'significance' to them. The inquirer needs to reconstruct this meaning empathetically. The significance of the eco-habitat is distinct and different from its objective properties, or the causal chains in which these properties are connected. A theory of understanding will represent the significant and objective features of the domain in a correct characterisation of the domain.

As mentioned elsewhere in this book, 'eco-habitat' is a key notion in the description of the domain of human ecology, that is, the domain where the interaction between humans and environment takes place. Though the notion is not derived from that of the 'ecosystem', which is central to ecology, 'eco-habitat' is conceivable only in a context of interconnectedness. If human actions or their consequences do not disturb the eco-habitat of human beings (at the local or global levels), the question of value or politics cannot be explicitly raised. A natural calamity can also affect the eco-habitat of a people. However, such cases, unless the causes of the disaster are traceable to human actions, they cannot be covered by human ecology. However, when human actions have some perceived or traceable impact on the events occurring in the domain of human ecology but are found to have no negative effect on the eco-habitat of the people concerned, then this instance is covered by human ecology (conservation efforts can be cited as an instance). In those instances, the value aspects of the events are not absent but are not normally brought to the notice of the human agents. When events occurring in the domain are perceived to be, and really are, normal, that is, they do not disturb the interconnectedness of the ecosystem, then that situation is valued for its own sake. What the science of ecology conceived of as the equilibrium of the system of interaction between living beings and their environment is valued for its normalcy, that is, subjectively by the human agents involved, without having any explicit theory of value from which it could be deduced. Whereas ecology has a theory of ecosystem that accounts for the equilibrium as well as the disturbance of this equilibrium (in most cases), this is felt by human agents in the form of their lived experience, as the normal course of events in their eco-habitat. For instance, when people in a locality suddenly find that the water in their wells is no longer drinkable because of the presence of a chemical, they perceive this as abnormal. This is an event that has a negative effect on their eco-habitat. What they have valued implicitly, in the sense of being normal, is now perceived to have been threatened. Value-dimension is involved in the situation in two senses. On the one hand, if some human actions have led to this situation (disturbance of eco-habitat), the value orientation of such agents can be viewed as insensitive to the value that eco-habitat has for the affected people. On the other hand, the affected people themselves had a value orientation towards the eco-habitat in the sense explained above.

It will be illuminating to see how 'the political' is implicated in such a situation. Not only clash of interests but also clash of values may lead to a situation in which eco-habitat problems become politically impregnated (environmental conflicts form a case in point). By clash of interests, we mean different agents come into conflict over the same resources. In a conflict of values, different groups confront each other on the basis of the different values they attribute to living or non-living parts of the environment. Sometimes the values and interests of one group, both of which are diametrically opposed to the values and interests of another group, may enter into conflict with each other. When their eco-habitat is disturbed, the affected people will find themselves in conflict with agents who initiated activities that led to such disturbances. In this context, we may speak of the dominant agents whose actions bring about negative changes in the eco-habitat of people who are the affected agents. Actions of the dominant agents relevant to our analysis are such that either (1) they are aware of the consequences of their actions or (2) they are not. When the disturbance of eco-habitat occurred as an unintended consequence of their actions, then the responsibility for their actions does not lie with them. But, if either they continue with the actions or do not find them to be wrong, they are held responsible for their actions. If they were aware of the consequences of the actions that led to the eco-habitat imbalance of the affected agents, then they themselves are responsible for the outcome of the actions. Dominant agents are those who, while responsible for their actions, enjoy the legal sanctions to act in the way they do or have powerful political clout for carrying on with their activities. In both senses the situation is politically implicated: in the first sense, by being legally entrenched in the polity; in the second sense, by being politically influential. In the case of affected agents, if they fight for their right to protect their eco-habitat, then that struggle is political in two senses: (1) if the situation arises because the laws of the land are silent or not clear about the legitimation of the actions of the dominant agents, then the struggle demands a change of situation through legislation and (2) if the actions of the dominant agents are not legally protected, but get support from and through political lobbying, then the affected agents can try to pressure the government by means of civil society movements to deliver justice to them.

Politics involves relations of power between agents with respect to their positions in the field in which they act. When the question of authorisation of resources arises in a field, the power relations between agents become strained. When such authorisation of resources is legally entrenched, the *political* describes the arrangement of institutions pertaining to the field. Resolving to keep the existing arrangement or recognising the need to change it can both arise from material interests of the agents as well as from their value orientation. In the context of eco-habitat, in most cases, the values the inhabitants attribute to the status quo of the eco-habitat and their interest in it are same. The political question in this context is whether the affected agents have the authority to make changes in the arrangement or to preserve the preferred one in their eco-habitat. It is simultaneously a question of whether the dominant agents have the authority to change the arrangement in the eco-habitat to suit their own interest.

The same instance of the disturbance of the eco-habitat can be viewed as an event that needs to be explained scientifically. This is the epistemic dimension of the event. Situating the event in a pattern of events can provide an explanation of why and how that particular event took place. Human ecology is specifically equipped to conduct research in this domain to provide explanation of events that take place there. Human ecology thus addresses the epistemic dimension of the domain. The question whether human ecology can give an account of the event in the domain without taking into account the political and value dimensions is a different one. The answer could be simpler than expected. Value orientation could enter into the explanation of the event as an antecedent condition of the actions that led to the event; the political nature of the actions also could be similarly treated. In both cases they enter into the description or explanation as objective references. Value judgements or political standpoints do not themselves form part of the account. When the human actions that led to the event in question are not directly linked to it, or their relation to it is not evident, a scientific account plays an important role in revealing this relation and thus identifying the causal chain. When the dominant agents are the prospective affected agents, then the consequences of their actions are also hidden from them. In such contexts the human ecological account can anticipate the consequences of the actions by predicting the event. In this respect, the function of the human ecological account is not substantially different from other natural and social sciences. The epistemic dimension is so crucial in the representation of the domain that without it a clear and distinct image of the event in question cannot be formed. Without such an image, it will not be clear how to figure out what happened in the case of an environmental change or issue.

An instance wherein the three dimensions discussed previously are implicated is exemplified as follows. In the conventional approach, while the possibilities of the construction of a dam in a particular place are usually studied depending on the geological and the geographical peculiarities of the region (mostly scientific), the issues that affect the people of the region often receive no proper consideration. This approach of the government will also be reflected in the strategies it adopts for tackling political (or environmental) struggles that might follow as a means of resistance to the government's decision to construct the dam. Generally, the struggle or the movement is not understood as a political problem, that is, as a problem internal to the policy adoption; rather, it is treated as a problem external to the decision-making process. In fact, the environmental struggle brings forth a number of relevant questions with a bearing on the questions of value (ethical) and political aspects. The question of value implies a worldview, an attitude towards nature and life of both the government and the people involved in an issue. The value dimension of the government is crucial in dealing with any environmental conflict, since this will determine the actions taken by the former towards the affected agents and dominant agents who are also parties in the issue. Typically, self-interests such as greed and the resulting instrumental approach of a few who have power over the weak influence the decisions, and this would have an adverse impact on the latter and on nature. Apart from that, there may be questions of political significance like the rehabilitation of those who are to be displaced, the actual benefits of the plan, justification regarding the sum spent for the project and the environmental cost compared to the actual social need, the political interests behind it and others which require careful scrutiny. Along with these, questions belonging to the knowledge realm prompt us to obtain an explanation about the social or environmental processes under discussion. That is, a detailed study about the issue in question will expose a pattern of the events that occurred both naturally and as motivated by human (social) agents, which will form an explanation for the present state of affairs. Hence, a study based on the value orientation of the people who form parties to the issue in question, an understanding of the socio-political contexts of the issue and an objective representation of the physical conditions of the issue would only provide us with the insights necessary for making a fair decision relevant to the situation and resolving the issue systematically, rather than technically managing it.

To conclude, for a characterisation of the domain of human ecology, these three analytically separable dimensions – value, political and epistemic – can be integrated into one single, comprehensive approach. Such an integral approach is necessary to understand what is going on in the domain, because the occurrences in the domain are entangled in human actions and therefore can occur as 'problems' internal to human life. Though this may not be true of all cases, in cases in which occurrences have direct consequences for the eco-habitat of human beings or at least affect the normal life of them, they are represented as problems that stand in need of urgent solution. Solution of such a problem triggers further human actions, this time subject to decision-making on the part of the agents concerned, the dominant, the affected and the arbitrator. Though in some cases the dominant agent could be government itself, usually it enters into the decision-making as an arbiter. The submission of Part V is that the data for the perusal of such arbitration, or decision-making, or policy-drafting can be provided by a characterisation of the domain, or events in the domain, outlined here. In many cases, the guidelines for making recommendations can ensue from such a characterisation. Therefore, what one may need for making policies that govern human actions in the domain in the context of problems arising in the domain is an understanding of what really goes on in that domain. Thus, the outline of the theory of understanding provided in this part of the book recommends a multidimensional approach to the study of the domain of human ecology.

BIBLIOGRAPHY

Aarssen, L. W. 1997. 'On the Progress of Ecology', *Oikos*, 80(1), 177–8.
Adams, C. C. 1935. 'The Relation of General Ecology to Human Ecology', *Ecology*, 16, 316–35.
Agarwal, B. 1998. 'The Gender and Environment Debate', in Keil, R., Bell, D. V. J., Denz, P. and Fawcett, L. (eds.), *Political Ecology: Global and Local*. New York: Routledge, 193–219.
Ali, S. 1997. *The Book of Indian Birds*. New Delhi: Oxford University Press.
Allchin, B. and Allchin, F. R. 1968. *The Birth of Indian Civilization*. Penguin Books.
Anon. 1982. *Undeclared Civil War: A Critique of the Forest Policy*. New Delhi: Peoples Union for Democratic Rights.
Applegate, R. D. 1999. 'Diversity and Natural History Observation in Ecology', *Oikos*, 87(3), 587–8.
Arndt, H. W. 1981. 'Economic Development: A Semantic History', *Economic Development and Cultural Change*, 29(3), 457–66.
Ashworth, W. B. Jr. 2000. 'Emblematic Natural History of the Renaissance', in Jardine, N., Secord, J. A. and Spary, E. C. (eds.), *Cultures of Natural History*. Cambridge: Cambridge University Press, 17–37.
Asian Development Bank. 1991. *Guidelines for Social Analysis of Development Projects*. Manila: ADB.
Asian and Pacific Women's Resource Collection Network. 1992. *Environment*. Kuala Lumpur: Asian and Pacific Development Centre.
AtKisson, A. 1989. 'Introduction to Deep Ecology', an interview with Zimmerman in *IN CONTEXT* # 22, Summer.
Baier, A. 1985. 'What Do Women Want in a Moral Theory', *Nous*, 19, 55–6.
Bapat, J. 2005. *Development Projects and Critical Theory of Environment*. New Delhi: Sage Publications.
Barikor-Wiwa, D. 1997. 'The Role of Women in the Struggle for Environmental Justice in Ogoni', *Cultural Survival Quarterly Issue*, 21(3), Fall, 46–9.
Barrows, H. H. 1923. 'Geography as Human Ecology', *Annals of the Association of American Geographers*, 13, 1–14.
Bartelmus, P. 1986. *Environment and Development*. London: Allen and Unwin.
Bauer, P. 2002. (1991). 'Foreign Aid: Central Component of World Development?' in Corbridge, S. (ed.), *Development Studies: A Reader*. New York: Oxford University Press, 359–68.

Beane, W. C. 1977. *Myth, Cult and Symbols in Sakta Hinduism: A Study of the Indian Mother Goddess*. Leiden: E. J. Brill.

Becat, J. 1974. 'La vallée d'Évol. Vivre en Haut Conflent', *Conflent*, 67, 1–59.

Behera, M. C. 2006. 'Introduction', in Behera, M. C. (ed.), *Globalising Rural Development: Competing Paradigms and Emerging Realities*. New Delhi: Sage Publications, 13–53.

Beinart, W. 1999. 'African History, Environmental History and Race Relations', Inaugural lecture delivered at the University of Oxford, 6 May, 9.

Bennett, J. W. 1996. *HE as Human Behavior: Essays in Environmental and Development Anthropology*. New Brunswick, NJ: Transaction Publishers.

Benton, L. M. and Short, J. R. 1999. *Environmental Discourse and Practice*. Wiley-Blackwell.

Berry, A. (ed.), 2003. *Infinite Tropics: An Alfred Russel Wallace Anthology*. New York: Verso.

Biehl, J. 1991. *Rethinking Ecofeminist Politics*. Boston, MA: South End Press.

Biehl, J. 1993. 'Dialectics in the Ethics of Social Ecology', in Zimmerman, M. (ed.), *Environmental Philosophy: From Animal Rights to Radical Ecology*. NJ: Prentice-Hall, 374–89.

Birch, C. and Cobb, J. 1981. *The Liberation of Life: From the Cell to the Community*. Cambridge: Cambridge University Press.

Blaikie, P., Cannon, T., Davis, I. and Wisner, B. 1994. *At Risk: Natural Hazards, People's Vulnerability and Disasters*. London: Routledge.

Blea, C. 1986. 'Animal Rights and Deep Ecology Movements', *Synthesis*, 23, 13–14.

Blewitt, J. 2008. *Understanding Sustainable Development*. London: Earthscan.

Bookchin, M. 1979. 'Ecology and Revolutionary Thought', *Antipode*, 10(3)/11(1), 21–32.

Bookchin, M. 1982. *The Ecology of Freedom: The Emergence and Dissolution of Hierarchy*. Palo Alto, CA: Cheshire Books.

Bookchin, M. 1986. 'Murray Bookchin: A Green Course', interview by Satish Kumar, *Resurgence*, 115, March/April, 10–13.

Bookchin, M. 1993. 'What Is Social Ecology', in Zimmerman, M. (ed.), *Environmental Philosophy: From Animal Rights to Radical Ecology*. NJ: Prentice-Hall, 354–73.

Bookchin, M. 1996a. *The Philosophy of Social Ecology: Essays on Dialectical Naturalism*. New Delhi: Rawat Publications.

Bookchin, M. 1996b. 'The Concept of Social Ecology', in Merchant, C. (ed.), *Key Concepts in Critical Theory Ecology*. New Delhi: Rawat Publications, 152–62.

Botkin, D. 1990. *Discordant Harmonies*. New York: Oxford University Press.

Boy, D. 2002. 'France', *Environmental Politics*, 11(1), Spring, Routledge, 64–5.

Browne, J. 2001. 'History of Biogeography', in *Encyclopedia of Life Sciences*. John Wiley and Sons Ltd. www.els.net.

Brulle, R. J. 2000. *Agency, Democracy and Nature: The U.S. Environmental Movement from a Critical Theory Perspective*. Cambridge, MA: MIT Press.

Bryant, R. L. and Bailey, S. 1997. *Third World Political Ecology*. London: Routledge.

Buckingham-Hatfield, S. 2000. *Gender and Environment*. London: Routledge.

Butler, J. 1990. *Gender Trouble, Feminism and the Subversion of Identity*. London: Routledge.

Callicott, J. B. 1980. 'Animal Liberation: A Triangular Affair', *Environmental Ethics*, 2, 324–5.

Card, C. 1985. 'Virtues and Moral Luck', Unpublished paper read at the American Philosophical Association Meeting in Chicago, Spring, 1–2.

Carew-Reid, J., Prescott-Allen, R., Bass, S. and Dalal-Clayton, B. 1994. *Strategies for National Sustainable Development*. London: Earthscan.

Carlassare, E. 1996. 'Essentialism in Ecofeminist Discourse', in Merchant, C. (ed.), *Key Concepts in Critical Theory Ecology*. New Delhi: Rawat Publications, 220–34.

Carr, S., Douglas, O. and Onyeagucha, U. 2001. 'The Ogoni People's Campaign over Oil Exploitation in the Niger Delta', in Thomas, A., Carr, S. and Humphrey, D. (eds.), *Environmental Policies and NGO Influence*. London: Routledge.

Carson, R. 1962. *Silent Spring*. India: The Other India Press.
Caswell, H. 1988. 'Theory and Models in Ecology: A Different Perspective', *Ecological Modeling*, 43, 33–44.
Catton, W. R. Jr. and Dunlap, R. E. 1978. 'Environmental Sociology: A New Paradigm', *The American Sociologist*, 13, 41–9.
Cheney, J. 1987. 'Eco-Feminism and Deep Ecology', *Environmental Ethics*, 9, Summer, 140 2.
Chettri, N., Deb, D. C., Sharma, E. and Jackson, R. 2005. 'The Relationship Between Bird Communities and Habitat: A Study Along a Trekking Corridor in the Sikkim Himalaya', *Mountain Research and Development*, 25(3), 235–43.
Cittadino, E. 1990. *Nature as the Laboratory, Darwinian Plant Ecology in the German Empire, 1880–1900*. New York: Cambridge University Press.
Clements, F. E. 1916. *Plant Succession*. Washington, DC: Carnegie Institution.
Collard, A. and Contrucci, J. 1988. *Rape of the Wild: Man's violence Against Animals and the Earth*. London: The Women's Press.
Collins, G. F. S. 1921. *Modifications in the Forest Settlements: Kanara Coastal Tract*, Part I. Karwar: Mahomedan Press.
Commoner, B. 1971. *The Closing Circle*. New York: Alfred A. Knopf.
Conkin, P. K. 2007. *The State of the Earth: Environmental Challenges on the Road to 2100*. Hyderabad, India: Universities Press (India) Private Limited.
Cooper, M. 2003. 'Transformation in Contemporary Russia', lecture given at UCLA, 28 March.
Cowen, M. P. and Shenton, R. W. 1996. *Doctrines of Development*. London: Routledge.
Cronon, W. 1983. *Changes in the Land: Indians, Colonists and the Ecology of the New England*. New York: Hill and Wang.
Crosby, A. 1988. 'Ecological Imperialism: The Overseas Migration of Western Europeans as a Biological Phenomenon', in Worster, D. (ed.), *The Ends of the Earth: Perspectives on Modern Environmental History*. Cambridge: Cambridge University Press, 103–17.
D'Eaubonne, F. 1996. 'The Time for Ecofeminism', in Merchant, C. (ed.), *Key Concepts in Critical Theory Ecology*. New Delhi: Rawat Publications, 174–97.
D'monte, D. 1991. *Storm over Silent Valley*. Ahmedabad: Center for Environment Education.
Daly, M. 1978. *Gyn/Ecology: The Metaethics of Radical Feminism*. Boston, MA: Beacon Press.
Dampier, W. 1982. 'Ten Years After Stockholm: A Decade of Environmental Debate', *Ambio*, 11(4), 215–31.
Darling, F. F. 1967. 'A Wider Environment of Ecology and Conservation', *Daedalus*, 96, 1003–19.
Darwin, C. 1859. *The Origin of Species*. New York: Appleton.
Denevan, W. 1966. 'The Aboriginal Cultural Geography of the Llanos de Mojos of Bolivia', in *Ibero-Americana*, 48. Berkeley, CA: University of California Press, 74–6.
Des Jardins, J. R. 2001. *Environmental Ethics: An Introduction to Environmental Philosophy*. Canada: Wadsworth.
Devall, B. and Sessions, G. 1985. 'Deep Ecology', *Resurgence*, 113, November/December, 18–21.
Devall, B. and Sessions, G. 1998. (1985). 'Deep Ecology', in Pojman, L. (ed.), *Environmental Ethics: Readings in Theory and Application*. New York: Wadsworth, 144–8.
Devi, T. V. Geetha. 2012. 'The "Political" Dimension in the Protest Movements of the Indigenous Groups', in Menon, V. (ed.), *Environment and Tribes in India: Resource Conflict and Adaptation*. New Delhi: IGRMS, Bhopal through Concept Publishing Company, 180–7.
Dhavalikar, M. K. 1988. *The First Farmers of the Deccan*. Pune: Deccan College.
Diehm, C. 2002. 'Arne Naess, Val Plumwood and Deep Ecological Subjectivity: A Contribution to the "Deep Ecology- Ecofeminism Debate"', *Ethics and the Environment*, 7(1), 24–38.

Dowie, M. 1995. *Losing Ground: American Environmentalism at the Close of the Twentieth Century*. Cambridge, MA: MIT Press.
Doyle, T. and McEachern, D. 1998. *Environment and Politics*. London: Routledge.
Dryzek, J. S. and Schlosberg, D. 1999. *Debating the Earth: The Environmental Politics Reader*. Oxford: Oxford University Press.
Du Pisani, J. A. 2006. 'Sustainable Development – Historical Roots of the Concept', *Environmental Sciences*, 3(2), June, 83–96.
Dubos, R. and Ward, B. 1972. *Only One Earth: The Care and Maintenance of a Small Planet*. New York: W. W. Norton & Company.
Duncan, O. D. 1959. 'Human Ecology and Population Studies', in Hauser, P. M. and Duncan, O. D. (eds.), *The Study of Population*. Chicago, IL: University of Chicago Press, 678–716.
Dunlap, R. E. and Catton, W. R. Jr. 1979. 'Environmental Sociology', *Annual Review of Sociology*, 5, 243–73.
Dunn, C. P., Sharpe, D. M., Guntenspergen, G. R., Stearns, F. and Yang, Z. 1991. 'Methods for Analyzing Temporal Changes in Landscape Pattern', in Turner, M. G. and Gardner, R. (eds.), *Quantitative Methods in Landscape Ecology*. New York: Springer-Verlag, 173–98.
Dyball, R. 2010. 'Human Ecology as Method', in Brown, V., Harris, J. and Russell, J. (eds.), *Tackling Wicked Problems with the Transdisciplinary Imagination*. London: Earthscan, 273–84.
Eaton, D. 2002. 'Incorporating the Other: Val Plumwood's Integration of Ethical Frameworks', *Ethics and the Environment*, 7(2), 153–80.
Economic and Political Weekly. 1985. 'Sabotaging Relief for Bhopal Victims' (Editorial), XX (27), July 6.
Edwards, M. 2008. (1989). 'The Irrelevance of Development Studies', in Chari, S. and Corbridge, S. (eds.), *The Development Reader*. New York: Routledge, 305–11.
Ehrlich, P. and Ehrlich, A. 1968. *The Population Bomb*. New York: Ballantine Books.
Eisler, R. 1988. *The Chalice and The Blade: Our History, Our Future*. San Francisco, CA: Harper & Row.
Elliott, L. 1998. *The Global Politics of the Environment*. London: Palgrave Macmillan.
Erickson, C. 1980. 'Sistemas agrícolas prehispánicos en los Llanos de Mojos', *América Indígena*, 40, 731–55.
Erickson, C. 2000. 'An Artificial Landscape-Scale Fishery in the Bolivian Amazon', *Nature*, 408, 190–3.
Escobar, A. 1992. 'Reflections on "Development": Grassroots Approaches and Alternative Politics in the Third World', *Futures*, 24(5), 411–36.
Escobar, A. 1997. 'Planning', in Sachs, W. (ed.), *The Development Dictionary: A Guide to Knowledge as Power*. Hyderabad: Orient Longman, 176–94.
Eyre, S. R. 1964. 'Determinism and the Ecological Approach to Geography', *Geography*, 49, (Part 4, 225), 369–76.
Fagerström, T. 1987. 'On Theory, Data and Mathematics in Ecology', *Oikos*, 50(2), 258–61.
Farber, P. 1982. 'The Transformation of Natural History in the Nineteenth Century', *Journal of the History of Biology*, 15(1), Spring, 145–52.
Ferguson, J. (with Larry Lohmann). 2008. (1994). 'The Anti-Politics Machine: "Development" and Bureaucratic Power in Lesotho', in Chari, S. and Corbridge, S. (eds.), *The Development Reader*. New York: Routledge, 322–31.
Fleming, D. 1972. 'Roots of the New Conservation Movement', *Perspectives in American History*, VI, 7–91.
Foley, G. 1988. 'Deep Ecology and Subjectivity', *The Ecologist*, 18(4/5), 119–22.
Foster, D. R. and Aber, J. D. 2004. *Forests in Time*. New Haven, CT: Yale University Press.
Foster, J. B. 2003. (2002). *Ecology Against Capitalism*. Kharagpur, India: Cornerstone Publications.
Foucault, M. 1972. *The Archaeology of Knowledge, and the Discourse on Language*. New York: Pantheon Books.

Fox, W. 1984. 'Deep Ecology: A New Philosophy of Our Time?' *The Ecologist*, 14(5–6), 194–200.
Fox, W. 1989. 'The Deep Ecology – Ecofeminism Debate and Its Parallels', *Environmental Ethics*, 11(1), 5–25.
Fox, W. 1990. *Towards a Transpersonal Ecology: Developing New Foundations for Environmentalism*. London: Shambhala.
Frank, A. G. 1995. 'The Underdevelopment of Development', in Corbridge, S. (ed.), *Development Studies: A Reader*. London: Arnold.
Gadgil, M. and Guha, R. 1992. *This Fissured Land: An Ecological History of India*. New Delhi: Oxford University Press.
Gadgil, M. and Guha, R. 1995. *Ecology and Equity: The Use and Abuse of Nature in Contemporary India*. New Delhi: Penguin Books.
Gadgil, M. and Thapar, R. 1990. 'Human Ecology in India: Some Historical Perspectives', *Interdisciplinary Science Reviews*, 15(3), 209–23.
Gale, F. P. and M'Gonigle, M. R. (eds.), 2000. *Nature, Production and Power: Toward an Ecological Political Economy*. Edward Elgar.
Gettys, W. E. 1940. 'Human Ecology and Social Theory', *Social Forces*, 18(4), 469–76.
Ghai, D. (ed.), 1994. *Development and Environment: Sustaining People and Nature*. Oxford: Wiley-Blackwell.
Gibbs, J. P. and Martin, W. T. 1959. 'Toward a Theoretical System of Human Ecology', *The Pacific Sociological Review*, 2(1), Spring, 29–36.
Giddens, A. 1979. *Central Problems in Social Theory: Action, Structure and Contradiction in Social Analysis*. London: Palgrave Macmillan.
Gilligan, C. 1982. *In a Different Voice: Psychological Theory and Women's Development*. Cambridge, MA: Harvard University Press.
Glaeser, B. 1995. *Environment, Development, Agriculture: Integrated Policy Through Human Ecology*. London: UCL Press Limited.
Glazebrook, T. 2002. 'Karen Warren's Ecofeminism', *Ethics and the Environment*, 7(2), 12–26.
Goldsmith, E. 1992. 'Economic Development: A False God', in Bahuguna, S., Shiva, V. and Buch, M. N. (Contributing Authors), *Environmental Crisis and Sustainable Development*. Dehra Dun: Natraj Publishers.
Goldsmith, E., Allen, R., Allaby, M., Davoll, J. and Lawrence, S. (eds.). 1972. 'A Blueprint for Survival', *The Ecologist*, 2(1).
Golley, F. M. 1987. 'Deep Ecology from the Perspective of Environmental Ethics', *Environmental Ethics*, 9(1), Spring.
Goode, J. P. 1904. 'The Human Response to the Physical Environment', *Journal of Geography*, 3, 333–43.
Goode, J. P. 1911. 'A College Course in Ontography', *Annals of the Association of American Geographers*, 1, 111.
Goodin, R. E. 1992. *Green Political Theory*. Polity Press.
Gottlieb, R. 1993. *Forcing the Spring: The Transformation of the American Environmental Movement*. Washington, DC: Island Press.
Goudge, T. A. 1958. 'Causal Explanations in Natural History', *The British Journal for the Philosophy of Science*, 9(35), 194–202.
Goulet, D. 1995. 'Authentic Development: Is it Sustainable?' in Trzyna, T. C. and Osborn, J. K. (eds.), *A Sustainable World: Defining and Measuring Sustainable Development*. Sacramento, CA: International Centre for the Environment and Public Policy, California Institute of Public Affairs.
Graham, L., Yackel-Adams, A. A. and Odell, E. A. 1999. 'Devaluation of Non-Experiments in the Current Ecological Paradigm', *Wildlife Society Bulletin*, 26(4), 1002–6.
Graham, M. H. and Dayton, P. K. 2002. 'On the Evolution of Ecological Ideas: Paradigms and Scientific Progress', *Ecology*, 83(6), 1481–9.

Grey, W. 1986. 'A Critique of Deep Ecology', *Journal of Applied Philosophy*, 3(2), 211–16.
Grey, W. 1993. 'Anthropocentrism and Deep Ecology', *Australian Journal of Philosophy*, 71(4), 463–75.
Griffin, S. 1978. *Woman and Nature: The Roaring Inside Her*. New York: Harper & Row.
Gross, M. 2004.'Human Geography and Ecological Sociology, The Unfolding of Human Ecology, 1890 to 1930 – and Beyond', *Social Science History*, 28(4), Winter, 575–605.
Guha, R. 1983. 'Forestry in British and Post-British India: A Historical Analysis', *Economic and Politic Weekly*, in two parts, 29 October, 1882–1896 and 5–12 November, 1940–48.
Guha, R. 1989. *The Unquiet Woods: Ecological Change and Peasant Resistance in the Himalaya*. New Delhi: Oxford University Press.
Guha, R. 2000. *Environmentalism: A Global History*. New York: Oxford University Press.
Guha, R. and Martinez-Alier, J. 1997. *Varieties of Environmentalism: Essays, North and South*. New Delhi: Oxford University Press.
Gurley, J. G. 1976. *China's Economy and the Maoist Strategy*. New York: Monthly Review Press.
Gurukkal, R. 1994. 'Ecological Perspective of Development', in Joy, K. P. (ed.), *Eco- Development and Nature Conservation*. New Delhi: AIACHE, 71–86.
Hall, C. A. S. 1988. 'An Assessment of the Historically Most Influential Theoretical Models Used in Ecology and the Data Provided in Their Support', *Ecological Modelling*, 43, 125–7.
Hannigan, J. A. 2000 (1995). *Environmental Sociology: A Social Constructionist Perspective*. New York: Routledge.
Hannigan, J. A. 2014 (1995). *Environmental Sociology: A Social Constructionist Perspective*. New York: Routledge.
Haq, G. and Paul, A. 2012. *Environmentalism Since 1945*. New York: Routledge.
Haque, M. S. 1999. 'The Fate of Sustainable Development Under Neo-Liberal Regimes in Developing Countries', *International Political Science Review*, 20(2), 197–218.
Hardin, G., 1968. 'The Tragedy of the Commons', *Science*, 162(3859), 1243–8.
Harle, V. 1978. *The Political Economy of Food*. Hants: Saxon House.
Hart, G. 2001. 'Development Critiques in the 1990s: *culs de sac* and Promising Paths', *Progress in Human Geography*, 24(4), 649–58.
Hawley, A. H. 1944. 'Ecology and Human Ecology', *Social Forces*, XXII, 398–405.
Hawley, A. H. 1968, 'Human Ecology', in David L. Sills (ed.), *International Encyclopedia of the Social Sciences*. Vol. 4. New York: The Macmillan Co. and the Free Press, 328–37.
Hayes, E. C. 1906. 'Sociological Construction Lines: V', *American Journal of Sociology*, 12, 45–67.
Hayes, E. C. 1908. 'Sociology and Psychology, Sociology and Geography', *American Journal of Sociology*, 14, 371–407.
Hayes, E. C. 1914. 'Effects of Geographic Conditions upon Social Realities', *American Journal of Sociology*, 19, 813–24.
Hays, S. 1997. 'From Conservation to Environment: Environmental Politics in the United States Since World War II', in Miller, C. and Rothman, H. (eds.), *Out of the Woods: Essays in Environmental History*. Pittsburgh, PA: University of Pittsburgh Press, 101–26.
Hirschman, A. O. 1967. *Development Projects Observed*. Washington, DC: Brooking Institution.
Hjelmar, U. 1996. *The Political Practice of Environmental Organizations*. Aldershot, UK: Avebury.
Hofstadter, R. 1963. *The Progressive Movement, 1900–1915*. Englewood Cliffs, NJ: Prentice-Hall.
Hope, A., Timmel, S. and Hodzi, C. 1984. *Training for Transformation: A Handbook for Community Workers*. Gweru: Mambo Press.
Horkheimer, M. and Adorno, T. 1972. *Dialectic of Enlightenment*. New York: Seabury Press.
Horvat, V. and Tomašević, T. 2011. 'Green Parties in Europe: Potential Routes of Future Development', *Scientific Review*, July/December, 15–29.
Humboldt, A. and Bonpland, A. 1807. *Essai sur la Géographie des Plantes*. Paris: F. Schoell.

Huntington, E. 1919. *World-Power and Evolution*. New Haven, CT: Yale University Press.
Hutchings, V. 1994. 'Support Your Local Village Green', *New Statesman and Society*, 7, 293, March 11, 20–2.
Hutchinson, J., Clark, G., Jope, E. M. and Riley, R. 1977. *Early History of Agriculture*. Oxford: Oxford University Press.
Jackson, C. 1995. 'Environmental Reproduction and Gender in the Third World', in Morse, S. and Stocking, M. (eds.), *People and Environment*. London: UGL Press, 109–30.
Jaggar, A. 1983. *Feminist Politics and Human Nature*. Totowa, NJ: Rowman & Allanheld.
Jardine, N., Secord, J. A. and Spary, E. C. (eds.), 2000. *Cultures of Natural History*. Cambridge: Cambridge University Press.
Jax, K. 2001. 'History of Ecology', in *Encyclopedia of Life Sciences*. John Wiley and Sons Ltd. www.els.net.
Jeffreys, K. 1995. 'Progressive Environmentalism: Principles for Regulatory Reform', *NCPA Policy Report* No. 194, June, 2.
John, B. 1999. *Environment and Social Theory*. London: Routledge.
Kalland, A. and Persoon, G. (eds.), 1998. *Environmental Movements in Asia*. Surrey: Curzon.
Keil, R., Bell, D. V. J., Denz, P. and Fawcett, L. (eds.), 1998. *Political Ecology: Global and Local*. New York: Routledge.
Khagram, S. 2005. *Dams and Development: Transnational Struggles for Water and Power*. New Delhi: Oxford University Press, 43–9.
King, A. and Schneider, B. 1993. *The First Global Revolution: A Report by the Council of the Club of Rome*. New Delhi: Orient Longman.
King, Y. 1983. 'The Ecology of Feminism and the Feminism of Ecology', *The Journal of Social Ecology*, Harbinger, 1(2), 16–22.
King, Y. 1996. 'Feminism and the Revolt of Nature', in Merchant, C. (ed.), *Key Concepts in Critical Theory Ecology*. New Delhi: Rawat Publications, 198–206.
Kingsland, S. 1995. *Modeling Nature: Episodes in the History of Population Biology*, 2nd edn. Chicago, IL: University of Chicago Press.
Knight, J. 1998. 'The Forest Grant Movement in Japan', in Kalland, A. and Persoon, G. (eds.), *Environmental Movements in Asia*. Surrey: Curzon, 110–30.
Koppes, C. R. 1988. 'Efficiency, Equity, Esthetics: Shifting Themes in American Conservation', in Worster, D. (ed.), *The Ends of the Earth: Perspectives on Modern Environmental History*. Cambridge: Cambridge University Press, 230–51.
Kormondy, E. J. and Brown, D. E. 1998. *Fundamentals of Human Ecology*. Pearson Education.
Kosambi, D. D. 1970. *The Culture and Civilization of Ancient India in its Historical Outline*. New Delhi: Vikas.
Krech, S., Mc Neill, J. R. and Merchant, C. (eds.), 2004. *Encyclopaedia of World Environmental History*. Vol. I. London: Routledge.
Kuzmiak, D. T. 1991. 'The American Environmental Movement', *The Geographical Journal*, 157(3), 265–78.
Lahar, S. 1991. 'Ecofeminist Theory and Grass Roots Politics', *Hypatia*, 6(1), 28–45.
Leopold, A. 1949. *A Sand County Almanac*. New York: Oxford University Press.
Levins, R. 1966. 'The Strategy of Model Building in Population Biology', *American Scientist*, 54, 421–31.
Lewis, M. 2003. *Inventing Global Ecology: Tracking the Biodiversity Ideal in India, 1945–1997*. New Delhi: Orient Longman.
Leys, C. 1996. *The Rise and Fall of Development Theory*. Bloomington, IN: Indiana University Press in Smelser, N. J. and Baltes, P. B. (eds.), 2001. *International Encyclopedia of Social and Behavioral Sciences*. Vol. 6. New York: Elsevier.
Lineton, J. 1975. 'Pasompe' Ugi': Bugis Migrants and Wanderers', *Archipel*, 10, 173–201.

Lippelt, H. 1991. 'The German Case: DIE GRUENEN, Short History-Basic Ideas', Paper presented to the Conference on Ecological Movements and Sustained Development in Latin America and Europe, Institute for Latin America Studies, University of London, November, 5.

Lloret, F., Calvo, E., Pons, X. and Diaz-Delgado, R. 2002. 'Wildfires and Landscape Pattern in the Eastern Iberian Peninsula', *Landscape Ecology*, 17, 745–59.

Loehle, C. 1983. 'Evaluation of Theories and Calculation Tools in Ecology', *Ecological Modeling*, 19, 230–47.

Lopes, P. and Begossi, A. (eds.), 2011. *Current Trends in Human Ecology*. Newcastle-upon-Tyne, UK: Cambridge Scholars Publishing.

Lorde, A. 1984. *Sister Outsider*. Freedom, CA: Crossing Press.

Luke, T. W. 1988. 'The Dreams of Deep Ecology', *Telos*, 65–92.

Luke, T. W. 1997. *Ecocritique: Contesting the Politics of Nature, Economy and Culture*. London: University of Minnesota Press.

Lundberg, P. 2004. 'Theoretical Ecology', in *Nature Encyclopedia of Life Sciences* Nature Publishing Group. www.els.net. doi:10.1038/npg.els.0003264.

Macfadyen, A. (ed.), 1974. *Advances in Ecological Research*. Vol. 8. London: Academic Press.

Macfadyen, A. 1975. 'Some Thoughts on the Behaviour of Ecologists', *The Journal of Ecology*, 63(2), 379–91.

Malinowsky, B. 1955. *Magic, Sciences and Religion*. Garden City, NY: Anchor Books.

Malthus, T. 1798. *An Essay on the Principle of Population*. London: J. Johnson.

Mamdani, M. 2000. 'Democratic Theory and Democratic Struggles (in Africa)', in Nnoli, O. (ed.), *Government and Politics in Africa – A Reader*. Harare: African Association of Political Science (AAPS) Books.

Marsh, G. P. 1864. *Man and Nature: Or, Physical Geography as Modified by Human Action*. New York: C. Scribner & Co.

Marten, G. G. 2001. *Human Ecology: Basic Concepts for Sustainable Development*. London: Earthscan.

Martin, C. 1986. 'The American Indian as Miscast Ecologist', in Schultz, R. C. and Hughes, J. D. (eds.), *Ecological Consciousness*. Washington, DC: University Press of America.

Mathur, H. M. 1995a. 'Introduction', in Mathur, H. M. (ed.), *Development, Displacement and Resettlement: Focus on Asian Experiences*. New Delhi: Vikas, 1–11.

Mathur, H. M. 1995b. 'The Resettlement of People Displaced by Development Projects: Issues and Approaches', in Mathur, H. M. (ed.), *Development, Displacement and Resettlement: Focus on Asian Experiences*. New Delhi: Vikas, 13–38.

McCormick, J. 1989. *Reclaiming Paradise: The Global Environmental Movement*. Bloomington, IN: Indiana University Press.

McKenzie, R. D. 1924. 'The Ecological Approach to the Study of the Human Community', *American Journal of Sociology*, 30, 287–301.

McKenzie, R. D. 1925. 'The Ecological Approach to the Study of the Human Community', in Park, R. E., Burgess, E. W. and McKenzie, R. D. (eds.), *The City*. Chicago, IL: University of Chicago Press, 63–79.

McLaughlin, A. 1995. 'The Heart of Deep Ecology', in Sessions, G. (ed.), *Deep Ecology for the Twenty-First Century*. Boston, MA: Shambhala, 85–93.

Meadows, D. H., Meadows, D. L., Randers, J. and Behrens, W. 1972. *The Limits to Growth*. New York: Universe Books.

Mellor, M. 2000. 'Nature, (Re) Production and Power: A Materialist Ecofeminist Perspective', in Gale, F. P. and M'Gonigle, R. M. (eds.), *Nature, Production and Power: Toward an Ecological Political Economy*. Edward Elgar, 105–17.

Mentis, M. T. 1988. 'Hypothetico-Deductive and Inductive Approaches in Ecology', *Functional Ecology*, 2, 5–14.
Merchant, C. 1992. *Radical Ecology*. New York: Routledge and Chapman and Hall Inc.
Merchant, C. 1993. 'The Death of Nature', in Zimmerman, M. E., Callicott, J. B., Sessions, G., Warren, K. J. and Clark, J. (eds.), *Environmental Philosophy: From Animal Rights to Radical Ecology*. NJ: Prentice-Hall, 268–83.
Merchant, C. (ed.), 1996. *Key Concepts in Critical Theory Ecology*. New Delhi: Rawat Publications.
Meyer, M. and Singh, N. 2006. 'Two Approaches to Evaluating the Outcomes of Development Projects', in Rowlands, J. (introduced by), Eade, D. (series ed.), *Development Methods and Approaches: Critical Reflections*. New Delhi: Rawat Publications, 240–8.
Mies, M. 1986. *Patriarchy and Accumulation on a World Scale: Women in the International Division of Labour*. London: Zed Books.
Mies, M. and Shiva, V. 1993. *Ecofeminism*. New Delhi: Kali for Women.
Moran, E. F. 2010. *Environmental Social Science: Human-Environment Interactions and Sustainability*. Hoboken, NJ: Wiley-Blackwell.
Morgan, W. B. and Moss, R. P. 1965. 'Geography and Ecology: The Concept of the Community and its Relationship to Environment', *Annals of Association of American Geographers*, 55, 339–50.
Morgan, W. B. and Moss, R. P. 1967. 'The Concept of the Community: Some Applications in Geographical Research', *Transactions of Institution of British Geographers*, 21–32.
Morse, S. and Stocking, M. (eds.), 1995. *People and Environment*. London: UGL Press.
Muldavin, J. 2003 (1996). 'The Political Ecology of Agrarian Reform in China: The Case of Heilongjiang Province', in Peet, R. and Watts, M. (eds.), *Liberation Ecologies: Environment, Development, Social Movements*. London: Routledge, 227–59.
Muller-Rommel, F. 1994. 'Green Parties Under Comparative Perspective'. Working Paper No. 99. Barcelona.
Muller-Rommel, F. 2002. 'The Lifespan and the Political Performance of Green Parties in Western Europe', *Environmental Politics*, 11(1), Spring, 1–16.
Muller-Rommel, F. and Poguntke, T. (eds.), 1995. *New Politics*. London: Dartmouth.
Mumford, L. 1931. *The Brown Decades: A Study of the Arts in America*. New York: Harcourt, Brace and Company.
Murickan, J., George, M. K., Emmanuel, K. A., Boban, J. and Prakash Pillai, R. 2003. *Development Induced Displacement: Case of Kerala*, A Joint Study by Indian Social Institute, Bangalore and Loyola college of Social Sciences, TVM. New Delhi: Rawat Publications.
Naess, A. 1984. 'Intuition, Intrinsic Value and Deep Ecology', *The Ecologist*, 14(5–6), 201–3.
Naess, A. 1987. 'Deep Ecology', interview by Stephen Bodian, *Resurgence*, 123, July/August, 13–14.
Naess, A. 1988. 'Deep Ecology and Ultimate Premises', *The Ecologist*, 18(4/5), 128–31.
Naess, A. 1992. 'Deep Ecology', *Resurgence*, 151, March/April, 22–3.
Naess, A. 1995a. 'The Deep Ecological Movement, Some Philosophical Aspects', in Sessions, G. (ed.), *Deep Ecology for the Twenty-First Century*. Boston, MA: Shambhala, 64–83.
Naess, A. 1995b. 'The Deep Ecology "Eight Points" Revisited', in Sessions, G. (ed.), *Deep Ecology for the Twenty-First Century*. Boston, MA: Shambhala, 213–21.
Naess, A. 1998a. 'Ecosophy T: Deep Versus Shallow Ecology', in Pojman, L. (ed.), *Environmental Ethics: Readings in Theory and Application*. New York: Wadsworth, 137–44.
Naess, A. 1998b. 'The Shallow and the Deep Long-Range Ecological Movement', in Pojman, L. (ed.), *Environmental Ethics: Readings in Theory and Application*. New York: Wadsworth, 134–7.
Nandy, A. 1986. *Introduction: Science, Hegemony and Violence*. United Nations University, Unpublished manuscript.

Nash, R. 1967. *Wilderness and the American Mind*. New Haven, CT and London: Yale University Press.
Nederveen Pieterse, J. 2001. *Development Theory: Deconstructions/Reconstructions*. New Delhi: Vistaar Publications.
Nihart, L. K. 2000. 'Natural History and the "new" Biology', in Jardine, N., Secord, J. A. and Spary, E. C. (eds.), *Cultures of Natural History*. Cambridge University Press, 426–43.
Nisbet, R. 1980. *History of the Idea of Progress*. London: Heinemann.
Nordenskiold, E. 1916. 'Die Anpassung der Indianer an die Verhältnisse in den Uberschwemungsgebieten in Südamerika', *Ymer*, 36(2), 138–55.
Norgaard, R. B. 1988. 'Sustainable Development: A Co-Evolutionary View', *Futures*, 20(6), December, 606–20.
Noss, R. F. 1996. 'The Naturalists are Dying off' (Editorial), *Conservation Biology*, 10(1), February, 1–3.
O'Neill, M. 2000. 'Preparing for Power: The German Greens and the Challenge of Party Politics', *Contemporary Politics*, 6(2), June, 165–84.
O'Riordan, T. 1971. 'The Third American Conservation Movement: New Implications for Public Policy', *Journal of American Studies*, 5, 155–71.
Obi, C. 2000. 'Globalization and Local Resistance: The Case of Shell versus the Ogoni', in Gills, B. (ed.), *Globalization and the Politics of Resistance*. New York: Palgrave Macmillan.
Obi, C. 2001. 'The Changing Forms of Identity Politics in Nigeria under Economic Adjustment: The Case of Oil Minorities Movement of the Niger Delta', Research Report No. 119, Nordiska Afrika institutet, Uppsala.
Obi, C. 2002. 'The Politics of the Nigerian Industry: Implications for Environmental Governance', in Osuntokun, A. (ed.), *Democracy and Sustainable Development in Nigeria*. Frankad Publishers for Friedrich Ebert Foundation.
Obi, C. 2005. 'Environmental Movements in Sub-Saharan Africa: A Political Ecology of Power and Conflict', Programme Paper no. 15 on Civil Society and Social Movements, United Nations Research Institute for Social Development, January.
Odum, E. P. 1971. *Fundamentals of Ecology*. Philadelphia: Saunders College Publishing.
OECD. 1989. Seminar Report, *Focus on the Future: Women and the Environment*. London: International Institute for Environment and Development.
Ordway, S. 1953. *Resources and the American Dream*. New York: The Ronald Press.
Park, R. E. 1918. 'Education in Its Relation to the Conflict and Fusion of Cultures: With Special Reference to the Problems of the Immigrant, the Negro and Missions', *Publications of the American Sociological Society*, 13, 38–63.
Park, R. E. 1936. 'Succession: An Ecological Concept', *American Sociological Review*, 1(2), 171–9.
Park, R. E. 1961. 'Human Ecology', in Theodorson, G. A. (ed.), *Studies in Human Ecology*. New York: Harper & Row, 22–9.
Park, R. E. and Burgess, E. W. 1921. *Introduction to the Science of Sociology*. Chicago, IL: University of Chicago Press.
Pearce, D. 1991. *Blueprint 2: Greening the World Economy*. London: Earthscan.
Peet, R. 1998. *Modern Geographical Thought*. Wiley-Blackwell.
Peet, R. and Watts, M. 2003. (1996). 'Liberation Ecology: Development, Sustainability and Environment in an Age of Market Triumphalism', in Peet, R. and Watts, M. (eds.), *Liberation Ecologies: Environment, Development, Social Movements*. London: Routledge, 1–45.
Peng, K. K. 1992. 'The Third World Environment Crisis: A Third World Perspective', in Bahuguna, S., Shiva, V. and Buch, M. N. (Contributing Authors), *Environmental Crisis and Sustainable Development*. Dehra Dun: Natraj Publishers, 15–30.
Pepper, D. 1984. *The Roots of Modern Environmentalism*. London: Croom Helm.

Peters, R. H. 1991. *A Critique for Ecology*. Cambridge: Cambridge University Press.
Petulla, J. M. 1977. *American Environmental History: The Exploitation and Conservation of Natural Resources*. San Francisco, CA: Boyd & Fraser Publishing Co.
Pielou, E. C. 1981. 'The Usefulness of Ecological Models: A Stock-Taking', *The Quarterly Review of Biology*, 56, 17–31.
Pinchot, G. 1947. *Breaking New Ground*. New York: Harcourt Brace.
Pino, J. and Roda, F. 1999. 'L'ecologia del paisatge: un nou marc de treball per a la ciència de la conservació', *Bulletí de la Institució Catalana d'Història Natural*, 67, 5–20.
Platt, J. R. 1964. 'Strong Inference', *Science*, 146, 347–53.
Plumwood, V. 1991. 'Nature, Self and Gender: Feminism, Environmental Philosophy and the Critique of Rationalism', *Hypatia*, VI (1), Spring, in Zimmerman, M. E., Callicott, J. B., Sessions, G., Warren, K. J. and Clark, J. (eds.), *Environmental Philosophy: From Animal Rights to Radical Ecology*. NJ: Prentice-Hall, 284–309.
Plumwood, V. 1994. *Feminism and The Mastery of Nature*. New York: Routledge.
Plumwood, V. 1996. 'Ecosocial Feminism as a General Theory of Oppression', in Merchant, C. (ed.), *Key Concepts in Critical Theory Ecology*. New Delhi: Rawat Publications, 207–19.
Pojman, L. (ed.), 1998. *Environmental Ethics: Readings in Theory and Application*. New York: Wadsworth.
Popper, K. R. 1959. *The Logic of Scientific Discovery*. New York: Basic Books.
Popper, K. R. 1961. *The Poverty of Historicism*. New York: Harper & Row.
Popper, K. R. 1983. 'A Proof of the Impossibility of Inductive Probability', *Nature*, 302, 687–8.
Possehl, G. L. (ed.), 1982. *Harappan Civilization*. New Delhi: Oxford and IBH.
Prasad, M. K., Parameswaran, M. P., Damodaran, V. K., Syamasundaran Nair, K. N. and Kannan, K. P. 1979. *Silent Valley Hydro-Electric Project: A Techno-Economic and Socio-Political Assessment*. Thiruvananthapuram: Kerala Sastra Sahitya Parishad.
Pratt, V., Howarth, J. and Brady, E. 2000. *Environment and Philosophy*. New York: Routledge.
Quarles vanUfford, P. and Giri, A. K. (eds.), 2003a. *A Moral Critique of Development: In Search of Global Responsibilities*. London: Routledge.
Quinn, J. A. 1939. 'The Nature of Human Ecology – Reexamination and Redefinition', *Social Forces*, 18, 161–8.
Quinn, J. F. and Dunham, A. E. 1983. 'On Hypothesis Testing in Ecology and Evolution', *The American Naturalist*, 122(5), 602–17.
Raffles, H. and WinklerPrins, A. M. G. A. 2003. 'Further Reflections on Amazonian Environmental History: Transformations of Rivers and Streams', *Latin American Research Review*, 38(3), October, 165–87.
Rahnema, M. 1988. 'A New Variety of AIDS and its Pathogens: Homo Economicus, Development and Aid', *Alternatives*, XIII, 117–36.
Rahnema, M. and Bawtree, V. (eds.), 1997. *The Post-Development Reader*. London: Zed Books.
Raina, V., Chowdhuri, A. and Chowdhuri, S. (eds.), 1999. (1997). *The Dispossessed: Victims of Development in Asia*. Hongkong: Arena Press.
Raju, S. 2003. 'Developmental Modernity: Man and Nature in the Discourse of Wealth and Labour', *Contemporary India*, 2(1), 45–74.
Rakestraw, L. 1972. 'Conservation History: An Assessment', *Pacific Historical Review*, XLI, 271–88.
Ramaseshan, R. 1984. 'Government Responsibility for Bhopal Gas Tragedy', *Economic and Political Weekly*, 19(50), December 15, 2109–10.
Rasmussen, K. and Arler, F. 2010. 'Interdisciplinarity at the Human-Environment Interface', *Danish Journal of Geography*, 110(1), 37–45.
Rees, J. 1990. (1985). *Natural Resources: Allocation, Economics and Policy*. London: Routledge.

Regan, T. 1981. 'The Nature and Possibility of an Environmental Ethic', *Environmental Ethics*, 3(1), 19–34.
Reiger, J. 1975. *American Sportsmen and the Origins of Conservation*. New York: Winchester Press.
Report of the Joint Committee set up by the Government of India and Government of Kerala. 1997 (1982). *The Silent Valley Hydro-electric Project: A Techno-Economic and Sociopolitical Assessment and Ecological Aspects of the Silent Valley*. Kochi: Kerala Sastra Sahitya Parishad (KSSP), 53–83.
Robinson, D. 1996. *Ogoni: The Struggle Continues*, World Council of Churches, Nairobi, Geneva and All Africa Conference of Churches.
Robson, B. T. 1969. *Urban Analysis*. New York: Cambridge University Press.
Rodda, A. 1993. *Women and the Environment*. London: Zed Books.
Rose, G. 1993. *Feminism and Geography: The Limits of Geographical Knowledge*. Cambridge: Polity Press.
Rosenzweig, M. L. 2003. *Win–Win Ecology: How the Earth's Species Can Survive in the Midst of Human Enterprise*. New York: Oxford University Press.
Rossetti, D. F. and De Toledo, P. M. 2006. 'Biodiversity from a Historical Geology Perspective: A Case Study from Marajo Island, Lower Amazon', *Geobiology*, 4, 215–23.
Roura-Pascual, N. 2005. 'Transformation of a Rural Landscape in the Eastern Pyrenees Between 1953 and 2000', *Mountain Research and Development*, 25(3), 252–61.
Sachs, W. 1990. 'On the Archaeology of the Development Idea', *Lokayan Bulletin*, 8(1), 7–36.
Sachs, W. 1997. 'Environment', in Sachs, W. (ed.), *The Development Dictionary: A Guide to Knowledge as Power*. New Delhi: Orient Longman Ltd, 35–50.
Sadik, N. 1992. *The State of World Population*. New York: United Nations Population Fund.
Salleh, A. K. 1996. 'Working with Nature: Reciprocity or Control?' in Zimmerman, M. E., Callicott, J. B., Sessions, G., Warren, K. J. and Clark, J. (eds.), *Environmental Philosophy: From Animal Rights to Radical Ecology*. NJ: Prentice-Hall, 310–19.
Sandbach, F. 1980. *Environment, Ideology and Policy*. Oxford: Basil Blackwell.
Sangvi, S. 2002. *The River and Life: People's Struggle in the Narmada Valley*. Mumbai: Earth Care Books.
Sarkar, S. 1986. 'The Green Movement in West Germany', *Alternatives*, XI, 219–54.
Saro-Wiwa, K. 1995. *A Month and a Day: A Detention Diary*. Lagos: Penguin Books.
Sayers, S. and Osborne, P. (eds.), 1990. *Socialism, Feminism and Philosophy: A Radical Philosophy Reader*. London: Routledge.
Schimper, A. F. W. 1903 (1898). *Plant Geography upon a Physiological Basis*. Revised and edited by Percy Groom and Isaac Balfour. Oxford: Clarendon Press.
Schmid, C. F. 1939, 'The Ecological Method in Social Research', in Young, P. V. (ed.), *Scientific Social Surveys and Research*. New York: Prentice-Hall.
Schmid, C. F. 1988. 'Research Techniques in Human Ecology', in Young, P. V. and Schmid, C. F., *Scientific Social Surveys and Research: An Introduction to the Background, Content, Methods, Principles and Analysis of Social Studies*. New Delhi: Prentice Hall of India Pvt Ltd., 432–71.
Schnaiberg, A. 1972. 'Environmental Sociology and the Division of Labor', Department of Sociology, Northwestern University, mimeograph.
Schnore, L. F. 1961. 'The Myth of Human Ecology', *Sociological Inquiry*, 31, 128–39.
Schrepfer, S. 1983. *The Fight to Save the Redwood: A History of Environmental Reform, 1917–1978*. Madison, WI: University of Wisconsin Press.
Schuurman, F. J. 1993. 'Introduction: Development Theory in the 1990s', in Schuurman, F. J. (ed.), *Beyond the Impasse: New Directions in Development Theory*. London: Zed Books, 1–48.

Scoones, I. 1999. 'New Ecology and the Social Sciences: What Prospects for a Fruitful Engagement?' *Annual Review of Anthropology*, 28, 479–507.
Scott, J. C. 2008. (1998). 'Seeing Like a State: Conclusion', in Chari, S and Corbridge, S (eds.), *The Development Reader*. New York: Routledge, 297–304.
Sen, G. (ed.), 1992. *Indigenous Vision, Peoples of India: Attitudes to the Environment*. New Delhi: Sage Publications.
Sessions, G. 1979. 'Spinoza, Perennial Philosophy and Deep Ecology', Paper presented to the first national "Reminding" Conference (Philosophy, Where Are You?), Dominican College, San Raphael, CA, 29 June–4 July.
Sessions, G. (ed.), 1995. *Deep Ecology for the Twenty-First Century*. Boston, MA: Shambhala.
Sheth, P. 1997. *Environmentalism: Politics, Ecology and Development*. New Delhi: Rawat Publications.
Shiva, V. 1991. *Ecology and the Politics of Survival: Conflicts over Natural Resources in India*. New Delhi: Sage Publications.
Shiva, V. 1992. 'Women's Indigenous Knowledge and Biodiversity Conservation', in Sen, G. (ed.), *Indigenous Vision, Peoples of India: Attitudes to the Environment*. New Delhi: Sage Publications, 205–9.
Shiva, V. 1996. 'Development, Ecology and Women', in Merchant, C. (ed.), *Key Concepts in Critical Theory Ecology*. New Delhi: Rawat Publications, 272–80.
Shiva, V. 2011. (1988). *Staying Alive: Women, Ecology and Survival in India*. New Delhi: Kali for Women.
Silveira, S. J. 2001. 'The American Environmental Movement: Surviving Through Diversity', *Boston College Environmental Affairs Law Review*, 28(2), Article 7, 499–500.
Simon, D. 1997. 'Development Reconsidered: New Directions in Development Thinking', *Geografiska Annaler*, 79B(4), 183–201.
Skolimowski, H. 1988. 'Eco-Philosophy and Deep Ecology', *The Ecologist*, 18(4/5), 124–7.
Small. A. W. and Vincent, G. E. 1894. *An Introduction to the Study of Society*. New York: American Book Co.
Smelser, N. J. and Baltes, P. B. (eds.), 2001. *International Encyclopedia of Social and Behavioral Sciences*. Vol. 6. New York: Elsevier.
Smith, F. M. 1952. 'Experimental Methods in Population Dynamics: A Critique', *Ecology*, 33(4), 441–50.
Stone, B. 1988. 'Development in Agricultural Technology', *China Quarterly*, 116, 767–822.
Strong, D. H. 1988. *Dreamers and Defenders – American Conservationists*. London: University of Nebraska Press, 83.
Sundar, N. 1998. 'Asna Women: Empowered or Merely Enlisted?' in Kalland, A. and Persoon, G. (eds.), *Environmental Movements in Asia*. Surrey: Curzon Press, 227–49.
Sutton, F. X. 1989. 'Development Ideology: Its Emergence and Decline', *Daedalus*, 118(1), 35–58.
Taylor, P. W. 1986. *Respect for Nature: A Theory of Environmental Ethics*. Princeton, NJ: Princeton University Press.
Theodorson, G. A. (ed.), 1961. *Studies in Human Ecology*. New York: Harper & Row.
Thomas, K. 1983. *Man and the Natural World, 1500–1800 (Changing Attitudes in England)*. London: Penguin Books.
Thornthwaite, C. W. 1940. 'The Relation of Geography to Human Ecology', *Ecological Monograph*, 10(3), 343–8.
Tokar, B. 1988. 'Social Ecology, Deep Ecology and the Future of Green Political Thought', *The Ecologist*, 18(4/5), 132–41.
Trainer, F. E. 1985. *Abandon Affluence!* London: Zed Books.

Udall, S. L. 1963. *The Quiet Crisis*. New York: Halt Rinehart and Winston.

United Nations (UN). 1992. *Results of the World Conference on Environment and Development: Agenda 21*, UN Doc. A/CONF.151/4. New York: United Nations.

United Nations (UN). 1993. *Report of United Nations Conference on Environment and Development*, Rio de Janeiro, 3–14 June, 1992. Vol. 1: Resolutions adopted by the conference. New York: United Nations.

United Nations Commission on Environment and Development (UNCED). 1992. *Agenda 21*. New York: United Nations.

United Nations Development Program (UNDP). 1996. *Human Development Report*. New York: Oxford University Press.

Van Wyck, P. C. 1997. *Primitives in the Wilderness: Deep Ecology and the Missing Human Subject*. New York and Albany: State University of New York Press.

Varley. G. C. and Gradwell, G. R. 1970. 'Recent Advances in Insect Population Dynamics', *Review of Entomology*, 15, 1–24.

Varma, R. 1874. *Our Industrial Status*, Trevandrum Debating Society. Cottayam, Trivandrum: CMS Press.

Vayda, A. P. 1983. 'Progressive Contextualization: Methods for Research in Human Ecology', *Human Ecology*, 11(3), 265–81.

Von Wright, G. H. 1997. 'Progress: Fact and Fiction', in Burgen, A. et al. (eds.), *The Idea of Progress*. Berlin: Walter de Gruyter, 1–18.

Wapner, P. 1996. *Environmental Activism and World Civic Politics*. New York: State University of New York Press.

Ward, B. and Dubos, R. 1972. *Only One Earth: The Care and Maintenance of a Small Planet*. New York: W. W. Norton & Company.

Ward, L. F. 1903. *Pure Sociology*. New York: Palgrave Macmillan.

Warming, E. 1909. (1895). *Oecology of Plants: An Introduction to the Study of Plant Communities*, trans. and ed. Percy Groom and I. B. Balfour. Oxford: Clarendon Press.

Warren, C. 1998. 'Symbols and Displacement: The Emergence of Environmental Activism on Bali', in Kalland, A. and Persoon, G. (eds.), *Environmental Movements in Asia*. Surrey: Curzon Press, 179–204.

Warren, K. J. 1987. 'Feminism and Ecology: Making Connections', *Environmental Ethics*, 9(1), 3–20.

Warren, K. J. 1993a. 'The Power and the Promise of Ecological Feminism', in Zimmerman, M. E. (ed.), *Environmental Philosophy: From Animal Rights to Radical Ecology*. NJ: Prentice-Hall, 320–41.

Warren, K. J. 1993b. 'Introduction', in Zimmerman, M. E. (ed.), *Environmental Philosophy: From Animal Rights to Radical Ecology*. NJ: Prentice-Hall, 253–67.

Warren, K. J. 2000. *Ecofeminist Philosophy: A Western Perspective on What It Is and Why It Matters*. New York: Rowman & Littlefield.

Watts, M. 1983. *Silent Violence: Food, Famine and Peasantry in Northern Nigeria*. Berkeley, CA: University of California Press.

Weber, T. P. 1999. 'A Plea for a Diversity of Scientific Styles in Ecology', *Oikos*, 84(3), 526–9.

Wehr, K. (ed.), 2011. *Green Culture*. London: Sage Publications.

Weiner, J. 1995. 'On the Practice of Ecology', *Journal of Ecology*, 83, 153–8.

Wheeler, W. M. 1910. *Ants: Their Structure, Development and Behavior*. New York: Columbia University Press.

White, C. L. and Renner, G. T. 1935. *Geography: An Introduction to Human Ecology*. New York: Appleton.

White, R. 1985. 'American Environmental History: The Development of a New Historical Field', *Pacific Historical Review*, 54(3), 297–335.

Whiteside, K. H. 2002. *Divided Natures: French Contributions to Political Ecology*. Cambridge, MA: MIT Press.
Williams, L., Roberts, R. and Mcintosh, A. 2012. *Radical Human Ecology: Intercultural and Indigenous Approaches*. Ashgate.
Williamson, J. 1993. 'Democracy and the Washington Consensus', *World Development*, 21(8), 1329–36.
Willis, K. 2005. *Theories and Practices of Development*. London: Routledge.
Wilson, E. O. 1992. *The Diversity of Life*. Cambridge, MA: Harvard University Press.
Wong, A. 1998. 'The Anti-Tropical Timber Campaign in Japan', in Kalland, A. and Persoon, G. (eds.), *Environmental Movements in Asia*. Surrey: Curzon Press, 131–50.
World Bank. 1994. *Making Development Sustainable: The World Bank Group and the Environment*. Washington, DC: World Bank.
World Commission on Environment and Development (WCED). 1987. *Our Common Future*. Oxford: Oxford University Press.
Worster, D. 1977. *Nature's Economy: The Roots of Ecology*. San Francisco, CA: Sierra Club Books.
Worster, D. 1988. *The Ends of the Earth: Perspectives on Modern Environmental History*. Cambridge: Cambridge University Press.
Worster, D. 1995. (1977). *Nature's Economy: A History of Ecological Ideas*. Cambridge: Cambridge University Press.
Young, G. L. 1974. 'Human Ecology as an Interdisciplinary Concept: A Critical Inquiry', in Macfadyen, A. (ed.), *Advances in Ecological Research*. Vol. 8. London: Academic Press, 1–105.
Zimmerer, K. S. 1994. 'Human Geography and the "New Ecology": The Prospect and Promise of Integration', *Annals of the Association of American Geographers*, 84(1), 108–25.
Zimmerman, E. W. 1951 (revised edition). *World Resources and Industries*. New York: Harper & Row.
Zimmerman, M. E. 1987. 'Feminism, Deep Ecology and Environmental Ethics', *Environmental Ethics*, 9(1), Spring, 21–44.
Zimmerman, M. E., Callicott, J. B., Sessions, G., Warren, K. J. and Clark, J. (eds.), 1993. *Environmental Philosophy: From Animal Rights to Radical Ecology*. NJ: Prentice-Hall.

Web/online sources

(Anonymous). 'Conservation, Preservation and Environmental Activism: A Survey of the Historical Literature'. www.cr.nps.gov/history/hisnps/NPSThinking/nps-oah.htm-48k.
Beck, R. and Kolankiewicz, L. 2001. 'The Environmental Movement's Retreat from Advocating U.S. Population Stabilization (1970–1998), A First Draft of History, "Causes 3 & 4"', June. www.mnforsustain.org/beck_environmental_movement_retreat_long3_causes2.htm.
Kendlebacher, 'A New World Order: Deep Ecology and Mental Environment', 69. www2.uah.es/iuen/friends_of_thoreau/documents_pdf/Julia%20Kendlebacher/Chapter%203_2.pdf.
Lewis, D. 2005. 'Anthropology and Development: The Uneasy Relationship'. http://eprints.lse.ac.uk/archive/00000253.
Light, A. 'Technology, Democracy and Environmentalism – On Feenberg's Questioning Technology'. www.abdn.ac.uk/philosophy/endsandmeans/vol4no2/ light.shtml.
Trumbore, S. A. 1996. 'A Case Against Deep Ecology', Unitarian Universalist Fellowship of Charlotte County, February 25. www.cyberstreet.com/trumbore/sermons/s624htm; www.audubon.org/nas/history.html-29k.

INDEX

Aarssen, L. W. 177
Aboriginal Tasmanians 60
Adams, C. C. 155
Africa 16, 28, 85, 86, 129–30; Movement for the Survival of the Ogoni People (MOSOP) 130–4
Agarwal, B. 56
AMDAL Commission 127, 128
American Antiquities Act 20
American conservationism 17
American conservation movement 21
American Ornithological Union 18
anarchism 29
anthropocentrism 67
anti-pollution movement, Gujarat 141–3
anti-tropical timber campaign 112–14
Arler, F. 7
Arndt, H. W. 83
Asia 16, 28, 85
Audubon Society 18
Australian Green party 145

Bali projects, movement against 125–9
Barrows, H. H. 158
Bauer, P. 91
Begossi, A. 7
Bennett, J. W. 6
Bentham, J. 35
'big D' development 90
biocentric equality 38, 39, 43, 44
biological sex 56
biospherical egalitarianism 38, 40–2
Birch, C. 39

Blueprint for Survival, A 30
Bookchin, M. 67–72, 74
Brandis, D. 16
Bretton Wood Conference 90
Brown, D. E. 7
Burgess, E. W. 154

Callicott, J. B. 41
capitalism 60
Carlassare, E. 55, 56
Carson, R. 30
causal relations 168
characterisation of the domain 3, 4, 10, 13, 151, 202, 203, 206
Chemical Oxygen Demand (COD) 142
Cheney, J. 41
Chettri, N. 183
Chicago school of sociological human ecologists 157
China 192
'Chipko' movements 110–11
Christian Franciscanism 36
Clean Air Act, 1970 32
Clements, F. E. 176
Closing Circle, The 30
Club of Rome 33–4
Coal Smoke Abatement Society 18
Coastal Zone Management Act 32, 33
Cobb, J. 39
Cochin China 19
Commoner, B. 30
Commons Preservation Society 17
conceptual-level engagement 100–3; deep ecology 100–1; ecofeminism 102–3;

reform environmentalism 100; social ecology 103
conflict resolution 42, 66
conservation movement 15, 16; American invention 16; legacy of 23
conservation/preservation dichotomy 23
constructionism 56
consumerism 51
counterculture 29
Cowen, M. P. 84
cultural conduciveness 22
cultural feminists 62

Daly, M. 55
Dayton, P. K. 176
D'Eaubonne, F. 59, 61, 62
decision-making 61, 66, 105, 205
deep ecology 4, 8, 9, 13, 14, 23, 36–52, 65, 66, 81, 100–2
deep ecology movement 13, 14, 36–52, 100–1; analysis 51–2; philosophical approach of 51
Devall, B. 43, 48
developmental modernity 93
development context, environment 83–99; development idea, trajectory 83–8; development interventions, nature and human life 88–95; environmental movements, emergence of 95–6
development ideas 4
Devil's Tower National Monument, Wyoming 20
dialectical naturalism 69
diversity of obligations 42
domain of human agency–environment interaction 3, 47, 74, 81, 102, 104, 151, 162, 194, 201, 203
domain of human agency–environment intersection 3, 10, 11, 151, 152, 194
domain of human ecology 3, 5, 6, 8, 11, 36, 51, 147, 162, 195, 201, 202, 203, 206
dominant agents 204
Dowie, M. 23
Dubos, R. 30
Duncan, O. D. 160
Du Pisani, J. A. 83
Dyball, R. 6

Earth Day 32
Earth First! 101
eco-communities 44
ecofeminism 9, 13, 14, 52–67, 102–3; analysis 67; ecofeminist solution 62–7
eco-habitat 202–4, 206
ecological anthropology 195

ecological degradation 24
ecological egalitarianism 39
ecological inquiry 156
ecological problems 68
ecology as science, status of: critical summary 175–7; making of ecology, historical perspective 169–75; methodological issues 163–6; models in ecology 166–9
economic 'aid' 91
economic development 83
economic failure 22
economic laissez-faire 17
Edwards, M. 92
efficiency school 17
Ehrlich, A. 31
Eisler, R. 58
Elton, C. 173, 176
Endangered Species Act, 1973 33
environment, defined 5–6
environmental catastrophes 32
Environmental Defense Fund 35
environmental degradation 64
environmentalism 16
environmental issues 24, 37; political dimension of 81–2
environmental movement 24
environmental movements, 'political' in 103–43; anti-pollution movement, Gujarat 141–3; biodiversity concern 105–9; deforestation and livelihood issues 109–16; development and displacement issues 116–34; people/state *versus* industry 141–3; people *versus* state 105–34; people *versus* state and industries 134–41; union carbide corporation, movements against 138–41; wood-based industry, movements against 134–8
environmental problems 6, 64, 67
Environmental Protection Agency (EPA) 32
environmental scenario: conservation movements 21–2; nineteenth-century conservation movement 15–20; preservation movements 21–2; of twentieth century 15–27
Environmental Social Science 7
environmental thought systems: conceptual-level engagement 100–3; deep ecology movement 36–52; ecofeminism 52–67; environmental movements, 'political' in 103–43; political process, 'political' in 143–7; reform environmentalism 28–36; social ecology 67–75; 'value' dynamics in 28–79
epistemic dimension 5, 202, 204, 205

Index

equity 17
Escobar, A. 90
'Essay on the Geography of Plants' 171
ethical conception, international relations 35
ethical dimension 5, 35, 73, 74
ethics 13–14; of freedom 73
Europe 25, 28, 85
explanatory framework 5

factor-by-factor approach 166
Fagerström, T. 167, 168
failure of 'development' model 92
Federal Water Pollution Control Act 1972 32
feminist environmentalism 56
Ferguson, A. 84, 91
feudalism 60
Fight for Conservation, The 21
Finnish Green League 144
Fischer, E. 59
Foley, G. 40
Fontenelle 84
Footpaths 17
Forest and Herbiage Protection Act 19
Forest Grant Movement 114–16
Forest Tree Act 19
'fountain of life' 22
Fox, W. 39
Frank, A. G. 85
French Forestry School, Nancy 20
Friends of the Earth (FoE) 35
Futehally, Z. 106

Gadgil, M. 185, 193
General Agreement on Tariffs and Trade (GATT) 90
Generelle Morphologie 154
German Green party 144
Gettys, W. E. 159
Gibbs, J. P. 156, 159
Gilligan, C. 62, 67
Glaeser, B. 7
global industrialisation 16
globalisation policies 4
Goode, J. P. 153
Gottlieb, R. 23
Goudge, T. A. 183
Graham, M. H. 176
Great Depression period 22
Greenpeace 35
Green party 82, 143–7
Green political parties 143–7; analysis 145–7

green projects 88
Green Revolution 87
Grey, W. 47, 49
Grinnell, G. B. 18
Grisebach, A. 172, 176
Gross National Product (GNP) 83
Gujarat Ecology Commission (GEC) 142
Gujarat Pollution Control Board (GPCB) 141, 142
Gurukkal, R. 89, 93

Haeckel, E. 19, 154
hard biocentrism 48
Hardin, G. 31
Hart, G. 90
Hawley, A. H. 156, 158
Hayes, E. C. 154
Heidegger, M. 36
Hjelmar, U. 17, 19
holistic perspective 11
Homestead Act of 1862 16
Household Responsibility System 192
human actions: ecological significance of 4
human actors 3
human agency–environment interaction 3
human agency–environment interacting sphere 6, 8, 10
human agency–environment interface 7, 11
human agency–environment intersection 3, 10, 11, 151, 152, 194
Human Development Index (HDI) 86
human ecological imagination 153–63; critical summary 161–3
human ecology 3–11, 36, 51, 147, 151–98, 201–6; case studies 184–94
human ecological theorising 5
human–environment interactions 4, 8, 10, 13, 81, 104, 201
Human Exceptionalism Paradigm (HEP) 160
human-induced environmental issues 4
humanity, collective values of 34
human–nature dualism 5, 65
human–nature relationship 51
hypothetico-deductive mould 164

India 16, 109–10; Narmada, victory of oustees 124–5; Save Narmada movement 116–23
Indian Forest Act 19
'indistinguishability' thesis 65
Indonesia: movement against Bali projects 125–9
inductive approach 165

Industrial Revolution 53, 89
Inland Waterways Commission 20
interdisciplinary methodology 7, 152, 184, 193, 201
International Monetary Fund (IMF) 90
intrinsic value 38, 40
Introduction to the Science of Sociology 154
Introduction to the Study of Society, An 153
involuntary relocation 96

Jan-Jagaran Yatra 119
Jan Vikas Sangarsh Yatrai 120
Japan 28, 112
Japan Tropical Forest Action Network (JATAN) 112, 113

Khedut Mazdoor Chetna Sangath (KMCS) 118
knowledge 151–2, 202
Koppes, C. R. 16
Kormondy, E. J. 7
Kropotkin, P. 30

Lake District Defence Society 17
Latin America 85, 86
Leopold, A. 18
'Limits to Growth, The' 33
Lok Adhikar Sangh 119
Lopes, P. 7
Lorde, A. 54, 55
Lotka–Volterra population models 167
Lovins, A. 35
Luke, T. W. 40, 44, 46, 48, 49, 51

Macfadyen, A. 168, 169
McKenzie, R. D. 158
McLaughlin, A. 38, 46, 47, 50
making of ecology, historical perspective 169–75; biogeography, role of 170–1; methodological shift 172–3; natural history 169–70; natural patterns, revival of 175; new ecology 173–4; plant ecology, origin of 171–2; theoretical ecology 174
Malinowsky, B. 49
Malthusian theory 31
Man and Nature: Or, Physical Geography as Modified by Human Action 15
Manav Adhikar Yatra 121
man/woman dichotomies 52
Maradia Hatao Ladat Samiti 142
Marsh, G. P. 15
Marten, G. G. 6
Martin, W. T. 156, 159

Medawar and Popper 166
Mellor, M. 57
Merchant, C. 53
methodological reflections 181–98; human ecology 194–7
Mies, M. 59, 64, 95–6
modern agricultural practices 49
modern environmentalism 30
modern environmental movement 25, 28
modernisation theory 85
Moran, E. F. 7
Morgan, W. B. 159
Morris, W. 17, 30
Moss, R. P. 159
Movement for the Survival of the Ogoni People (MOSOP) 130–4
Muir, J. 18, 21, 22
Muldavin, J. 191
Mumford, L. 30
multidimensional approach 11, 201–6

Naess, A. 37–46, 50
Narmada Asargrasta Sangharsha Samiti (NASS) 119
Narmada Bachao–Nimad Bachao Andolan 119
Narmada Dharmagrastha Samiti 118
Narmada Ghati Navnirman Samiti 118
Narmada Yojana Vichar Samiti 119
National Audubon Society 18
National Conservation Commission 20
National Environmental Policy Act (NEPA) 32
national forest–wilderness system 18
National Reclamation Act 20
National Trust 17
natural history, case studies 181–4
Natural History of Selborne 170
Natural Resources Defense Council 35
nature-based conflicts 24
nature feminists 53
neo-liberalisation 4
New Environmental Paradigm (NEP) 160
New Left 29–31
Nimad Bachao–Narmada Bachao Samiti 117
nineteenth-century conservation movement 15–20
North America 16, 25, 28, 85
Northern environmental groups 25

Oecology of Plants: An Introduction to the Study of Plant Communities 172
'Oeconomy of Nature, The' 170
Only One Earth 30
Open Spaces Preservation Society 17

Ordway, S. 31
Organization of Petroleum Exporting Countries (OPEC) 35
O'Riordan, T. 21, 22
overpopulation 65
Owen, R. 30

Park, R. E. 154, 155
pastoralism 60
Patkar, Medha 119, 122
patriarchal economy 61
personal creativity 29
Pesticides Act 1972 33
Petrified Forest National Monument, Arizona 20
Pielou, E. C. 167
Pieterse, N. 84
Pinchot, G. 20, 21
Plant Geography upon a Physiological Basis 172
Plumwood, V. 60
poisonous waste 29
political dimension 4, 5, 9, 10, 81, 96, 104, 146, 147, 201
political ecology 195, 196
political process, 'political': Green political parties 143–7
Popper, K. R. 164
Popperian deductive model 165
Population Bomb, The 31
poverty 92
power factor 104
power relations 3
progressive era conservation thinking 17
pseudo replication 165
psychological behaviourism 158
pure femininity 54

quality-of-life issues 9, 28
question of 'political' 100–50
Quiet Crisis, The 30
Quinn, J. A. 157, 159, 163

radical ecofeminism 53
radical feminists 54
Raffles, H. 183
Rahnema, M. 92, 96
Raju, S. 93
Rasmussen, K. 7
reform environmentalism 8, 13, 14, 28–36, 100; analysis 35–6
Renaissance period 84
Renner, G. T. 158
Resources and the American Dream 31

Rhine–Rhone canal project 145
Robson, B. T. 157
Roosevelt, F. D. 22
Roosevelt, T. 19, 20
Rostow, W. W. 85
Royal Forestry Commission in 1871 19

Salix herbacea 40
Salleh, A. K. 61, 64
Sandbach, F. 29
Sand County Almanac, A 18
Schimper, A. F. W. 172
scientific conservation 19
Scott, J. C. 92, 93
Scottish Rights of Way Society 18
Selborne League 17
self-development 29
self-identity 70
Self-realization 38, 40, 43, 44, 48
Sen, A. 86
Sessions, G. 43, 48
Shenton, R. W. 84
Shiva, V. 57, 58, 89, 94–6
Sierra Club 18, 19
Silent Spring 23, 30
Silent Valley Hydroelectric project 105–9
Silveira, S. J. 29
Small, A. W. 153, 161
Smith, A. 83, 84
Snowy Mountains Programme 7
social agents 3
social conflicts 81
Social Darwinism 17
social ecology 9, 13, 67–75, 103; analysis 74–5; ecological outlook 72–4; evolutionary perspective 69–72
social/ist ecofeminists 55
social system 6
soft anthropocentrism 48
South Africa 16
South Asia 86
Southern environmental groups 25
spiritual ecofeminism 54
spiritual enlightenment 17
State of India's Environment, The 63
sustainable development 88
symbolic rituals of sacralization 46
synecology 172

Thapar, R. 185, 193
Third World countries 24, 86, 88–90, 94, 96
Thornthwaite, C. W. 159
Torrey Canyon 32
'Tragedy of the Commons, The' 31

transdisciplinary inquiry 7
Transley, A. 176
Trumbore, S. A. 44, 45, 49

Udall, S. L. 30
union carbide corporation, movements against 138–41
United Nations Development Programme (UNDP) 86
United States 16, 18, 23, 24; baby boom in 28; Earth Day in 32
utilitarianism 35

value conflicts 39
value-dimension 203
'value' dynamics 28–79
value judgements 5, 74, 205
value objectivism 37
value orientation 67, 205
Vayda, A. P. 189, 195
Vincent, G. E. 153, 161

Ward, B. 30
Wards, L. F. 154
Warming, E. 154, 172
Warren, K. J. 66
Weber, T. P. 168
Weiner, J. 166, 167, 169, 176

Western Europe 28
White, C. L. 158
White, G. 18, 170
White, R. 24
Whiteheadian ecological ethics 39
Wilderness Society 18
wildlife refuges 20
Williams, L. 7
Williamstown Alpine Club 17
WinklerPrins, A. M. G. A. 183
woman–nature connection 53, 54
women: daily lives of 63; ethic of care 62; household, consumers of energy 64; participation in cultivation 58; responsibility conception 62
wood-based industry, movements against 134–8
Wordsworth-Ruskin lineage 17
World Bank (IBRD) 90
world resolutique 34
World War II 83
World Wildlife Fund 35
Worster, D. 24

Yale Forestry School 20
Yellowstone National Park 19
Yosemite National Park 21
Young, G. L. 157, 158